Project Sanctuary III
Created by
Silvia Hartmann

3rd Revised Edition 2003
ISBN 1-873483-98-8

Published by
DragonRising
United Kingdom

Project Sanctuary III

© Silvia Hartmann 1996/2003

3rd Revised Edition

Published By DragonRising

18 Marlow Avenue, Eastbourne

East Sussex BN22 8SJ

United Kingdom

+44 (0)1323 729666

http://DragonRising.com

services@DragonRising.com

Other Publications By Silvia Hartmann:

Adventures In EFT

Advanced Patterns Of EFT

In Serein

Oceans of Energy

Printed and Bound by Antony Rowe Ltd

Dedications & Acknowledgements

There would be no Project Sanctuary III without the following:
Richard Bandler, NLP and DHE.
Charles Faulkner, Metaphors Of Life
Derek McCarthy-Baker, Commissioner of Project Sanctuary I
Ananga Sivyer, Instigator of Project Sanctuary III

With Gratitude To These Originators who contributed patterns:
David Grove
Connirae Andreas
Win Wenger
Richard Bandler
Tad James

And those who have played and learned in the Sanctuary realms with me:
Marilyn Pawson
Steve Collins
Nicola Quinn
Chrissie Hardisty

Thank you all!

Table Of Contents

Introduction To The First Edition, 1997

Welcome To Project Sanctuary!

I salute you - you might or might not know this yet, but you are about to take a journey into a world like no other.

Your world, your mind, your internal Universe.

Compared to the deepest oceans, the widest expanses of the galaxies or what sleeps beneath the miles of ice on our Earth's poles, this is a region as uncharted as no other. At its outer edges, it touches the very fabric of time and space itself.

It is the realm of infinite possibilities, of dreams, and most importantly, of magic - the realm where thought creates just like it did in the olden days.

Do you remember?

It doesn't matter if you do or if you don't, or if your knowing of such things is more like a feeling of homesickness that sweeps over you now and then, even though you are already safe and sound in your own home.

Project Sanctuary is here to help you remember. It is here to help you re-awaken your sleeping dragons, your lions and your powers to be and do.

You do not need to join a monastery, or to take to meditation in a big way. You don't need to study for years or take more courses and classes, and you don't need a PhD to start the journey.

Project Sanctuary is natural and it will come easy to you, because it will help you remember. There is nothing new here. This is a reminder for those who wish to be reminded, those like myself, who need to remember - for if we didn't, this world would make no sense and there would be no sense in struggling to live here at all.

Welcome to the journey.

Silvia Hartmann

November 1996

Introduction 2002

Welcome to the third edition of Project Sanctuary.

So here we are, six years later.

I don't think any of us who played with Project Sanctuary as we did when I first got the idea could have begun to know what we had on our hands with this.

I certainly didn't.

I thought it was a lot of fun, very satisfying to do, immensely helpful with many clients and in many different situations and although I always used it, it took second seat for a while to my journey through the new Energy Psychology techniques, or Meridian Therapies.

Once in a while I wondered why I was picking up techniques faster and in more depth than others around me but it was not until I was asked to produce a Bibliography that I saw in black and white before me what Project Sanctuary had meant for my personal development as an author, and beyond that, what it had done for me as a person.

It has changed my understanding of creativity and how I view the Universe. It has taught me compassion for myself and also taught me how much more I can do than I thought I could. It is directly responsible for the genesis of the Sidereus Foundation, the Starfields patterns, PowerFields, Guiding Stars and literally hundreds of creative therapy and personal development patterns which I have since never stopped generating.

Further, my own giant Project Sanctuary, otherwise known as In Serein, is due to this manual here before you.

The process code-named 'Project Sanctuary' is a big thing, a really big deal.

I kind of guessed that it was way back when I first wrote it. I had a notion that it was but I really didn't know how big. There was a tremendous temptation to rewrite this manual from scratch with the wisdom of hindsight. I thought about it for a long time and then finally decided that it is right it should stand as it is, for it was written from a space of newness and exploration that I then shared with the others who had not undertaken this particular journey before. I have made a few minor adjustments to this new edition and confined myself to addition of extra chapters and further interesting and helpful patterns.

Other than that, I have left my old self alone to speak as she did at that time and respect her view at that part of her journey.

Not everyone who reads Project Sanctuary 'gets it', 'it' being the inordinate scope of this process and just what you can do with it if you want to, or indeed, what **it does for you** if you will let it.

Not everyone takes to it and makes it their own. All I can say is that I hope you are one of those who does.

With best wishes, Older Silvia, October 2002

1 - THE DEPARTURE GATE

1/1 - Global Metaphor Immersion Training?

Welcome to the wonderful world of Global Metaphor Immersion Training!

Now, first of all, relax. 'Global Metaphor Immersion Training' is just a phrase.

But what it is, is a process about you

Totally, completely, and only about you.

If you want to, you can take the ideas in this book and begin to create a brand new mindscape of your very own - a personal Sanctuary for you to simply enjoy or to use at will to make changes in your life.

In this process, you are completely in charge.

You create your world and you find out about yourself, at your own speed, in your own time and no sooner than you are ready.

Moreover, the Universe that you will discover and co-create will hold within all the wonderful resources you have always heard other people have, but couldn't really find within yourself - a gateway to magic, to healing, to creativity and inspiration, and the starting point for a life so much better that you might find it hard to conceive of right now.

Sounds too good to be true?

Well, let me tell you a few of my personal beliefs.

Firstly, I absolutely believe that every single one of us, bar major neurological damage, has the potential to out-Leonardo Davinci, and to out-Albert Einstein.

After all, we only use about five percent of our brains. By my reckoning that means that to be a genius, you only have to bring about another 2% or so on line. Surely, that must be well within reach and easy to do.

Secondly, I absolutely believe that as a species, we seem to have a habit of making things far more complicated and far harder than they need to be. Over and over again in my own life I have had major and minor revelations that have helped me overcome all sorts of problems, and the answers were always surprisingly simple and often even embarrassingly so. Moshe Feldenkreis's 'elusive obvious' continues to be elusive - but only because we like to make life hard for ourselves, if given half a chance.

I am therefore making it my life's aim to find more ways in which to prove that **there is gain without pain** - in fact, that if someone isn't in pain, he or she might find it a lot easier to remain focussed, relaxed and to make faster and better gains on their life's journey.

There is one last belief that has helped me a great deal, and it underlies much of what you're going to be exploring - and that is that **there is more to the world than meets the eye.**

We know so frighteningly little about even simple functions of the human brain, never mind the whole neurology, and never mind the human mind, that one should really **keep a very, very open mind** indeed about a whole vast range of possibilities that could exist.

With this mindset, I'm sure you agree, the sky need not be the limit, nor space the final frontier.

So what, you might well wonder at this point, is holding us back?

1/2 - The Freudian Nights

This vexed question of "What is holding people back from utter brilliance?", when put to therapists and their clients produces answers such as "The injured child within" - "Faulty childhood programming" - "Negative self beliefs" - "Pre-birth trauma" - "Karmic blockages from past lives", etc. etc. etc.

Now this is all good and true. And it is also true that every single conceivable form of therapy has helped some people at some time - no matter how esoteric or bizarre, and no matter how unlikely or theoretical.

However, having been very seriously engaged in Personal Development and the Human Potential Movement both on a personal as well as a professional level, I found the following things that troubled me.

1/2/1 - Re-Active Development

It seemed to me after some years that people were forever running after their problems, like some weird flock of sheep that never stayed together - as soon as one had been rescued from a ditch and returned to the herd, the next one would require attention. So, as soon as one

18

problem ceased to invite attention for whatever reason, a new one would appear - and like the distraught shepherd in the very shallow metaphor above, the person who sought development never seemed to be able to rest on a decent bunch of laurels.

As a result of this permanent 'running after the problems', little space was left for active future planning, or for what I would call Pro-Active Personal Development. But that was not the worst of the problems.

1/2/2 - The Piecemeal Approach

More and more, I began to see clients in my practise who had done all kinds of work with the aid of therapists, and counsellors, and books, and tapes, and lectures and circles and practise groups. Some clients had done therapies that I hadn't even heard about!

And yet, here they were, sitting on my couch, with their lives a total shambles, unhappy, dissatisfied, miserable, exhibiting anything from problems in relationships via addictions of all kinds to eczema, asthma and cancer. Yes, they had certainly made gains along the way, and had a much better understanding of the causes of their troubles, but had it made them any happier?

One client in particular reminded me of ...

Imagine you buy an old house with a view to doing it up. It's in bad repair all around but it has a lot of potential, was a bargain, and you've got the rest of your life to sort it all out and make it a pleasure to come home to of a night time.

Right. So you go in, and you put down new carpet. Next, you hack out the old fire place and paint the ceiling - oops, now the carpet's ruined. Oh dear, must stop and see to the attic, it's started to rain and there's a leak. While we're up there, how about installing a new hot water tank? Oh dear, the floorboards were rotten, and it fell through two ceilings below, burying the new wall paper in the lounge and the carpet to boot. And while the floor in the attic collapsed, the roof supports collapsed as well so now the rain's coming in again.

That, in metaphorical form, was what the client had done in personal development terms over the last twenty years or so.

Any builder can tell you that this kind of approach is not only hopelessly inefficient and very expensive, but that you'll never get it done - because you keep creating new problems all the while.

What this old house needs is to have some kind of **overall strategy**, logically levelled down from the most important structural work at the top, right down to a little nail to hang up the last picture right at the bottom.

It was then that I realised that if my clients were to make true, long lasting, long term gains towards being more happy and fulfilled and contributing human beings, something was desperately needed to provide this supporting structure - but the only place that seemed to offer something like that at the time were organised religions and cults, not the psychotherapy scene.

1/2/3 - A Rag Bag Of Techniques

Nowadays, fast fix therapies are all the rage. Hypnosis, meditation workshops and NLP for example offer the "One session and all will be well" kind of approach. This, once again, has led many into problems.

Each counsellor has their own ideas, their own style, and their own worldview. As clients move from counsellor to counsellor, from system to system, and from technique to technique, they end up with a whole mixed rag bag of other people's beliefs, values and attitudes, mostly problem specific, often contradictory and sometimes even down right conflicting.

Thing is, **a mind once stretched by a new idea never regains its original dimensions,** and so, unless the memories of all those techniques and ideas were to be somehow surgically removed, they remain within the client's mind, running their little subroutines, and generally adding greatly to the confusion.

Also, something I've really thoroughly understood recently, is that *problems are, generally speaking, only symptoms of something completely unrelated* that needs the attention - like someone limping from the left hip, but he's only doing that because a vertebra in the neck is out of line, thus causing the spine to twist, thus causing the visible limp.

Further, I think that the interconnectedness and ecology in human minds is such that virtually everything is either connected with everything else, or at least impacts just about everything else - a bit like this friend of mine who put a new engine into his old car, and the whole thing started to shake itself into its rusty parts because the rest of it couldn't cope with the increased power output.

Needless to say, the more the client's done in the way of counselling and personal development in general, the worse this kind of confusion becomes, and all these techniques, styles and approaches need to be integrated in some way - but how?

Something else came out of this idea that personal development needs to be viewed in a **more holistic context** altogether - and this was the idea that as a person grows and changes and meets challenges in their life, they would also need ...

1/2/4 - Long Term Continuity

Anyone who has ever been involved in the care of anyone else knows how important long term continuity is - children in orphanages, residents in old people's homes and patients in hospitals all exhibit stress and even bereavement related symptoms when their carers change.

This was one great thing about the old therapy forms - because they went on forever, there was *consistent and long term continuity of care*, often twenty years or more with the same therapist.

I gave this some thought and came up with a simple solution, as you will find out in a little while. But there was one more aspect that I felt needed to be addressed.

1/2/5 - Send In The Priests!

The greatest single development in my personal opinion on the scene in the last few decades is the **re-emergence of spirituality as an acknowledged human need.** I cannot begin to express my gratitude to the quantum physicists for being able to express that spiritual matters and magic have been allowed to rejoin even the strictly scientifically minded once more.

The fact that standard organised religion in this country has ended up less spiritual than the Body Shop corporation has also led to people once more having to **confront their own spiritual issues** which may arise quite unexpectedly and without being able to resort to standard pat phrases for their resolution - and gratefully I congratulate this trend.

The more esoteric domains of the personal development movement have long made good use of spirit guides, angels and other higher beings, thus adding a tremendous dimension to the world in which we live, which has for many proved to be intensely healing and reconciling. Once again, here too are conflicting beliefs, values and attitudes, and a

truly holistic and integrative mind healing system would have to be able to incorporate the unseen realms seamlessly and elegantly in the overall structure.

These main five points - *Pro-Activity, A Planned and Structured Approach, Finding A Framework For Techniques, Continuity and Spirituality* - were my main points on the shopping list to find an approach that would really work for my clients, long term, no matter what the problem, no matter who or what the counsellor or therapy approach, no matter what the circumstances, and no matter what went on in their external lives.

At the time I was searching for such an approach, there was a particular form of therapy that I always found to be most fascinating and truly remarkable in its results.

2 - Re-Learning The Oldest Language

2/1 - The Babel Of Self

As a species, we have a major problem.

Consider this:

I was watching a TV show about a starship the other day.

The Captain and the First Officer were completely at odds about what strategy would get them out of trouble.

The Captain believed that the ship should go to the heart of the enemy's territory and fight it out. To this end, she ordered everyone to work on the weapons systems and for the ship to go at full speed towards the enemy. But as soon as her watch was over, the First Officer ordered the ship to be turned about, to get as far away as possible from the enemy, and for everyone to stop working on the weapons systems and to start working on the defensive array instead.

After three days of flat out racing and frantic shifts working around the clock, the ship was found by the enemy exactly where they had started out in the first place, with the crew totally exhausted and with neither the weapons nor the defences in working order.

It occurred to me that this is a lot like how many people I know spend their lives, and that this little story really illustrates very well how our unconscious and our conscious desires, if at odds, create just this kind of exhausted stalemate.

On the starship, the problem was communication between the Captain and the First Officer. For us, that's the same problem.

We've got two minds who don't even speak the same language.

How often have you had what I would call a really profound dream, you just knew it was important somehow, but were left with no idea what the message was supposed to be?

Dream Dictionaries, I suspect, are probably a bit like the famous Hungarian Dictionary in the Monty Python sketch - not only could the translation for, "What is the time?" be something like, "I'm going to murder you with a toothpick" but worse, we wouldn't even know until we got smacked in the face!

I have had my experiences with trying to translate one language into another. At school, I must have missed something important and thus failed to comprehend Latin. It didn't make any sense and I didn't have a clue about the underlying structure of the language. This, by the way, is absolutely true and not a metaphor to support my approach to Metaphor Therapy.

In tests, we were allowed to use a dictionary to help us with translating passages. I ended up looking up each word in a sentence, writing them down on scraps of paper and then trying to arrange them in an order that would make some kind of sense out of the whole thing. I understand that, to this day, some of my more outrageous 'translations' are standard jokes amongst the common room staff of that particular school, and even twenty years later the long retired ageing Latin master started to laugh uncontrollably upon spotting me in the supermarket on a recent visit to my home town.

Now you may be forgiven for thinking that I was just not very good at languages. I have to tell you that I am in fact German and came to the UK about 18 years ago. English, and the words you will be reading in this book, are my second language. The simple reason for the fact that I learned English easily and can now express myself fluently is that *I learned it by immersion*, just as children learn their native tongue.

I learned by trial and error, practise, and by following examples. Latin, on the other hand, was trying to learn by what I shall forthwith term the "Dream Book Strategy" - or the Monty Python Hungarian dictionary approach, for that matter.

For this reason, I would suggest that you try the following, different approach in working with your self generated internal metaphors and symbolic representations - namely,

> **to resist attempting to translate them,**

> **to put aside any preconceived notions of what something "might mean" or represent,**

> **and, most importantly, to stop trying to work out the meaning of symbols by taking them out of the grammatical context of the whole story, be it a dream or waking meditation -**

> **because as soon as you do that, they may well become <u>entirely meaningless</u>.**

Instead, we're going to immerse ourselves and learn like children do, by trial and error, with experimentation, and by copying what seems to work for others, until the time has come, when we are entirely familiar with the underlying structure at a totally unconscious level, and **we can really and fully begin to have complex and meaningful two way conversations with our selves.**

2/2 - Metaphor As A Language

Metaphor Therapy in all kinds of guises has been employed for longer than we can know. Whether it's the heroic tales of old, educational stories such as Aesop's fables, Tarot Decks, working with dreams, inner journeys, meditations, or, as some suspect, past lives - profound concerns can be addressed in a very holistic way when working with metaphors. I was - and still am - particularly impressed with Charles Faulkner's work on life metaphors.

He points out that metaphors are the basic organising process for the way we live our lives, and that these underlying unconscious metaphors are made visible in the form of the artefacts we surround ourselves with, the clothes we wear, the relationships we form and the language that we use - in fact, **we materialise our internal metaphors by the very way we live our lives.**

To give an example, someone who might have a troublesome relationship may be operating from the basic metaphor "Relationships are War" - and would be living this out by fighting with his significant others, having an army type structure in the way he brings up his children, and whatever therapy this man did, **as long as this deep underlying metaphor remained in place, he would always be driven back to the behaviours it demanded within its own context.**

What I liked especially was the gentle and cohesively holistic transformations that occurred when such underlying metaphors were changed.

I had a client whose life's metaphor was: "Life is Like An Inner City Jungle". He imagined himself in a grey and smoggy city, where starving tramps were trying to warm themselves by burning oil drums, dirty children begged in gutters, prostitutes stalked, sirens filled the air and with villains hiding behind every garbage bag and street corner who would kill you for your shoes. His 'real life' problems included continuous conflicts with the law and authorities, inability to sleep, being extremely aggressive when challenged; he couldn't trust anyone, had never had a steady relationship and was a petty criminal and drug user.

All of these behaviours made a lot more sense when viewed in context of the metaphorical domain of his life; as there were so many seemingly unrelated problems, I decided to do the metaphorical "world enlargement" in preference to a more directional approach.

I asked him to find the landscape beyond the city and pointed out that *as this was his metaphor, he could choose to change it.* He then went ahead and instigated a public order and restoration programme in his own internal metaphorical world, acting as the mayor of the town, and went to live in a lovely house on the green hills instead.

Incredibly, within 6 months, he had a job, a girlfriend, and had stopped using drugs - all of this for the first time in his life and without any further counselling. No-one who knew him could believe the change. Also, it was not as though the changes had taken place overnight.

With hindsight, it was very difficult to pin point just what had happened how and when - we had all woken up at some point and here he was, a different person. This was five years ago. He's married now, has two children and to all intents and purposes, the changes have stayed.

This young man was my first experience with Direct Metaphor Only Therapy.

From then on, whatever the problem and whatever the techniques employed, I went ahead and always finished the session with a little metaphor discussion about life in general as well. Not everyone who took part at that time had miraculous transformations, but there were many little 'convincers' along the way, such as:

> A lady whose original problem was panic attacks. She was also unhappy at work, but had been in the same unhappy job for 25 years. In her metaphor she was living in a house with no access to any roads or ways, either in or out. I had her build a road and within a fortnight she had found a new job she thoroughly enjoyed.

> Another lady (a stop smoking client) who desperately wanted to move to the country but it somehow wasn't happening - whenever she got close to making the move, there was a family disaster of some kind, or money or health problems; for twenty years this had been going on and she was expressing doubts as to whether she'd ever achieve her dream as she was getting on in years. She imagined herself looking at her dream house but there was a barred gate and a high metal fence all around over which she could not climb. In the end, I gave her a magic wand to use on the gate so she could finally get in. Four months after the session, she send me an invitation to a house warming party. She had moved into 'Magpies', a lovely old farm house in the country.

A young man who was hard working but found life very hard and depressing (asthma was the problem he came to see me about). He saw himself going around and around in a giant treadmill down an endless road. I had him stop it and get out. Quite miraculously, just a few weeks later he received a highly unlikely invitation to take an interesting and much better paid job in Spain, which he accepted without hesitation.

Lastly, a borderline agoraphobic gentleman who had envisaged himself living in a walled monastery. Once we found a door to the outside world, he went ahead and got himself his first passport of his life as he felt the unheard of desire to take a day trip to France - he was 49 at that time.

I could go on and on and on with such examples, but I think you're beginning to get the pattern.

What fascinated me then and still fascinates me today is how *unlikely* the changes are that occur following even such a clumsy exercise in speaking to the person's unconscious beliefs **directly in metaphorical terms**. The changes are unlikely and many of them completely illogical. A few even defy belief - it seemed in some cases as though the entire Universe conspired all of a sudden to help the person following a metaphorical change on the inside.

So here then were the glimpses of a system for change that was:

gentle,

easy to do,

fun even, according to many clients,

often very profound in its repercussions

and, most importantly, was fundamentally under the person's individual control - **they were finding their own solutions to their own problems** instead of being told what to do and how to do it.

I decided to try some variations on the theme and began offering all my existing clients a free metaphor session, just to see what would happen and where it would lead us.

The resulting strategy and practises you will find in the rest of this book.

2/3 - Introducing The Sanctuary

Many hypnotic inductions, meditations and guided journeys take as their starting point the idea of an inner sanctuary - a safe and protected space that would allow you to leave all your cares behind for a while, to simply be surrounded with peace and beauty, a place all of your own you can call your inner home where you can finally let go of all your barriers and inhibitions and simply be your self.

In some approaches you are advised to imagine a favourite place in nature; in others, more detailed instructions are given to help the user co-create an inter-dimensional meadow, say, an enchanted forest, or a moonlit beach.

As I was in my experimental frame of mind, rather than starting to seriously mess with people's operating life metaphors, I thought it a good idea to have a closer look at their internal sanctuaries first.

A second compelling reason for working with the sanctuary idea was that many of my clients really never got their heads around the idea that **home is within the self**, rather than with another person, or in a particular place. Some were forever going somewhere or doing something in order to "find themselves" - I'd rather always believed that *"wherever you go, there you are."*

I've got to tell you this story: One of my clients, a rich, middle aged bachelor, who, frankly, came to see me quite regularly basically because he didn't have any friends or family and enjoyed my company, and to this end tended to make up various imaginary complaints which we both knew were just an excuse to come and have a good old chat, travelled a lot to help fill his time and get rid of some of his money. He was quite a cynical person and one time, following a multi-thousand pound adventure excursion to India, told me how he had sat on an elephant, watching the sun come up over the Himalayas and feeling "rather bored".

Talk about "wherever you go, there you are"! Can you imagine it! Sitting on an elephant in the Himalayas at sunrise - what a breathtakingly, indescribably amazing experience. Yet it did nothing for him, and so he might as well have sat at Eastbourne Pier on a rainy November day.

To me, this really summed up how desperately important it is to go inside to solve problems before you start going to the Himalayas, because if you do it the other way around, you're just wasting your time - and a considerable amount of money.

2/4 - Contacting Sanctuary

How do you find your own Sanctuary? That's quite simple. In a moment, put down this book and allow yourself to imagine a place that would feel like a Sanctuary to you personally, somewhere where you would feel completely safe, and completely happy.

Say the word 'Sanctuary' out loud and simply experience what this word represents to you. Don't argue with yourself about your choices at this point - this is your first lesson in accepting thing the way they currently are.

Stop and do this now.

If you are one of these people who, like myself, would rather get on with the text right now and think 'Oh, I'll do this later', know that it only takes a minute or two and know to understand that the rest of the book will be far more enjoyable and useful to you. So, and as you want to get your money's worth from this text, don't you?

Stop reading and do it now!

Say the word 'Sanctuary' out loud and simply experience what this word represents to you. Don't argue with yourself about your choices at this point - this is your first lesson in accepting things the way they currently are.

When I first said this word, it was a sensation of deep longing, a longing for something that seemed impossibly far away, unattainable. A place of rest. A place of peace. Of security, where you can be yourself in all ways, completely accepted, with nothing demanded of or from you, with nothing to do and no-one to be but simply yourself.

A place where you are protected from all and everything.

That is the meaning, to me, of the word 'Sanctuary'.

Aspects of this were always in my goals and in my dreams, in my hopes for the future. It is true that I have sought this vibration of Sanctuary in people, in landscapes, in buildings for as long as I have known.

But what it is, in truth, is a state of being, a state of mind and of body we can begin to attain as we begin to heal within and without, as we begin to relearn about our own true resources, as we begin to once again take charge of our own selves.

From wherever you currently are, and to help us get a sense of what it is we need to give ourselves to heal, restore and relax into a different way of being, our first exercise in Sanctuary is to evoke a representation of an environment, a place and a time where we can firstly stop and take a break, a much needed well earned rest from our lives as they are.

So now, let us consider what kind of place, what kind of time springs to your mind when you think of a place that would be your perfect Sanctuary?

What happens if you ask people to tell you about their inner Sanctuary?

Enough material for a creative artist to paint a picture a day until they drop dead from exhaustion!

Here are just some descriptions of the many, many I have heard:

> I'm living in a giant tower rising high from a small rocky island in a stormy sea.

> It's a small prison cell. Thick, thick walls of bedrock stone. I'm safe here.

> A piece of meadow, about the size of a small back yard, with a dark forest all around it.

> An oasis in an eternal desert under a night sky filled with a thousand falling stars.

> An endless beach but the sea has receded and gone dry.

> A fairy castle in the middle of an enchanted lake filled with fish-like dragons.

> A white marble gazebo on a mountain top so high that the clouds are like a sea below.

> An enchanted garden with a high wall around it.

> It is like a beach hut on the shores of an endless ocean and nothing and no-one else around.

> A nice old house, but it really needs doing up.

On a plateau of a giant glass mountain that rises high from a desert.

As you read through these, I would now advise you of the **prime directive** of metaphorical work for me:

Don't think for a moment you have any idea what's going on!

After a short period of time, I gave up trying to analyse 'what it might mean' altogether, and with good effect.

I don't think that our analytical minds can comprehend at all what's happening, what it's all supposed to mean, and that *the first step towards true conscious/unconscious communication is to accept things as they are*, and to proceed mostly on feeling, trust and intuition.

If it feels good and right and true, do more of it. If it doesn't, back off and try something else.

Allowing your own feelings and intuitions to guide you instead of fighting with yourself and hopelessly trying to work what's happening in a conscious fashion is also a great time saver.

I mean, you could spend the rest of your life discussing with your client what a fairy castle in the middle of an enchanted lake filled with fish-like dragons might represent. You might be right, you might be wrong, and you'd probably never know; and, in the meantime, you'd get side tracked into God knows what kind of detail and at the end of the day, nothing much would have been accomplished.

I'm sure that by now you have an idea of your own Sanctuary space. If you have not, simply answer the following questions quite quickly and without thinking too much to localise your special space-of-mind so you can go there, know where it is, find it again and begin to work with it.

What kind of landscape?

What time of year?

What time of day?

What else is important to have it be there?

* **3rd Edition Note:** *I have appended the 'Project Sanctuary Virtual Introduction Evening', a short paper I wrote 4 years after the original text to be able to give Internet visitors a flavour of what Project Sanctuary is all about. If you are having trouble with finding a space to begin the exercises in this manual, you might like to read/do this now. You can find it in the Addendum.*

Now, once we have a representation of this Sanctuary space, it might be interesting to ask the following questions:

> How do you like it?
>
> How does it feel being there?
>
> Are there aspects that you could improve?
>
> Is there anything not there that you would like to be there?

* **A Safety Note:** *If you do this with anyone other than yourself, be incredibly careful how you ask these questions. It is very possible that* **you install the thing you ask about**, *as in order for the other person to think about the thing you asked about, they will need to create an internal representation of it.*

On the other hand, if you wish to install something later on that you feel is missing, a question such as, "Where is the water?" will instantly create it. Magic!

2/5 - A First Exploration

2/5/1 - Size & Restrictions

You might have noticed that most of the examples of inner Sanctuaries were very limited in size, although most were set within a limit-less space. Often there is a direct boundary, such as the moat around the fairy castle, the sea around the island with the tower on it, and very obviously in the prison cell example.

People who are trapped, tightly enclosed or walled in some way need to find a way out first before they can even ascertain what kind of landscape surrounds them; and making a connection with the surrounding countryside in the form of a doorway, gate or bridge might become the first priority.

In other cases and especially if defence was a major concern, I would just ask for the area that was covered by the Sanctuary to be enlarged if it was particularly small or, let's face it, just plain boring.

I mean, a gazebo made from marble on a mountain top is pretty romantic, but it's not even comfortable for sitting in, never mind all the other things that will be going on there eventually. By the way, when I mentioned this to the client, he did admit that he didn't use it much for that reason, as he always felt strangely cold and stiff only a few minutes into his meditations!

Not all Sanctuaries need this enlargement straight away. Before we go any further, however, they should be big enough so that there's something to look at, something to explore. Later on, as the Sanctuary's owner grows in confidence, it may well have developed into an entire world. But let's take one step at a time.

2/5/2 - What is already there?

Having a walk around the Sanctuary consciously is a very interesting experience.

To start with, we'll change nothing, just see what there is and what there isn't.

To my great amusement, quite a few clients reported clutter of all kinds, left over from various personal development techniques they engaged in, sometimes many years ago. Weird wire mesh 'belief screens', trees with doors in them to access a past life, figures of eight engraved in the floor from a 'cutting the ties that bind us', sundials, elevators that go nowhere, strange plants, and even materialised Reiki symbols floating about - with some people a process not unlike clearing out a garage would eventually be required.

Many report obvious trouble spots, such as a black swamp in one corner, or shrivelled foliage on plants, or a dried up well, a scary forest etc. These items will have to be dealt with as one of the first priorities.

Not everyone seems to be alone in their own Sanctuary. Creatures and people of all imaginable shapes, forms or levels of existence can be found wandering about.

Then, there are natural features of the landscape and the vegetation; further, the man made features such as buildings, gardens etc.

Finally, there's the climate, the temperature, the time of day and the season to be considered.

After we've had a good look at all of these things, it's time to return to Earth and take note of what has been discovered.

At this point, most people want to dive straight in and want to make changes right away. Although I applaud this enthusiasm, I think it might be a good idea to sit back for a moment, and to access the first important resource that will be of tremendous help in the Sanctuary restoration project.

2/6 - Getting Help

Do you believe in Guardian Angels? I personally think that's a particularly nice and supportive belief to hold, especially when the going gets rough. Do they really exist? I don't know ... enough yet to make a firm declaration one way or the other. I've certainly had experiences that would support my belief, but you know how it is - whatever belief you hold, you'll find experiences to support it.

What I do know is that 'a bit of help from a friend' is a most wonderfully welcomed gift, and in the context of building a full, working Sanctuary it's actually a necessity.

So, depending on the beliefs the owner of the Sanctuary may hold, now is the time to call on any of the following:

A guardian angel

A spirit guide

An 'advisor' part

A wise person they may have met or admired in their life

A friend

An imaginary friend

A fictional character from novels, fairy tales, plays, TV or movies.

An ever growing number of folk these days already have a guide, and you should certainly use these ones, as they are a tremendous resource. Most people who do not have one yet will more than readily manifest such a guide as soon as this is put to them.

So, for your own Project Sanctuary, turn within and check if there is someone there already who will be your guide, or if you will have to call someone in to do this very important job for you at this point.

A very few people might need extra help from their own unconscious minds to bring forth someone they will be able to trust completely, to advise them.

Use the following simple questions to elicit the guide (no hypnosis required).

Don't think about it, just answer really quickly - if you think about it too hard you will be overcrowding the channels through which your unconscious mind is trying to communicate.

You can also use a pendulum or even toss a coin to find the answers to these questions - either way, here they are:

Is it human?

Is it a he or a she?

How old?

How are they dressed?

What is their name - and accept the first thought that springs into your mind.

Notice something special about them - something personal that distinguishes this individual from others of their kind.

What do you like most about them?

If you do this exercise with others and they refuse to co-operate or keep insisting that they don't know or nothing comes to them, to ask them about a fictional character from books, TV or movies they think they'd like to have as an advisor or helper may be an option; if the worst comes to the worst, you can lend them someone else's guide for the interim, although that is very rarely necessary.

People who snort at the idea of guides altogether will usually accept a pseudo scientific explanation along the lines of, "You have learned many, many things all through your life. It is now held to be true even by scientists that everything you've ever learned is stored in your unconscious mind. All we're going to do is to create a kind of interface that will allow you to access this knowledge fully whenever you need it." - and promptly, a client of that nature went ahead and manifested a Star Trek-like hand held communications device into which he could input his questions. Oh well - horses for courses!

2/7 - Guides and Their Uses

2/7/1 - Interfaces To Inner Resources

As my own main guide is male, I'm going to take the liberty to use the 'he' for the following - but remember, talking animals, tricorders, angels, glowing fire balls, hermaphrodites and females are just fine as well.

When faced with the Sanctuary 'as is', only a few people experience flat out and unambiguous delight.

Most feel the urge to make changes of one kind or the other right away, but are unsure what to change, in which order, and most especially, what to change it into. And that's where they will need the guide as a sounding board for their ideas.

This is a very important aspect, because what we're doing is building **interfaces to access inner resources** and to begin weaning ourselves off of running to a counsellor, therapist or guru every time we're stuck with something.

In general and as a rule of thumb, you can have communications and conversations with absolutely everything in the realms where we are working with Project Sanctuary. Every item has a meaning, an existence, an identity and can be talked to, be it a river, a rock or a tree.

Guides are special in that they are **created specifically** to guide you and to help you. In this context they help with the following:

2/7/2 - Decision Making

If you've ever seen someone choosing wallpaper for their sitting room, you'll know what I mean when I say that making profound decisions that may well have long lasting effects on the very structure of your personality isn't as easy as it may seem.

Therefore, the guide comes in handy to help *clarify purposes and outcomes, and as a useful safety check* on the more drastic types of decisions.

2/7/3 - As a Teacher and Interpreter

As the guide is at the very least **through** the unconscious mind, if not directly **of** the unconscious mind, he is also one of the first direct contacts with that realm, and will serve as a teacher to help us communicate with that part of ourselves more easily in the beginning stages of this process.

It is very important to realise that guides, whatever their shape, form or appearance are a first bridge to a veritable wonderworld of undiscovered talents. Riches and treasures of unknowable proportions are there and your guides can help you find them within yourself.

In communicating with the various guides you will notice that they don't speak like we do, not exactly, even if they speak directly to us and use words and phrases, body postures and other signs and signals.

It is even possible that, in the very act of seeking to communicate with a guide, our unconscious minds learn something about our conscious selves - it has been our experience with Project Sanctuary processes that this is indeed so, and the more these communications take place, not only is it easier to understand what is being presented, but the presentation seems to become much more direct, much more easily understandable as time goes on.

2/7/4 - Re-Assurance and Support

Over and over, clients have expressed their relief at having someone to turn to within themselves - so the guide can help alleviate fears, relieve stress, and offer gentle and steady support to help the owner of the Sanctuary grow and expand safely, always on call, 24 hours a day, without complaint, without fail.

As with all and every mental and physical skill or ability, the more you use your guide, the more 'manifest' it becomes, the more real, if you will. I have personally had occasions where in a moment of distress one of my special guides 'just turned up' and was right there in the room, offering their presence and their support. It was quite extraordinary and welcomer than I can tell you here; I've always preferred it in real life when help was given without my having to ask for it first. Indeed, there are so many times and circumstances when one doesn't think to ask; sometimes I'm too distressed or upset and lose access to all the many resources that I normally know I have at my fingertips.

For a guide to manifest autonomously and automatically in **direct response** to an emergency situation could possible be a life saver one day; it is certainly all by itself a very good reason why one should talk to one's guides on a regular basis and get to know them very well indeed.

An Important Note: *If anyone experiences their guide as overly talkative, demanding, disruptive, turning up without having been asked to do so repeatedly, too vague, unhelpful or too dominant, or they just don't like them at all, ask them to sack him and find a better one. True communication can only exist between equal partners, and the guide is supposed to be helpful and guide, not tell the client what to do on the one hand, or waffle on esoterically on the other.*

OK. Now we have an internal helper, and a Sanctuary that might not be all that it could be. So what's next?

2/8 - What's Missing?

What have we got, and what do we want?

The first important decision is to be clear on what this Sanctuary space should be like. And it's intriguing to note how difficult this is for most people. After all, if you can have anything you ever wanted, it throws up this vexed question of **"What DO you want?"** Not only teenagers have a hard time with that one!

Some people have been so browbeaten by life, they don't even know anymore what they like. Sure, they can tell you what they should be doing, or ought to be having, but their own feelings have become so detached they can't tell you what it is they want if they've only got themselves to consider, minus an audience, a society, neighbours, family or peers. Sometimes it is therefore necessary to ask them what they don't like, and then find a positive answer by process of elimination.

An easy way of getting some starting points is to ask what concepts, feelings and sensations are particularly valuable and pleasurable - and then to find a metaphorical representation for these, such as:

Tranquillity - a still, deep pool; clouds; gentle rain; birds flying.

Peace - a wide grassland at dusk with the stars just becoming visible high above; a sandy beach with palm trees; a slow drifting river; a nightingale singing.

Happiness - lots of brightly coloured flowers and birds singing in the trees; sun sparkling off a lake; a playground with laughing children; a large diamond.

Strength - a mountain range; a dragon; a waterfall; a pride of lions, a glacier.

Love - a beautiful garden; a single red rose; two white swans; a herd of wild horses.

Energy - a sparkling waterfall; lightning; a bull; a volcano; a soaring tower.

Abundance - a cave full of crystals; gold fish in a pond; a golden statue; a field of ripe wheat; an ocean.

Freedom - the wide blue summer skies; a thunderstorm; a dolphin; an emerald.

Note how different many of these are, and these are only a few examples - the permutations on these themes are really endless. Know that these kind of representations are **absolutely specific** (idiosyncratic) to the person themselves, and if you work with others, never, ever push your own preferences or ideas of what 'loyalty' should be made to look like. Also, don't argue with any person's choices in this matter - and especially not your own. If someone's unconscious mind wants to materialise 'friendship' as a three headed scaly dragon and they feel good about this, so be it.

At this point, let's also be clear that this Sanctuary space we are creating is **very fluid and open to all kinds of changes** at any point, if you should choose. I recently painted my bedroom violently purple all over - originally, I'd just wanted that colour on one wall, and it kind of spread onto the ceiling and all around the room. (Oh, and by the way, if you now start to wonder 'what that might mean' about me as a person, be warned! Any such thoughts and I'll come haunting you on the astral plane tonight!!) Anyhow, the room ended up looking like nothing you've ever seen; most family, friends and acquaintances informed me that I had made a terrible mistake - but all of them relaxed visibly when I told them that **it could be changed quite easily** by applying another colour at a later date.

2/9 - Time To Get Started!

Do you remember that story about restoring a house? The most urgent is not necessarily the most important, so at this point, using what we have learned from our 'walkabout', we're going to make a plan, borrowing a Time Plan system. In this system, we have 4 different priority levels which are tackled one at a time, starting at the top:

First, that which is both urgent and important.

Second, that which is important but not urgent.

Third, that which is urgent but not important.

And fourth, that which is neither urgent nor important.

Allow yourself to be guided exclusively by intuition. Always remember that we are dealing with a realm that the conscious mind does not yet understand, and that logic here is often more of a hindrance than a help.

Therefore, **find out what needs attention most desperately**, right away, and most importantly. This is most easily accomplished by looking around and taking note of what you **want** to do as the first priority.

For some, this might be dealing with a 'black spot', for others, a clear problem is built into the very structure of the Sanctuary that needs to be addressed before we can go any further.

At this point, people often express dismay at the magnitude of the task ahead.

I remember especially one man - let's call him Bob - who had found a completely overgrown, walled in garden, where everything was either thorny weeds or dead, the ponds and fountains clogged up with sludge and algae and dead leaves, all the manmade structures were collapsed and in ruin, and it was a case of Bob standing there, shaking his head and simply not knowing where to start. But luckily, Sanctuary renovation is nothing like working in a real situation. For a start, and seeing that he was so forlorn, I felt he needed some practical help; and so I asked him to call in anyone who would come and aid him in this enterprise.

To his astonishment, the first to materialise were his long dead paternal grandparents who had been farmers, ready equipped with various gardening tools. Past friends he had known forty years ago joined the party, army chums, family members, his wife and children amongst them, as did some people he had never met before, until there were about a hundred willing helpers standing all around him, waiting for him to tell them what to do.

They had to wait a little while longer, because by this time he was in tears. He'd forgotten how many people had wished him well over the years and he had, until that point, considered himself unloved, friendless, and lonely.

He then reported to me that he had that one thought go through his mind, faintly at first, then stronger and stronger until he could "virtually hear it" - "Clear The Weeds!"

And so they set to, and many hands make light work. A mountainous heap of weeds formed in one corner of the garden, which would in time become good compost for the new generation of plants. He thanked everyone most sincerely, and they wished him well and left happily.

Well, it was a start. Bob told me later that he had, on his way home, stopped off at a gardening centre to look at the plants there to help him get some ideas of how he wanted to design his new garden - something he had never before taken even the slightest interest in. Like so many others, there was a new-found excitement about him and an enthusiasm that was quite new to him.

Of course, there are hundreds of different ways of achieving fast and efficient transformations - all that's required is that it should feel right to the individual person.

2/10 - Transformational Magic

Make no mistake - Project Sanctuary is all about **learning and change**. You could call it growth or healing, too, but that's change just as well, only in other words.

The whole object of the exercise is to learn something that will give you the ability and the tools you need to repair what once was broken; to put things to right that once had gone wrong; to recover what was stolen or lost or simply abandoned; to retrieve what was misplaced in time or space and to make your whole self work better all around.

Even those who do Project Sanctuary with the focussed desire for outward and inward bound exploration or to go straight for retrieving their magic or other essential resources, skills, talents or information find invariably that before we can get onto that, some major repair work or change work needs to be done first and as a very high priority.

Now, the greatest disservice in the realms of Project Sanctuary is to think the same as we do here in our daily dealings in The Hard.

Here, it takes much effort to carry big heavy boxes up a steep rocky hill beneath a merciless burning sun.

The Project Sanctuary realms are not like that.

They are quantum realms where time, space, gravity, friction and so forth don't actually exist at all and they seem to exist ONLY because **we assign such qualities** to the objects, spaces, creatures and all that reside here.

However, we have thought in terms of The Hard for a very long time, all our lives in fact, and we need to relearn to think differently when we are dealing with these spaces in which Project Sanctuary resides.

So, and when for example we are faced in Sanctuary with a giant mountain that is blocking our path, our natural and automatic tendency is to 'think hard' i.e. come up with solutions that would be appropriate to a real hard mountain. Such solutions would be to possibly climb it, find a pass, find an underground cavern system so one might travel beneath it instead, use a flying machine to get over it and solutions of this nature.

However, a Sanctuary mountain is NOT made from granite but from the fabric of time and space instead and therefore, it could be instantly made to never have been there at all - just for the price of a single thought of intention that this should be so.

To begin with, this is quite a strange thought and what we need to do to get used to the qualities and sheer possibilities in these realms as well as to begin to understand the many differences in the 'laws of nature' that govern our ordinary reality and the Project Sanctuary spaces, we need to bridge this and begin to 'think magically' instead.

In the following sections, I am going to give some ideas that bridge between our old and new thinking and so we begin to learn that overgrown gardens, grey wastelands and rocky hill tops can be tackled in a whole different way.

2/10/1 - Magic

That is the easiest way, but not everyone likes it - it's somehow 'too easy'. Our friend Bob in the example above could have just imagined holding a magic wand, closed his eyes, stated the desire for the weeds to be gone, and then touched the wand to the ground. The magic could have whirled around the garden, doing the job within seconds. If someone would like to use magic to move a mountain, drain a swamp or whatever and they're not too sure whether it's appropriate, remember that's what the Guide is for: ask for clarification.

I would like to point out that the ability to ask for and to accept plain, simple Deus Ex Machina magic in the Sanctuary realm is the first starting point to be asking for and accepting the possibilities of true magic in all their many other Worlds.

2/10/2 - Magic By Proxy

Of course, in the Sanctuary, the owner is the main magician. Not everyone feels comfortable with this idea to start with, but might have no problem in passing the job on to someone else who'll do the magic for them.

Elves, dwarfs, wizards, helpful animals, magical creatures, angels or even a representation of a real person they consider magical and up to the task can all be employed to this end.

There is also the interesting option of creating magical beings for a specific task. These are also known as servitors and can be incredibly useful as they are tasked and send out to do your bidding in their own time, and whilst you give your attention to something else.

2/10/3 - Quantum Time

Time in the Sanctuary is as liquid and fluid as everything else. So, a mountain could virtually be eroded by rain and a hundred thousand years can pass in the blink of an eye. This is handy when planting trees, for example, re-populating rivers with fish or when 'growing up' inner children.

As your intention is what rules paramount in this space, you set the rules for time in every way, should you choose to do so.

Checking the evolution of a process you have set in action over time, then longer and longer time still, can certainly give you insights on what should be there as the seed at the beginning and make it a lot easier to decide on what it is you're trying to do, and how you are planning to do this.

2/10/4 - Time Travel

Sometimes there may have been a time before everything fell to rack and ruin. In this case, a bit of time travel can be the most efficient way to undo the harm by going back into the past and dealing with that which caused the problem in the first place. It is often one of my first choices, especially when faced with a multitude of problems that would take too long to tackle individually.

For more advanced users, time travel can become very interesting when you don't just go back and forwards in time but also sideways and across. This clearly leads into Multiverse spaces which hold **alternatives** that may never have been considered before.

2/10/5 - The Sci-Fi Approach

For those who feel this way inclined, machinery - both terran and alien - can be used to create the miracles required. Someone who had to deal with a vast desert of quicksand used a large spaceship with massive lasers to fuse the sand so that there would be a firm foundation for him to build on.

Aliens with special powers, crystalline entities or human Super Heroes - like the Marvel Comic Characters, Superman etc. - have also helped out in the past, and with one particularly problematic youngster, bringing in the Power Rangers was the turning point for both of us.

2/10/6 - Construction Crews

If you feel a need to re-create the pyramids, there's nothing to stop you from hiring the entire original cast of thousands to do it for you whilst you sleep. Every kind of large scale project that has ever been undertaken in human history (and you need not confine yourself to the current chapter, Atlantean and Lemurian skilled crews are out there waiting for you to call on them as well!) can be undertaken for you, should you wish to order it done; ranging from bridge building to desert re-planting or large scale industrial de-contamination.

2/10/7 - DIY (Do It Yourself)

Sometimes there seems to be a real need for becoming 'physical' and moving something brick by brick, as it were. One client who had a very small meadow enclosed by traditional stone walls, reported that they spent a whole evening hacking away, pushing, carrying, shoving to create an opening - sitting on their couch, eyes closed, and sweat pouring off them! Another wanted badly to take a shovel and, in the wilderness, start to dig the foundations for their kingdom - without anyone's help, just them doing it. A friend of mine reported having spent two whole weeks, every night before going to sleep, painstakingly covering a rock face in murals. Well, whatever turns you on ... (!)

2/11 - Doing It Right

Is there a right way and a wrong way to do these things?

Yes. There is only one right way to do it, and that is to do it so **it feels congruently right and completely appropriate to YOU**.

The wrong way for you is to do anything that feels wrong to you, or to do it as you think it 'ought to be done'.

Here is now the time and the place to let go of any 'musts', 'shoulds', and 'ought to's' and to turn to wants, needs and 'I can do' instead.

I would also suggest at this point that it is extremely important to **be true to yourself** and not to pretend you're more enlightened than you really are.

No-one, including the soul mates from the healing group, will ever know what goes on within your Sanctuary space; so if in truth you'd rather have a huge pot of gold and twelve scantily clad nymphomaniac nymphs than an enlightened pink angel oozing unconditional platonic love, please feel absolutely free to go for it.

Trust yourself to know what is good for you and what you need, right here, right now.

If you're unsure about a particular situation, leave it, or freeze frame it by stopping time for a time, and ask for general guidance from the good old Universe, question your Guide specifically, or both.

There's no need to hurry. Rome wasn't built in a day, and it's been God knows how many years that your Sanctuary has been as it is now, so a few more days won't make much difference.

2/12 - The Ecology Of Project Sanctuary

Project Sanctuary is a way of making the existing ecology of your systems visible and directly noticeable as you explore what there is, see possible problem areas, become aware of things that are not as they should be, and begin to make some changes.

The changes you make have, of course, ripple-on feedback effects. These follow-on effects are also termed 'ecology' in many schools of human psychology because it is a fact that the human mind and the human body in all its strata, levels and layers are incredibly **interlinked**

47

- what happens in one part of this system necessarily affects other parts of the system, often in a most unpredictable fashion.

Here is an example that is both a metaphor as well as a real, true story. In the 70's some people thought it was a good idea to straighten the river Rhine to cut off some travelling time for the commercial shipping industry as it wound its way in many loops through the lowlands on its way to the sea.

They were then thinking just 'river' and 'travelling time'. I guess such a thing had never been attempted before on this scale and so there was no precedence to warn them or say 'Well aren't you forgetting something here, guys?', before they sent in the big diggers.

This is what happened. The river became way too fast and silted up immediately, making it quickly too shallow for the bigger boats. This also eroded the banks and destroyed entire eco-systems on the way. The water table in various areas collapsed entirely and whole towns fell into holes in the ground, as they were no longer supported by the water from beneath; in other places sea water got into the water table and poisoned vast tracts of agricultural land. Loads of species died out. They had created true ecological nightmare that affected so much, it was scary. It cost billions not to put it to rights but just to fire-fight the whole thing into some kind of functionality once more and this is still going on in many ways today. What there once was cannot be retrieved or recovered, and what there is now is of debatable use in the greater scheme of things.

This is 'hard' ecology.

When you make changes to your own internal ecology, this will happen too - and in the process it will teach you immediately and with direct feedback what the strands of connection that hold your internal worlds together are really like.

To learn about your own ecology is one of the most amazing as well as useful endeavours you could want to engage in, and there is another point of course, which I will repeat a number of times throughout this book, namely to remember that:

Project Sanctuary is a quantum realm in which you can learn in absolute safety.

Should you create an ecological disaster like the straightening of the river Rhine, you are NOT stuck with the terrible repercussions. You can change it immediately back to the way it was before and you have the opportunity to learn in absolute safety a very important lesson, and then you can go back and try a different approach, a different solution to the problem in hand, one that won't hurt your ecology but that works **with** your ecology to produce an outstanding and **ecological** solution.

At this point, it might be nice for you, if you haven't already done so by now, to go inside and check out your very own Sanctuary, and get an idea of what you will want to do, in what order, and how to do it. If you're ready, start making some changes for the better - expand it a little, clear it up, deal with any structural problems.

Then go and simply be there for a while - is it beginning to feel truly good?

Even a small and incomplete Sanctuary, if it feels like 'coming home', is a perfect place to rest awhile whenever you need it.

But it can be far more than that. Far, far more.

3 - Dwelling In Perfection

Before we go into the specific uses of the Sanctuary - and there are many! - let us just briefly back up and talk about a few basics.

Firstly, remember that it is **created by** you, within you, **for you**.

It is for all of the many yous, as you will find out sooner or later.

It's a safe meeting place where you will begin to **make direct contact** with your unconscious mind, past selves, inner children, forgotten, neglected and 'repressed' parts of your self, and your higher aspects too.

A very profound space, if you will.

But this doesn't mean that you have to make a song and a dance to get there.

You might have wondered how I got people to tell me about their Sanctuaries, and you might be forgiven for thinking that perhaps they were under deep hypnosis, that I had them meditating for hours, or undergoing heavy duty inner odysseys complete with joss sticks, 60-beat a minute music and blue lights.

Nope. All of the above strategies are designed to get the conscious mind out of the way, and that's not what I want. I want the conscious mind to be right there, remember everything, and become actively involved in the process of communicating.

Now of course there's the theory that anything that pre-supposes trance, causes trance - and having someone riding an imaginary dragon up the flank of an extinct volcano in their mind is certainly pre-supposing trance. However, I tend to lean towards the idea that we're in some kind of trance all the time anyway, only we're mostly not aware of it.

What you need to understand is that you do not have to do any major league meditating in order to work with your own Sanctuary - you just need to give it your attention, just need to think about it.

Just close your eyes for a moment, and you're there - and even when you're not there, you are aware of it, and may 'think' about it every so often. It really is that easy. I've gotten hundreds of people to tell me about their favourite places, their favourite things, what kind of house they would build if there was no restriction on time or resources of any kind, just over a cup of coffee, or even complete strangers on a train.

Everyone can do that, and most people daydream anyway about what kind of car they would like some day, fantasize about perfect relationships or plan their retirement activities.

It does help somewhat to talk about it out loud. If you've ever told someone about a dream, you might be familiar with the fact that it becomes clearer in your own mind as a result, and you remember more details as you speak. So if there's a friend or a family member who would like to share in the excitement that is building and regenerating your own personal Sanctuary, by all means go ahead and talk with them about it.

But you could also make notes, write a diary, do an architectural plan, or paint pictures about the main features and events (I do that all the time - talk about inspiration!), write poetry about it, or collect pictures from magazines and travel brochures, if you want.

All - or any - of this can help **make it more real**; but it's just as good if you want to keep it to yourself and strictly only in your own head.

When Bob went to the garden centre to look at plants for his Sanctuary, he breached the unspoken invisible divide between so called 'real life' and the unconscious realms - something that was previously thought to be the domain of creative folk and those with special talents only.

In magic, this is called 'acting in accord'.

It means that on top of the psychic - inner - work, a physical act of some kind - outer work - is performed which will make it easier for the outcome to manifest itself - **to make it become real.** This is not as esoteric as it may sound - many therapies have aspects of symbolical practical actions embedded within, even in the guise of homework exercises; and Milton Erickson used to send clients on 'tasks', such as climbing a mountain.

This kind of behaviour is a signal to the unconscious that *we are willing to do something* - even if we're not quite sure what it means. And in return, the unconscious responds by being more communicative, more freely forthcoming with suggestions, ideas and intuitions.

The invisible divide is beginning to become more transparent.

Every time you think of your Sanctuary, it becomes more real and easier to access. It's easy and a natural process, and anyone can do it. And believe me, I have worked with people who haven't even dreamed as far as they were concerned in 50 years or more - just like Bob.

Every time you use your Sanctuary for some of the things we're going to be looking at in a few minutes it becomes easier, more profound, more meaningful. There is no need for 3D hallucinations, so if you have trouble visualising things, don't worry about it. Just think about what you would like, and where you would like it.

Also, keep an eye open for what you see around you. If there's some kind of countryside that really "makes your neurology sing" as Richard Bandler terms it, take it home and build it in. A colour, a song, a particularly fascinating species of animal, a dream house, a special scent, fabrics that make you dissolve with pleasure when you touch them, even a beautiful car or a beautiful person - make them a part of your Sanctuary, until such time as when you think about it, you can feel yourself smiling within at the beauty of what you have allowed yourself to create for you to enjoy.

And, by the way, if you thoroughly enjoy lighting candles, taking salt baths and putting on the New Age music for your 'meditations', go ahead. There's nothing wrong with it. It's just not necessary to restrict one's Sanctuary activities to weekly meditations in order to have access to the profound help and amazing experiences which await within.

Now that we've covered the basics, let's have a look at what could be there if you wanted it to be.

3/1 - Sanctuary Features

What does a fully equipped, hi-spec Sanctuary have on offer?

Well, as you perhaps know by now, **anything** you want. Here, for once, is a space that is exclusively your own, without being bound by any kinds of limitations other than those which exist within yourself.

As you might well discover in due course, this will certainly throw up your own beliefs of what can and cannot be had, and will come to represent *a map of your own expectations.*

One lady had a forest growing near the central area which she didn't like to visit because she was quite sure that "there were probably wolves and things in the darker parts". Her guide, who was accompanying her on a little stroll, pointed out that, "If there's wolves, it's only because you've put them there!"

Sanctuaries, their surrounding landscape and their various features and functions are of course completely individual. However, here are some features that seem to be generally popular. Some of these were invented by the users, others have come out of various personal development approaches.

In the next sections we will be looking at a number of features you might like to consider for inclusion in your own personal Sanctuary.

3/2 - A Shelter For You

One of the first things which most people consider to be essential is the protection of a dwelling, a shelter of some kind which has been a first priority for humans for at least 10,000 years.

I didn't actually have a house or any kind of man made structure in my own Sanctuary for a very long time, preferring to lie about amidst the various wonderful natural features - in my Sanctuary, you can lie in long grass and need never worry about bugs, ants or any suchlike inconveniences! However, one day it suddenly occurred to me to build one, and that was the start of a very interesting exercise. It never occurred to me to create some kind of magic palace; the eventual structure was a modern affair, half built into the backing hill, which looked as though a spacecraft had crashed and bonded with the rock to form a fluid unit.

As any dream book will have you know, various parts of a house are meant to represent various parts of the self.

I would urge you now to leave all such considerations behind and simply create something that **feels wonderfully right** for you.

I've known a couple of people who wanted a house but didn't feel they could cope with the many decisions involved in building one from scratch, so they manifested an inner architect and inner interior designer instead and let them get on with it.

One of these eventually had a massive row with their inner interior designer because they didn't actually like what had happened and made them change it all again!

Whichever way you go about building a house, what it looks like and what it contains, it'll be alright. You can always send in a couple of inner workmen with some 'One Coat' Dulux and try something else, or simply erase the old structure and start from scratch somewhere else. There are no limits.

3/2/1 - Fun Rooms

Since the Sanctuary is all about feeling good, I've heard of a few interesting 'fun rooms' that I personally would never have considered installing, and so I submit these for your consideration.

One lady told me that she'd build a massage parlour, fully staffed with lightly oiled, near nude gentlemen of Mediterranean origins. Now that's not my scene, I must say, but the thing is that this particular lady feels great when she's had a massage and been "pampered" - she said it made her feel relaxed and happy.

And that's what the Sanctuary is supposed to do; remember, you're only to please yourself.

Sarah had been suffering from bulimia on and off for years. She felt that after any kind of large meal, she would either have to throw up to "relieve the tension" or she would exercise herself into a state of near exhaustion. She told me that recently, she had been on a long car journey with her husband. They'd stopped at a roadside inn, where the most amazing portion of food was served - it was delicious, and she ate it all up. But back in the car, the familiar feeling of tension began to build up in her stomach, and she began to panic, thinking that she couldn't possibly make her husband stop the car and go through either a regurgitation or an exercise ritual. So she closed her eyes, pretended to go to sleep, went to her Sanctuary, and installed a gym in one of the rooms in her house. She got onto an exercise bicycle and then a rowing machine in her mind, and, as she worked out, "I could feel the tension receding, the pressure in my stomach beginning to lessen, and lessen, and then it was completely gone. I was so very grateful, but astonished too. This is the first time since I was about 13 that I could keep an entire huge meal down without having to go through a long physical trauma in order to relieve it. I felt absolutely fine for the rest of the day. I kept thinking, 'I don't believe it, this really, really works.' "

Games rooms, collection rooms, even a beauty parlour - whatever takes your fancy, whatever you enjoy - have fun!

3/2/2 - Topical Dwellings

Although at first it can be expected that you will have only one central dwelling in your Project Sanctuary central space, such as a dream house, fairy castle and so forth, as your internal landscapes expand and develop, you are likely to find different dwellings for different purposes.

Holiday homes such as beach huts, mountain or forest cabins for example are specific places for resting and restoration, contemplation or to be used for special projects - think of an author who hires a lodge somewhere quiet in the pleasing countryside to complete a novel, for example, or an artist who goes to a special location and hires a studio for a series of special paintings or sculptures.

In this context, you can widen the idea of dwellings for special purposes to include camping trips, or sleeping out in the open in particular locations, in a magical cave or a magical forest grove.

Going to work, sleep or rest in a particular dwelling, shelter or location can be a tremendous help with inspiration and creativity in problem solving, but also simply provide a balance or energy that is in short supply in our ordinary waking lives.

Sandra, 42, reports going through a period in her life where every night as she went to bed, she would close her eyes and, in her Project Sanctuary setting, begin to walk across a coastal landscape of dunes, making her way to a beach hut. It was old, originally had been painted blue but was bleached out from the sand, sun and salt in the air and it did not contain anything other than a comfortable bed, upon which she would lie, draw a blanket over herself and fall asleep, listening to the sound of the wind and the waves on the shore.

"I really don't know what that was or why I needed it, but I really did need it. It was so restful, so **right** it is really hard to describe. I was really there. It went on for nearly 3 months that I would go there and just lie in the beach hut, going to rest, being able to rest in total safety there. Even now, and this must have been nearly three years ago now, I remember the place so well, it was as real as anywhere I've ever been and a great deal more useful at that."

3/3 - The Realms Beneath

Most people have some form of subterranean structure and one or more access points to it. These may take the form of caves, cellars, dungeons, lower levels of their house, or even a multi dimensional portal. One person had a pretty innocent looking door and entrance hall, but when you went through another door, you would find yourself at the top of a high escalator, looking down on what appeared like a giant magical shopping mall - levels and levels of stores, departments, shops, cafeterias etc.

Richard, on the other hand, experienced the unconscious realm as a cluttered and cobweb-choked dungeon-like cellar, with dim lurky things in shadows, a slimy, slippery floor, and the junk and garbage of the ages piled high in every room, corner and even in the passage ways. He took one look and slammed the door on it, duly overwhelmed by the amount of work he thought it would take to restore some semblance of order.

This is a pretty common problem. Mostly when faced with that kind of clutter, the Sanctuary owner seems to revert to 'real world' thinking and envisage themself for a dreary eternity, sifting through the rubbish, carting stuff here and there, as though it was a real house clearing job that required a lot of brawn rather than brain.

Think magically!

If you wanted to, you could just literally snap your fingers and all would be repaired, sorted, filed and arranged.

But oh no. Not a single person felt that this was appropriate, that there was some kind of hard work and suffering required and that it would take literally forever.

Fine. I suppose with all the kind of rubbish we've been fed all our lives along the lines of, "If the medicine isn't bitter, it won't work" - "Life is a vale of tears" - "No pain, no gain" and so on and so on and so on, it's hardly surprising that such a simple solution would be "like cheating", as one person put it.

So, if this happens to you, go as far as you can towards:

at least starting on the job in some form, shape or size, thus declaring your intent to *do something about it*; and,

get all the help that you can allow yourself to have at this point; it could be in the form of a tribe of hard working dwarfs, robots, relatives, giant ants, I don't care what you would like, just choose someone or other who can get on with the job even if you're not there.

I personally like the idea of putting someone intelligent in charge of such a cleaning crew, because you don't want to misplace items that might turn out to be important, and the filing and storage systems must make some kind of sense in the context of the overall structure and operation. It can be quite amusing to set something like this in action and then just visit every so often to check on the progress that's being made.

3/4 - Subterranean Treasures & Surprises

Ed found, whilst wandering through his subterranean structures, a large room with a sandy floor. In the middle of the floor was a very large pool, and in the pool lay a most beautiful sleeping golden dragon.

Many others have reported intriguing finds of this nature. Treasure chambers overflowing with sparkling gems and shining gold are certainly something very exciting to discover, someone else found what appeared to be a whole warehouse full of exciting children's toys; another a fully stocked medicine room with every possible substance and healing medicine ever invented; yet another discovered an art gallery with the most amazing paintings and beautiful sculptures.

See, the good ol' unconscious domains don't just contain darkness and weirdness. There's a great deal of wondrousness and beauty there too. And, remember what the guide said to the lady, "If there's wolves, it's because you've put them there."

3/5 - Dealing With Dark Rooms

Modern 24th century personal force field shield technology is a great bonus when exploring slightly - or intensely - scary parts of the subterranean regions. Taking body guards, spirit animals and protective magic along can all be very useful indeed to *give you the confidence* you need to allow yourself to look into the 'Dark Rooms'. A tip - a seriously huge torch that will shine pure white light at great intensity works extremely effectively to dis-spell just about anything that might lurk. If you take a few coloured filters along, you might even be able to overcome problems with a spot of direct colour therapy!

If the whole thing sounds still beyond you, do what a client of mine did once - instead of entering the room himself, he sent Richard Bandler (Co-developer of NLP) in first - and, as expected, the demons ran, screaming, all the way home! One lady who could not even begin to face a particularly unpleasant set of characters locked up under a giant stone slab found an arbitrator in the form of a friend's guide to establish first tentative lines of communications.

Should the room indeed turn out to be inhabited by some creature of the night or other, don't worry too much about it. They feed only on negativity - fear, anger, hate. If you can be cheerful, or even loving, they can be set free. After an initial knee-jerk fear response, feel sorry for them - what a miserable existence they must have led, incarcerated like that, with only their own miserable company for God knows how long.

You can trust me on this.

I've accompanied many on their travels into dark rooms, and it was never as bad as had been expected. Your job is not to fight these guys, or to destroy them, but to find a *way to heal and transmute them so they may be set free*. You will find much more information about the specifics of re-habilitating internal dark offenders in the following chapters.

Finally on the subject of Dark Rooms I would say that such places never reveal themselves to someone who isn't yet ready to deal with them. If you find one, take it as a message that your unconscious mind considers you ready now, and that you now have all the resources you need to resolve and heal this particular situation.

3/6 - The Library

As every student knows, a well-stocked library is a tremendous resource; and, as every student knows, a badly catalogued library, no matter how well stocked, is just a lot of very frustrating and basically useless paper and binding.

I've often used a library metaphor for people complaining of having a 'bad memory' - standard joke first, "Well, you remembered the time and you found your way here - yet again! How bad can it be?"

So, here it goes. I see memory retrieval as getting a question, and then going to a little guy behind the desk and saying to him, "Hey, I need the answer to ..." As he turns away to go look for it, I shout, "Well, go on then, what's the bloody answer?" , thus stopping him from actually being able to go away and retrieve it.

The more I shout at him, the less he's able to do his job until he folds his arms and refuses to budge at all.

I use that idea all the time to good effect. Even in the middle of a lecture, if I can't remember a name or something, I think of the poor little man and let it go - and within seconds, it's there, upon which I stop and give grateful thanks and acknowledgement. Before, I used to 'rack my brain' and would wake up in the middle of the night, finally getting the answer to something I'd asked hours earlier and then moaning and groaning about the inefficiency of it all! My little man has been getting faster and faster recently, and I have hardly ever any problem now with any kind of memory retrieval - thanks to a much better internal staff relationship scheme!

But back to the internal library. It might need re-organising, updating, cross-referencing or similar work done on it; one lady was horrified to notice that some of the books were in danger of falling apart or crumbling into dust and felt the strong need to start a restoration programme at once and before more damage was done; or it may be glorious just the way it is.

By the way, you needn't confine yourself to books. A musician client had a section with CD's, vinyl and audio tapes; another client had a library plus video library. Quite a few people use computer terminals and hi-tech search options to find what they're looking for.

How or if you're going to use the library is really up to you, but before we leave the library I would just draw your attention to some particularly interesting books:

3/6/1 - The Book Of Beliefs

This is a great big leather bound book in which your beliefs are written when they are decided upon, with blank pages for new beliefs to be added.

You could have a book of decisions instead; either way, you can erase old beliefs from the books and write in new ones which are more supportive.

If you use affirmations as a real world activity, putting these into an appropriate book in your internal library can certainly be very helpful for the affirmations to succeed. Someone I know actually gave up writing affirmations for real and hired a little monk who would sit in the library 8 hours a day, writing the statements in beautiful calligraphy over and over again.

3/6/2 - The Book Of Shadows

This is the title of journals kept by magicians all through their training and mastery years and these books would, upon their owner's death, contain their life's work and many useful and original magic spells.

We all have small and large revelations of some kind or another; virtually every day, there's a little insight, a new piece of understanding, or simply something that struck our curiosity. Putting these into your personal Book Of Shadows is an interesting and beneficial experience; looking up past revelations and understandings can be of tremendous use in many situations.

3/6/3 - The Book Of Dreams

Most people experience what I call a 'profound dream' every so often - a dream that is so vivid and stays in your mind so strongly that you can recall it even years after you had it, just as though it was something that had 'really happened'.

Placing such a dream in the form of a symbol, a description or even a picture into a dream book or, in more modern terms, to make a video or CD-Rom library of such important dreams, at the very least signals the unconscious that you are willing to take note. You can then look up past dreams and find your understanding of what's going on increasing as time goes by.

One young man, Steven, used radical technology instead - he installed a computer filing system for dreams with an automatic search function to determine recurrent symbolism, subjects, archetypes and situations. Now that's not my cup of tea, but it did work for him and helped him figure out what he was supposed to do about a recurring nightmare all by himself and with no assistance from me or anyone else.

My personal dream book has both pictures and brief descriptive comments; I was looking through it the other day and there was a progression of interspersed dreams I had never noticed before - a particular kind of animal had gone through a complete transformation over the period of five years and a series of nine seemingly unrelated dreams.

This is one of the nice things about Sanctuary work - once urgent problems have been resolved, you have time for idle exploration and fascinating little voyages of discovery that will always end up teaching you something important about yourself.

4 - THE WISDOM OF WATER

4/1 - The Innocent Energy

Water is the source of all life. Nothing would be happening on this planet of ours without it, very practically speaking. In all forms of magic and religion, water is of prime importance as one of the key elements from which all else is constructed.

I personally have a special fondness for water. It is one of the first introductions in energy work I use for the concept of 'the innocent energy' - many healers try to heal with love, for example, which is a very powerful and dangerous form of energy both to handle and to receive. There are many systems in a person which respond badly to the application of love; think of the equivalent of a vampire bursting into flames under the noonday sun.

Water is not like that; it is structurally very different. Here is a quote which explains this perhaps better than any amount of theoretical discussion might.

The speaker in this case is an executioner and a torturer, and he says:

"I have no idea where I am but wherever I am, I am alone here and this is a relief as intense as the cold rain that bathes me steadily on, never caring if it fell on me, or on a stone beyond, or on a blade of grass, or on a smouldering wet fire that, if you stirred it somewhat, would contain bones, and teeth."

Water is an example of a natural energy. Unlike anything even remotely connected to human values and endeavours, water is entirely innocent. It is innocent when it brings joy, life and fertility to landscapes, and just as innocent when it rises up and washes away an entire civilisation.

It doesn't care whether it falls on a torturer or on their victims, or on a blade of grass and therein lies the power of the innocent energy of water. Whatever your connection with water, it is life and therefore it comes as no surprise that Sanctuaries are famous for their imaginative water features.

Something you might also like to consider is that different manifestations on the general theme of water have very different and highly specific energies, vibes or feelings attached to them. Just allow yourself to imagine the very real difference in your internal experience between swimming in a swimming pool, a lake, a river, or an ocean. For this reason, it might be an idea to have more than just one kind of water present.

Here are just a few examples for you to consider.

4/2 - The High Energy Of Waterfalls

Is there anything more energising, refreshing and clearing than standing beneath a real waterfall in the sparkling sunlight? I have one that I use to rinse away all kinds of negativity, right down to the cellular level. In my opinion, every Sanctuary should have one.

4/3 - Still Ponds and Lakes

Lovely for meditating, still, deep ponds and pools, perhaps reflecting the moon in a clear velvet sky, in a variety of shapes and sizes are certainly a nice thing to have around. You can of course have these inside structures as well as on the outside, and one lady described hers as a 'spirit pool'.

4/4 -The Healing Pool

One of the very favourite and most useful features in my own Sanctuary is a healing pool, filled in my case with a kind of bubbly carbonated, mineral enriched, deep turquoise warm water. The edges are shallow for ease of sliding in and the centre is deep enough to float suspended or immerse completely.

Both for myself and any injured parts, visitors or anything/anybody that requires deepest relaxation and healing, I have found this to be invaluable and I would urge you to install a healing pool to your own desires and specifications as one of your first priorities.

4/5 - Oceans

As the Sanctuary expands into a world, seashores and their accompanying oceans tend to turn up - or rather, reveal themselves. These are full of life, power and energy of a very special kind and their water experiences are totally unlike those of the fresh water features. Oceans will of course provide a meeting realm with all manner of sea creatures. These days it sounds a bit naff, but I have swum with my internal dolphins and it was great fun. Oceans also really rather pre-suppose islands and further realms beyond their reach; and sea going vessels and the like also belong to this realm.

4/6 - Rivers, Brooks and Streams

From an exciting rushing river to gentle little countryside streams, flowing water is wonderful to look at and to swim in if you feel so inclined.

Huge, powerful creatures such as the Amazon, the Nile or the Danube are amazing to behold and have enormous repercussions on the surrounding countryside; these represent the most advanced and evolved state of 'river-ness', whatever that may be.

Underground rivers are particularly exciting. Gliding on their still blackness to goodness knows what you might find is a powerful experience; and creatures and features you encounter there are amongst the most unusual and magical you find anywhere in a Sanctuary.

4/7 - Wells & Springs

I reckon that wells and springs are on the 'must have' list of water features somewhere quite near the top. The mythology around these natural fountains is legion; and the mythological creatures who are said to dwell there are amazing. Also, wells and springs bring a lusciousness and a fruitfulness to the area around them that makes it easy to spot them from miles away - hence the habit of the people of old to build shrines and temples there.

This is also a water that begs to be drunk - thus, once again, very different from any other water you might already possess. Down the ages, people have travelled vast distances to drink from a certain well to cure all manner of ills and diseases.

Of course, you can have more than one well, including a wishing well, if this hadn't occurred to you before; at any rate, whether you're after prosperity, health or creativity, wells can be extremely helpful in providing you with just the tonic you need.

4/8 - Estuaries

I've always been particularly fascinated by estuaries - the place where a river slowly becomes one with the sea. Estuaries have their very own ecology and are considered to be a landscape in their own right. In this context I would suggest that, with the mingling of fresh and salt water, they are also waterscapes in their own right.

4/9 - Lakes and Lochs

I knew someone who had a huge African lake as one of their main features, absolutely teeming with the most exotic of wild life. (But, I trust, minus mosquitoes!)

Still mountain lakes, or park-like civilised lakes with little romantic islands can be fun as well.

Lochs are perhaps the most magical in the 'large body of fresh water' department, and of course, you know what lives in a loch!

Magic of a different kind can be experienced by lakes formed in meteor craters and old volcanoes. In fact, a couple of people who had a troublesome volcano ended up turning it into such a lake with many practically beneficial effects for them and their loved ones.

4/10 - Artificial Bodies Of Water

Swimming pools, Jacuzzi's, sunken baths, fish ponds, and especially set ups with decorative fountains can be used to cheer up any kind of Sanctuary lay out. The Chinese hold goldfish to be a symbol of wealth, so stock up your aquarium!

Canals and aqueducts are fascinating too and can be created to ferry water to a previously parched region.

Dammed rivers (God! Doesn't that sound like "damned rivers"!) are something that doesn't feel good to me personally, but you never know - for you such a thing might be just the job to generate energy, create a recreational lake and stop lower lying land from being continuously flooded.

4/11 - Water From The Sky

I love the rain. I've always felt it purifies, cleans the air, and everything looks so much greener and brighter after a heavy rainfall, it's as though the entire world has been through the car wash.

So in my Sanctuary, rain is very welcome and I've in fact used it to rejuvenate, clear and energise parts of the landscape that needed it. Others have used rain to create new bodies of water, put out fires, cut pathways into mountain ranges, still volcanoes and turn deserts into flowering meadows.

Snow too can have its uses. It can preserve and, in its rightful place (such as on mountain tops and the like) or rightful time (I like a white Christmas in my Sanctuary) can create the most breathtakingly beautiful landscapes you've ever seen. It isn't ever much of a problem because it can be easily melted by bringing in the sun.

Hail, on the other hand, is one of those natural phenomena that I haven't yet found a great deal of practical use for. Because of its tendency to flatten and smash things, it goes against my idea that you should be kind to everything in the Sanctuary and find a way to transmute and develop, rather than to fight, injure or destroy. But, as all things in nature have a place, no doubt there will come a time when I figure that one out and hail can then be welcomed home and integrated too.

To conclude this section on water, I would just point out that in a way, all these different manifestations are linked and part of a larger system.

The well becomes the brook, the brook the river, the river the river giant, the river giant the estuary, the estuary the ocean, the ocean the clouds, the clouds the rain, the rain the subterranean rivers and finally, the well. I would therefore suggest that eventually all your water features *will find their connections and become a completely integrated, fluid whole.*

5 - THE PLANT KINGDOM

5/1 - Inviting The Plant Kingdoms

Any Sanctuary would be a sad place indeed in the absence of representatives of the plant kingdom.

Some of the saddest people I have met had representations of dust bowls, grey wastelands and stony deserts inside, and they literally began to bloom once they turned their hand to gardening a little.

"Don't cast your seeds on stony ground" is good advice indeed. For any plant person to be able to thrive, there's got to be the four main conditions of light, water, soil and nutrients firmly established.

Thank the Lord gardening in the Sanctuary doesn't involve a shovel and a pick! Nor, for that matter, does it involve never ending misery such as lawn care - when my interdimensional meadows threatened to go out of control, I acquired a 'sheep per acre' instead; it makes for a nice pastoral scene as well as solving that problem once and for all. Later, I traded half the sheep for a flock of unicorns - well, why not?

It seems that most people instinctively go for a managed, garden-type affair near the centre of their Sanctuary, and more natural features further out, with real untamed wilderness towards the furthest realms, but remember to suit yourself completely and only ever do what's right for you.

5/2 - Gardens

I'm sure you're familiar with terms such as 'Garden of Remembrance', 'Garden of Contemplation' and the like. If you're a Gill Edwards fan, you probably already have a 'Garden of Prosperity' somewhere in your internal mindscape. Point is, that you can have a 'garden of absolutely anything' to represent concerns and experience solutions in good old metaphorical form.

A 'Garden of Relationships' - oh ho! Any weeds in there, m'dear? - a 'Garden of Health', or even, very specifically, a 'Garden Of My Bloody Ex Wife', for that matter! (Oh, by the way, if that really appealed to you, don't go stomping on the plants, no matter how much you feel like it at the moment. Put a high fence around it and deal with it when you're in a more enlightened frame of mind!)

This in itself is good fun, very beneficial and often highly thought provoking.

It becomes really transformational if you set these specialist areas into a kind of 'Garden Of My Entire Life' context, and then go ahead and create something that is pleasing as an overall effort, **embracing and bringing together the various sub-sections in a harmonious manner**, which after all is the purpose and key concept of the whole Sanctuary idea.

If you're not into gardening and haven't really got a clue about plants other than that there are red ones and yellow ones, you might either like to look at a few gardens from real life with a view to copying them to start with, or to turn the task over to the parts of you that have an affinity with nature. If you can't find such a part yet, you can most likely get a past life self to help, because for thousands of years people survived mostly by agriculture of some kind and there's bound to be a few of those in your karmic link. If the worst comes to the worst, a direct plea for help send to the Universe at large will bring forth a few itinerant gardeners from God knows where - it's amazing how many of these guys are out there, just dying to be of help and spending their boring astral lives hoping and praying that someone will finally ask for assistance.

5/3 - Parkscapes & Trees

It is possible that the parkscapes bring you into contact with the plant equivalents of giant rivers - the really big, really old, really impressive trees.

I'm sure you heard this tale about Aspen groves being the largest living organisms on earth, all interconnected below the soil level and in communication with each other. I reckon that trees everywhere, but most especially in the Sanctuary, should be treated with respect. Just because they don't talk doesn't mean they're not alive, aware, and important.

Trees can advise you, give you strength and comfort, and simply hypnotise you with their presence, their sounds and their sights.

According to dream dictionaries, various trees are supposed to represent various things, but I shouldn't bother with this if I were you. Invite the tree kingdom into your Sanctuary and allow yourself to be entranced by their sheer magic which is subtly different for every species and every individual within the species again.

Together and in groups, forests, or groves they also have further magic where the total is more and different than just the sum of the parts.

One more thing on the subject of trees. As you know, 'from little acorns mighty oak trees grow'. A popular way of creating new inner resources or to install, as it were, beliefs, values or attitudes in a very ecological manner is via the medium of tree planting.

Jenny, for example, felt she needed more strength. She came up with the idea of planting an acorn and dedicating it as her 'new strength'. It was interesting to note that she took quite a while to decide just where this needed to be in the context of the surrounding landscapes, garden and other features; I like that, because everything interconnects with everything else on some level. She duly planted the acorn, and, as it grew gently and steadily, she reported physically being able to feel a kind of excitement and energy building that she had never felt before.

Not just beliefs and attitudes can be addressed via the trees, but any kind of long term project that requires growth from a small start to an eventually magnificent structure.

Jason, who had just started out with his own business, planted Californian Redwood seeds in its honour - and the progress these little trees made, and the problems they experienced, reflected beautifully what was going on in real terms, in the real world. At one point, when he went to look at them, there had been an erosion of some sort and their roots were exposed; some had even fallen over. He build a protecting wall a little way above them on the hillside, and worried about 'what it might mean' all through the next two days and nights. Finally, he got up at 4am and felt compelled to look at his business plan. To his amazement, he found a simple addition error which, had he not discovered it, would have led to his business becoming seriously under funded when more orders started to come in. He told me later that he was so excited by this that he really had to stop himself from ringing me there and then!

5/4 - Greenhouses

Thelma, an elderly lady, created a greenhouse in which there grew the most wonderful and exotic medicinal plants. She had a whole host of minor health problems and just made plant labels for each one, got some pots and asked her unconscious mind to provide the seeds that were appropriate. In due course they arrived - delivered by a postie! -

and she planted them according to the instructions. Needless to say, the plants grew well.

An old and very wise Chinese medicinal plant expert arrived and advised her on what she had to do to turn the plants into potions, as in some cases it was the flowers, or the roots, seeds or leaves that had the cures within them and they needed to be processed in highly specific ways for maximum potency. As an aside, what was really interesting about this particular story was that once she had all the bottles with the cures, she experienced a strong reluctance to taking any of them - it turned out that visiting various health people and talking about diseases were her main occupations, and she was worried that she might really get cured by taking them!

Greenhouses can be excellent shelters and supportive environments for any weak or young or delicate plants. One lady who had done a visualisation exercise with someone else which involved imagining herself to be a plant had come up with a sad and shrivelled thing that, in spite of all of her best efforts on the inner mind front, remained miserable and droopy and distinctly unhealthy looking. Once she put 'her plant' into a custom made greenhouse with strictly controlled temperature and feeding routine, it began to thrive and was eventually 'hardened off' (a gardening term which denotes desensitising a plant slowly to living outside) enough to be planted in pride of place in the centre of her Sanctuary. This lady had suffered from eczema all her life and this receded more and more, until one morning, when the plant's first flower opened, it was completely gone.

5/5 - Orchards

Once, whilst just chilling out in my Sanctuary, it occurred to me that I was hungry and that there was nothing to eat anywhere. Now I could have manifested an instant banquet, but that didn't feel quite right and so I began to create an orchard instead.

To begin with, it just had boring old apple trees and the like; but later, I began to develop my own genetically engineered plant life. For example, I've got this tree-like affair that has, below the bark, a dry, slightly honeycomb like texture, is a delightful orange yellow in colour and tastes a bit like a mango. I can't get enough of the stuff, it's delicious! Tomato-sized strawberries and variations of nuts the like of which you've never met before are also present.

The orchard is a very popular feature with all manner of my astral visitors; if you feel like a healthy snack, you are free to come by and pick your own; it's expansive and there's enough for everyone. Just one thing - try not to scare the unicorns. They're a bit shy.

5/6 - Garden Architecture

In a Sanctuary, garden architecture can be much more than merely decorative. Gazebos, for example, can be portals to other planes of reality, distant star systems, past lives, the light, or any place within the entire Universe, time and space you would want to go.

They can also be arrival points for visitors of all kinds; and before you freak out, thinking that there may be all manner of unwanted astral folk pouring through without your permission, I would suggest that as it's your portal, it will only work when you will it to do so. **It is perfectly safe.**

Later on, you might feel you're ready to allow your unconscious self to also use the portal at will and to manifest whatever might need your attention in some way.

Quite a few people have a Stonehenge-type stone circle as a feature; and you can just about begin to imagine what powerful and wondrous opportunities a fully functioning version might present to you. By the way, Lazarus reckons that they were designed to be made of quartz crystal instead of rock - can you imagine the power of Stonehenge at its heyday, full size, at the equinox, and in crystal?

A lot of people are totally fascinated with pyramids; and there are all kinds of claims to their amazing powers for healing and transformation. You could have one of those, if you should want one.

Sculpture in general and statues in particular can also be added for beauty, interest or to represent some aspect of your inner self or other. There is a visualisation exercise in which you imagine that a great artist created a statue of you. If you are intrigued about your own perception of who or what you are, this might be an exercise you could find valuable; if you have already done this exercise, find the statue, bring it into your garden and then transform it so it is entirely to your liking and a fitting addition to the beauty and tranquillity of your Sanctuary.

Here's just a few more structures that have cropped up in the past for your consideration:

Windmills and watermills; Summer Houses; Towers; Churches; Temples of all shapes and sizes; Crystal Domes; Mushroom shaped houses; Playgrounds; Altars, to name just a few.

5/7 - Agricultural And Managed Landscapes

Whether to you personally a huge field of golden wheat is a symbol of abundance and prosperity, or whether you view it as an abhorrent example of post modern monoculture, there's a great deal of often forgotten emotion and meaning tied up in agriculture through the ages, even if you've lived in a city all your life.

Agriculture in its widest meaning doesn't just mean ploughing fields. There are managed forests, orchards we've mentioned before, vineyards, herb gardens, managed rubber trees in the midst of a tropical rain forest, fields of roses and sunflowers, and pastures too of all kinds; whatever takes your fancy, really.

You are free to choose to have any agricultural landscape, and you are free to do what you wish to do with them and have them serve whatever purposes they may serve you, I would just point out that you are not restricted to merely re-creating already existing agriculture; you can have an orchard of money-bearing trees, a hedge to harvest a never ending supply of magic wands, a managed forest of extraterrestrial giant singing orchids or meadows of freely growing crystals and diamonds, should you so desire; and do remember that no matter what the size of your agricultural endeavours, you need never worry about getting enough help at harvest time!

5/8 - Untamed Wilderness

These days it's rare to find places where people haven't yet changed the landscape into something of their own making (and this may be a beautiful park as well as a toxic wasteland). If you've stood in such a wild place, then you will be very familiar with how small it makes you feel, how vulnerable and how exhilarated at the same time.

Whether it's a huge roaming sea of grassland under an enormous sky, a forbiddingly beautiful expanse of mountain range, the ocean, an elder forest, an ancient heath, a blistering desert - I mean, wow! No wonder people get so frightened of these places that they'll do anything to make then more cosy and break their powerful spell!

The Gaia theory holds that our planet is more like a living organism than a dead football made of rock floating about in space. It holds that all the various habitats work together to keep the organism as a whole, as a functioning, self regulating ecology.

By definition I take this to mean that every kind of wilderness habitat you may encounter in your wider Sanctuary will probably have a contribution to make. Thereby, I get a little worried when, after the original central Sanctuary space has been park-scaped to the owner's requirements, they then go ahead and turn the whole internal planet into something you might have seen in a Sci-Fi movie or whilst driving through Milton Keynes - a spooky and kind of lifeless advertising agency's version of 'paradise, 1960's style'.

Sure, having a nasty black swamp smack in the middle of your Sanctuary isn't going to make you feel better; however, further out, a swamp might be needed in the overall ecology as a whole. Talk to any botanist or biologist about swamps, and they go into raptures about the interesting, varied and abundant life they support, and how clearing and draining them has had dreadful and far ranging effects on the ecology as a whole. I'm not suggesting here to not change things or to 'learn to love your swamps'. What I am suggesting is that whenever you begin to deal with the wider areas of untamed wilderness, to be firstly a little respectful to begin with, and secondly to **ALWAYS give serious consideration to the greater ecology** before you start waving your magic wand.

6 - THE MINERAL KINGDOM

Even people who scoff at the New Age fascination with pet crystals usually fall very quiet and reflective if you put a small piece of quartz, opal or gold into their hands.

It's difficult not to become thoughtful and reverent at their beauty and complexity, the sensation, feeling and weight they convey, their timeless age and purity.

One of the most amazing presents I've ever received was a small meteorite, which looked like a cigar end - brown, mottled and cylindrical. When I held it, I couldn't help but think that this little representative of the mineral kingdom had travelled amongst the stars, had seen the earth grow larger and larger on his approach, burning through the atmosphere and finally coming to rest on the downs not far from my home where he might have waited for hundreds of thousands of years before my friend found him.

I have the greatest respect for the mineral kingdom.

If you're ever stuck for strength, clarity and a timeless patient wisdom, you might like to look to this kingdom for assistance; if you're after beauty and abundance, it must be surely amongst your first choices.

Once again, I would like you to consider approaching the mineral kingdom with an open mind and without prejudice; many are the books on the meaning, properties and uses of the various crystals, minerals etc. and there are very few that agree on anything much past the basics.

Like any other relationship, what place you choose to accord to a mountain, a pearl or a rose quartz crystal for that matter, is a personal relationship between them and you; and like any other Sanctuary relationship, they are there to support you, help and guide you - all you have to do is want it to be so.

7 - CIVILISATION IN THE SANCTUARY

To start with, any Sanctuary tends to be a confined smallish mindscape and whatever primary dwellings and structures there exist within are all there is in the way of traces of civilisation.

Sooner or later, other areas of civilisation tend to appear, from tiny hamlets to giant cities via anything in between; most of these bring with them challenges in some form or the other, but as you know by now, these challenges are nothing compared to the resource you have for solving the puzzles and overcoming the problems elegantly and completely.

Sometimes the Sanctuary owner feels like building a city, community or dwelling of their own accord and for a particular purpose; this can be as easy or as time-consuming and involved a task as you might want it to be.

7/1 - Roads & Connections

The Roman Empire would have gotten nowhere without the road building crews they sent up ahead; the American West could not have been opened successfully without the railroads.

I have lost count of how many people, who experienced a kind of 'stuck-ness' in their lives, be it regarding relationships, jobs, or general dissatisfaction, went on to then experience an amazing unfolding of possibilities and opportunities once they'd started to put in a few connections with the outer reaches of their inner space, beyond the inner Sanctuary.

It didn't seem to matter much if they put in the equivalent of a medieval rutted track or a ten lane super highway, in every case this always 'led to something new', if you'll pardon the expression!

Although in Sanctuary terms transportation is not a problem in any way (as you can simply 'wish yourself' to wherever you want to go, fly yourself, ride a dragon or even a broomstick if that's what turns you on), there does seem to be a strong connection between forward movement towards new ends and aims and the building of such permanent infra structures.

Roads, however, do not have to be confined to strictly literal roads.

Jessica had always wanted to travel, but was 'stuck' with her young baby in a small council flat on social security. She surprised me by deciding very early on to have a railway station and a shining track, upon which a huge back steam engine with 'Oriental Express' type luxury carriages awaited her and her child. Being the very picture of a modern girl, I don't know where that came from, but it certainly worked for her; the Universe unfolded and just a couple of months later, she moved to London, found a new man and a job in a company that organises big club events which entails, she tells me, both travel and excitement in plenty.

You can travel on waterways too; in one case, a young man whose Sanctuary was a small island experienced the unfolding shift after creating a new bay complete with a harbour and ocean going vessels; someone else put in a number of airports; yet someone else again had so many rivers that they needed to build a lot of bridges before any kind of regular overland travel was possible.

On the topic of overland travel, I will always gratefully remember a gentleman of Oriental origin who connected various cities, dwellings and landscapes by an elaborate caravan route; a very romantic and stimulating idea, I thought; so I went ahead and stole that from him (Sanctuary features aren't yet trademark-able!) just so that every so often an exotic caravan would stop by my Sanctuary to trade my crystals and fruit for the most amazing and unusual artefacts, creatures, substances and materials.

However, I took that idea just one little step further - my own exotic caravan has a route that takes in most of the important planets in the Alpha Quadrant - well, why confine oneself to Planet Earth when there's so much more fun to be had when you take a larger part of the galaxy into consideration?

8 - DREAM SPACES

8/1 - Resolving Dreams

Anne, a fellow therapist and a good friend, dreamed of starving kittens repeatedly over a period of years. The dreams were frightening and depressing and always proceeded along the same lines:

She would be quite happy in some landscape or other, and then would come across a litter of near starved kittens of about 3-4 weeks old. They were skin and bones and obviously unloved and abandoned. After each dream she'd wake up scared and full of dread.

Dream books hardly mention kittens specifically and a cat is held to be some symbol of the female. That, as usual, didn't help a bit. She thought about it, wrote herself letters, discussed it with anyone who would listen, and still got no further in understanding the meaning of these dreams or what to do in order to stop having to have them.

As time went by, these dreams became more frequent and the kittens were in a ever more desperate condition. Now, when she discovered the nest, there were some dead already, and some even maggot riddled. She was getting desperate and very worried.

Finally she took up my suggestion to create a basic Sanctuary structure complete with guides and help built in. She designed a dream space - in her case something not unlike the holodeck on the starship Enterprise, in which the main points of the dream could be re-created.

Standing outside the holodeck, she gave the instruction, "Re-create kitten dreams" and the door opened and she stepped inside.

We were both shocked at what she found. Cages upon cages upon cages stacked up the walls of a large, large warehouse type affair, with dead or dying kittens in each. There were so many of them! Thousands upon thousands in that huge space - whatever was going on here, it was major.

Now, what to do? Anne expressed a real sense of urgency - some were still alive and they needed immediate attention. So, as I often do when faced with overwhelm in such situations, I suggested we call in whatever reinforcements would make themselves available.

A big crowd of people arrived right away - healers of all kinds, allopathic and holistic, real ones, imaginary ones and dead ones, a veritable army of astral healers. They began organising something like a conveyor belt process by which cage after cage was opened, the kitten extracted, put to one side if already dead and treated immediately if still alive. There was a feeling of working around the clock, although in real terms little time had passed, of course, and finally the situation was under control.

The exhausted team of healers heaved a sigh of relief and just stood about, chatting amongst themselves when, at the back of the hall, a glowing circle of bright light appeared. Out of the light came adult cats of all shapes and sizes, and each one gently picked up one of the injured kittens and then returned into the light. Then, that light source closed and another, less bright and more like ultraviolet light appeared. From it came ghost cats who went to the dead kittens lying in a row. On approach of the ghost cat, a small kitten shape detached itself from the body, and was lovingly carried away to the other light whilst the body simply dissolved away.

Anne was crying and shaking after it was all over; I was marvelling again at this piece of interesting conscious/unconscious communication - her unconscious had repeatedly presented a major concern; we'd consciously entered into the process by deciding to bring in the healers, and Anne's unconscious **had responded by finishing the story and bringing it to an amazing and very wonderful conclusion.**

I asked her to go home and to make a note in her diary of this day and to put in a corresponding date six months from there, to check back and to see what kind of changes had happened in her life, as I was as puzzled and intrigued by the whole affair as she was.

Firstly, she has never dreamed about kittens since - it's been about a year now. We can presume that whatever the issue was, it really had been thoroughly resolved. The most noticeable differences she found was firstly an intense increase in creativity of all kind - she hasn't stopped painting since and her paintings 'before' and 'after' are very different; the 'after' kind being much more vibrant, powerful and saleable.

She's completely redecorated her entire house and her income has doubled from very unlikely sources, such as all of a sudden finding an American publisher for a series of self-help books she wrote ten years ago. Is that because of the kittens? You know what I'm going to say by now - I've no idea! She's a happier person, that much I know, and when she goes to bed at night, she smiles in anticipation of what she's going to dream about.

8/2 - Placing The Dream

Having a dream space to recreate and address dreams is a really neat thing. As with all Sanctuary features, the more often you use it, the more real it becomes and the easier it is to do. A dream space could take the form of an amphitheatre, a movie house, a theatre, a stage, a film studio set, a clearing somewhere, or even a special room in your house or subterranean structure.

Sometimes, dreams take place in a very specific landscape, time of day, placement, if you will.

In these cases it is of the essence, for the structure and fabric of the dream to remain cohesive and the message or action that needs to be taken to be correct, that the **entire dream is fully re-created** and, in this case, you end up with a new mindscape in Sanctuary that is an addition to your usual Sanctuary spaces, an enlargement that might well need to be put into the context of the rest of your inner world by means of direction or connection - where is it? How do you get from Sanctuary to that space?

This is a most profound activity to be undertaking, namely to **connect** the dream space with your Sanctuary realms and to understand just what happens when you do. Apart from your own attention, what else will travel from one to the other? What happens to the ecology of both? What needs to be done, learned, changed, accepted, understood to have the dream space become a **full and active part** of the landscapes, or the universe in which both they and your Sanctuary exist?

Whether you wish to undertake this connection with some of your dream spaces depends often on the content and feel of the dream - if it is very frightening or seems threatening, you might prefer to leave that world encapsulated for a while longer. And this brings us to the topic of ...

8/3 - Frightening Dreams

If dreams are just too scary to recreate in a dream space at all, even in the encapsulated safe version, you can disassociate from them by watching them as a movie or video with some helpers around you; one gentleman dealt with a nasty recurring nightmare about zombies and vampires by using an editing suite such as you would find in a film production company, and replaced himself with a current screen action hero who could be trusted to deal with the problems quite easily.

A young child had the brilliant idea of turning a recurring nightmare into a cartoon - this translated it away enough from the original experience to take the emotional charge out of it and made it easier for him to find solutions.

Another person created a repeated dream-world in a bubble in space and visited it as though they were a ghost or an angel there - non-material in nature, being able to observe and move about but without being noticed themselves or in any kind of physical danger.

I know of two people who both dreamed of a giant floodwave coming towards them. One became a dolphin and moved into the wave; the other switched view points and **became the wave** - a most incredible experience, from their description.

A young gentlemen repeatedly dreamed of walking in a pleasant landscape that turned to marsh beneath his feet, then water in which he would drown. He took the dream into Sanctuary and as he sank into the water, transformed himself into a fishlike creature and found, much to his surprise, sunken treasure at the bottom of the lake the landscape had become.

We have mentioned this before, but I'd like to repeat that if you have any dream 'nasties', be they landscapes, creatures, people or whatever, be as kind to them as you can find in your heart to be. If you can't find any kindness whatever, keep them in some kind of safe and supporting holding area for them. This is an interim solution to allow the problem to be contained whilst you gather further resources or just think about what you will eventually do to set them free.

The most important thing with bad dreams is to move them forward however and let them run on to a satisfactory conclusion. By bringing in our conscious will it is easy to do and I have not heard of a single case where the nightmare came back in the same form, for simply, whatever the issue had been, it becomes resolved when you answer the call in this way.

8/4 - Beautiful Dreams

Nice or even amazing dreams are, incidentally, perfectly placed to suggest additions that make you feel better to your Sanctuary.

Lillian dreamed of meeting a man who just sat beside her and she experienced a sense of complete relaxation and peace, not having to speak to him or do anything at all, and that it was 'alright for him to be there' - a sensation and experience she had never had in real life before with any person, man or woman, or not so that she could remember. This experience gave her a baseline of what she wanted in her guides and companions and showed her a quality of relationship and way of being that became centrally important in her further dealings, first in Sanctuary and then in 'real life'.

Following a dream which involved a pair of white swans majestically gliding across a beautiful lake and which left her feeling intensely relaxed, joyful and light, Joanna added this feature to her Sanctuary, and reports that she has the same good feelings every time she visits there.

On the subject of chirpy birds, Rob had a dream featuring a giant albatross by which he was particularly enchanted and so he adopted the albatross and even created an ocean for him to fish in, and, when it occurred to him later on, a female for company. They went on to breed successfully and, last I heard, there were many of these amazing birds to be seen, soaring above a dramatic seascape.

9 - RELATIONSHIPS

9/1 - Individual Freedom Of Expression

I truly believe that each of us has all the resources - mental, spiritual and magical - to overcome absolutely everything the Universe wishes to test us against.

The main use of the Sanctuary as I see it is to allow us to have somewhere safe where we can rest, heal, experiment and grow, in our own time, in our own way. I have already said this in various different ways before, but here it goes again, this time in the form of a quote from Krishnamurti:

"I believe that the truth is a pathless land, and that it cannot be discovered through any teacher, leader, sect, religion, or organisation. Individuals need to discover for themselves their own unconditioned truth so that they may be truly free."

So how, when and why you will choose to use your Sanctuary and to what end is nobody's business but your own. You do what you want to and how you want to do it, in your own time, using as your resources and your guides those that you meet within.

It is important for you to know that you do not need to see a special counsellor, and that the process you have started will go forward under your own guidance for as long as you wish to make good use of it. The following chapters only contain suggestions and examples, they are not operating instructions. They may also very well be quite incomplete.

Although I have used these ideas for a good few years and with many very different people, each new person still brings with them new surprises and images that I couldn't have conceived of in a thousand years.

So, after this disclaimer, let's take a look at some of the uses we've found so far and how you can go about getting the kind of benefits we've been able to enjoy, starting with the area that, according to some, has the most profound effect on our lives.

9/2 - It's All A Part Of Me ...

Now if you ever want to truly boggle your mind, do as I have just done and, on a big piece of blank paper, write the heading 'Relationships'.

Wow. Where do you start?

Perhaps with the interesting quote: "You are the people you have met."

People are so damn complicated. You think you know someone, and then they turn around and rip the tenuous carpet of reality on which we are perched right from under us and send us reeling into confusion, anger, love and hate. Then they die on us and we suffer bereavement for the rest of our lives. What fun!

There is a school of thought that holds that everyone we have ever interacted with becomes a 'part' of us.

This belief is by no means confined to Gestalt Therapists and Neuro Linguistic Programmers.

It turns up in different guises also in various religions, in magic, and shamanism. In fact, the NLP technique of 'parts integration' - where negotiations are held with conflicting sub-personalities in order for them to change their often wicked ways - has been called 'voodoo without the dolls' by some. Another term for such sub-personalities that have somehow become detached and are now functioning independently is found in the idea of 'Soul Loss' - the same idea, just a different phrase.

I think the word 'parts' is alright to use, and it has made sense for me in the past to use the following belief system. So, every person you have ever had a relationship with exists within you as a memory, an internal representation, for short, as a part. The longer and/or the more intense the relationship, the larger the part, and the stronger this part's influence on the whole that is you.

As these parts are part of you, their function is generally held to be to serve you in some way, to aid you in your survival, growth and happiness.

However, many of these parts go about it in a way that is less than straightforward and often, they cause a lot of trouble by the means to their ends.

A heroin addict may have a part that wants him to be happy - and the happiest he ever is, is when he's on a fix. So this part might continue to drive the behaviour in all good faith that it is doing everything it can to make him happy. Of course, in the long run, it's going to make him extremely unhappy - only the part was formed inside when he was only 14 months old, it only lives for the now, and has never grown up to make wiser or more long term choices.

A part that might appear in an 'external' form could be a long forgotten parish priest who still spooks through someone's neurology and now makes having sex with the new girlfriend out of wedlock strangely impossible.

Now if you've never heard of these ideas before, you might be thinking "Oh my God! What a nightmare! All these people I thought I had finally left behind! And they're still there? Having a bearing on my life today? Aaargh!"

Certainly. But look on the bright side. It has its advantages too. It means - and that's just for starters! - *that you can settle any conflict with anyone*, no matter where they are, no matter if they're dead or alive or even imaginary, no matter if in the real world they would have you shot, safely and neatly in your Sanctuary and thus help to reduce conflict within yourself and give you more energy and freedom to go ahead and manifest the things you really want out of life.

Let's look at a few strategies to first of all begin to make peace with your most important relationship.

9/3 - Relationships With The Self

I am simply not the same person I was 20 years ago.

If I could travel through time and meet myself aged 18, she would not recognise me, and I would only recognise her because I've seen her in pictures.

I find it very hard to even remember what used to be important to her, and as far as her views on life, the Universe and everything go, it hurts my head to even begin to get into rapport with her now.

No doubt you too have made major steps in your life at one point or the other that have led you to be the person who you are today, perhaps more seamlessly than I did, perhaps even less so.

The point is that even without major traumas interfering and creating sub-personalities within the self that are then frozen in time and cannot go on to grow up with you, our minds are littered with past selves.

The more different they are from the way we are now, the more potential for expanding the self to something more than the sum of your parts exists - if they can be integrated, healed, communicated and made peace with in some way.

9/3/1 - Children & Babies

I sometimes can't help myself but cry when I hear what happens when people begin to bring lost, unloved and abandoned past selves into their Sanctuaries. Terrified children who were never consoled, hungry children who weren't fed, desperate children who no-one ever listened to, forsaken children wandering in wastelands, shrivelled babies starved of all nourishment, wild children who are so afraid of humans that they hide in the wilderness, angry, ferocious children more like beasts than humans, deformed and misshapen ones, beaten ones, abused ones - the metaphorical representations of the every day traumas of growing up in this so-called civilised society of ours.

But finally, here is now someone who can make it alright. Who can be the loving support they never had. Someone who truly understands them and forgives them. Someone who will never let them down and who loves them with all their heart.

You.

An impossible task?

No. You can bring them one at a time into your Sanctuary as you become aware of their existence. In this safe and healing space they will become well even if left to themselves over time; but of course, there are ways and means of speeding this process along. After the initial contact, older past selves can be employed to help look after them until they're fully grown; angels can heal, soothe and love, you can enclose them in loving light or even have your higher self give them love directly from The Source (God, Goddess, All There Is, The Universe).

Some people baulk at this next option, but others have found it very helpful to have more enlightened versions of the original parents take over the care of the child, this time doing it properly and raising it with unconditional love and regard. Representations of grandparents or other relatives can also be of help.

Inner child therapies of all forms and kinds have been popular for many years now, and rightly so. If you already have favourite approaches in this area, go ahead and use these - the Sanctuary space allows you to integrate everything you've learned, no matter where, and no matter when. Whatever processes you want to use to this end, I'm sure your internal systems will be the better for it.

What happens to these children after they have been healed? Well, some tell me the child simply dissolves into sparkles of light, others embrace the child and feel it become part of themselves once more, others still see the child remaining in the Sanctuary, playing happily amongst the beauty and safety there. Either which way, once you have done something like this, you will know that it is a profoundly emotional and profoundly freeing process which will in many small ways contribute to your well being from thereon in.

9/3/2 - Older Children & Teenagers

The transition from the childhood self to the adult self is marked by many inherent conflicts, even if the family in which you grew up was exceptionally supportive and your life exceptionally stress free and the others in your class and neighbourhood exceptionally nice.

Then there's the whole sorry area of sexuality - not that sexuality is sorry, but that the way it's been dealt with, expressed and experienced is more often than not a complete shambles of grand proportions.

Because of the intense emotions present at that time, residue is created that vibrates through the rest of an adult's lifetime.

I've heard people declare themselves sexually aberrant after just a single one unfortunate experience in their youth and then go forth and punish themselves with utter misery for the next 50 years or so.

We will look at how to deal with problem memories in the Sanctuary at a later date - for now, let's just stick with calling these poor young people home.

The nice thing about this age range is that they can speak for themselves, and will express amazing revelations to you if encouraged to do so. See, I don't think teenagers are irrational at all. They're intense, yes, and sometimes they haven't learned to reign themselves in like an adult would. They have also mostly not yet got a perspective of time which allows them to view any problem in a greater context - every problem is right here and it is mountainous. But whenever I've talked to any teenager, in real life or within someone's Sanctuary, I could always see that they were expressing real concerns that mattered to them, and most were damn right in their assertion that "nobody understands me" - the adults around them mostly didn't even try very hard.

The trick when dealing with younger selves is to make sure you step out of your enlightened wise adult persona and allow yourself to really remember what it was like at that time. How wearing the right hair slide was so incredibly important; how one look or a comment from someone at school could truly mean the end of the world; how wonderfully exciting it was to do the forbidden things.

A few people reported that upon meeting with their persona now, the younger self expressed dismay at what they had become; in these cases the drive and enthusiasm of the younger self can be just the tonic that was needed to start the now persona on the road to brighter and better things.

Generally however, younger selves are pretty amazed at all the things you can do; driving a car, doing your work, coping with children, whatever - either way, the 'injured teenager within' is a truly amazing experience, be it as simply a conversational partner, a mirror for you across time, or just as the means to overcome some problem that is bugging you now in your every day life.

9/3/3 - Adult Younger Selves

If you're 90, an adult younger self can be as old as 89 and still be classed as a 'younger adult self'. In this category, especially if you have been breeding, are many opportunities for soul loss, loss of self, conflict, and dispersal of energy - that's why such a lot of people have faded to grey by the time they're 55.

I find that it doesn't do to treat younger adult selves (or YADs, from now on) as too grown up. Any YADs that come to you for help or appear with a plea for resolution, or turn up as the result of your investigating a problem situation that has occurred in the real world, probably lack some of the basic nourishments - hope, trust, love, friendship, fun, creativity, sex, security.

Here's an example: Nick was an advertising man, good looking, very creative, highly paid, and globally hated by everyone at work. He'd had three tribunals already to do with such things as sexual harassment, bullying at work and the like, had 'gone through' 15 secretaries in less than three years, and the only reason the boss hadn't fired him years ago was that a talent like that was extremely hard to come by, and the highest paying clients of the firm demanded his services. Nick's private life was not much better; he lived alone and paid for whatever services he required in the housekeeping and companionship departments. Now, you might say, this does not sound like the personality structure of someone who would seek help from a holistic counsellor, and you'd be dead right there. His boss made him come and see me under threat of finally losing his job.

I could well imagine how his secretaries must have felt; he was a powerful, aggressive and unpredictable entity that easily filled my spacious room. So I said to him, "Let's talk about the injured child within", and he hit the roof like a rocket! When he saw that I was laughing, he calmed down somewhat and allowed me, under the guise of "Let's just get this over with and we'll tell the boss we've done all we could", to show him the paintings around my place, most of which have metaphorical themes.

Less than fifteen minutes later, he was freely hallucinating volcanoes, fire breathing dragons, magic chalices and all sorts, completely absorbed in his own inner world. Then, he sat up with a start and asked me if it was normal that there were two of him. Two of him? Yes, himself and another him - an evil twin. (I must confess to thinking at that point that if the Nick in my office was the good one of the two, I would certainly not have wanted to meet the other one!)

At any rate, conversation between the two wasn't getting anywhere, and in the end, they fought each other in a mediaeval setting, with lightning striking all around them. After slugging it out for the best part of half an hour - I must admit, the running commentary was fascinating and I had to remind myself to breathe every so often - Good Nick finally won out.

Real Nick stretched like a big cat and smiled happily.

"Wow." he said. "That was amazing. I haven't had so much fun in years! I feel great! No wonder so many people go to shrinks - can I come again next week? Please?"

The point is that just because a part manifests as a younger adult self or even, as in this case, an alternate adult self, doesn't mean that they are grown up, or sensible, or even rational. The way Nick dealt with this part was about as far away from my own understanding of how to do these things correctly as you can get, and at the time I had sincere doubts whether it was a good way to go about it. **In general, damaging or hurting any part of yourself damages and hurts you - because it's part of you, of course**. That's like "if thine eye offends thee, cut it out"; personally, I lean towards the alternative "if thine eye offends thee, do a quick sub modality change and then have an aromatherapy bath by candle light" instead.

Also, slaying a part right out as Nick had done can and usually does have long lasting repercussions in some form or the other, because the mind is an interactive system where everything is balanced and working together. Even when there's conflict, this conflict has been part of what was a functioning system of sorts for a very long time, and the outcomes of such invasive surgery are usually highly unpredictable.

Still, neither one of the three Nicks were adults yet in the true sense of the word, and something that will make changes and interventions easier for you personally is to really know that anything you do can be reversed at a later date if necessary. Even a part that had been killed off can be retrieved, if this should turn out to have been damaging, by 'time machine' type strategies; and it was this knowledge that made me allow Nick to go ahead with his desire to slay the alternate self. It was what he really wanted, and it had provided an incentive for him to begin to explore more of his inner world.

As an aside, and when he'd left, I gave very humble and grateful thanks to the Universe at large and metaphor therapy in particular - with that particular client, what could have worked as well?

Adult younger selves are, in my opinion, the forgotten ones as far as personal development is concerned. So much time is spent going through people's childhoods, it is simply not generally recognised how important lost or detached or denied adult selves are to a person as a whole.

Winny had cancer. She was very bitter about this because about four years ago she had changed her life completely. She had been grossly overweight since she had been a teenager, had not had much of a social life and generally was a very unhappy person. But apparently all that changed four years ago when she went to have her stomach stapled, began exercising and following a vegetarian diet. She lost over 120 pounds and 'became a new person'.

"This is so unfair," she said bitterly. "That fat cow I used to be would have deserved that, but not me. I'm a changed person, I'm better now."

It was, interestingly for me, very sad to notice how she was deriding her previous self. She didn't have a good word for her at all, she was just some hopeless fat loser she hated, and not just wished she had never been; but declared strongly that she had no relationship whatsoever with this younger adult self.

Now obviously I'm not suggesting you are going to get cancer if you treat your previous selves in that way; however, I have a strong notion that it is a most unhealthy thing to do if you're into the idea that the mind of a person is a landscape that connects across time and space.

If the above case story rings a bell with you, the time might come when you are ready to invite your past selves in for peace talks. It might be the best thing you ever do for your self.

9/3/4 - Future Selves

Future Selves can be a tremendous resource indeed. The very idea that there is a you in the future, who has successfully negotiated and survived every problem that you are so worried about today, and not only survived but even prospered, can be a real life saver when the going gets rough. Further, future selves can be amongst the best advisors and helpers on just about any issue you need clarification on - from whether to invest in a specific company, to how to deal with a current relationship.

Now, this presumes rather that the future self represents as prosperous, happy, and well. And this is the case for most people. Some, however, experience their future selves as less than happy in some way, and this can be even more helpful in a strange way.

Shelley, for example, got such a shock when faced with a disease ridden, miserable and bitter future self that it gave her the incentive to make dramatic changes in her life style; she used the changes that manifested in the future self as a guide line as to whether she was on the right track with her real world activities. At one point, and, after having started a particularly grim regime of vegan food combining and starvation, she went to her Sanctuary to find not her future self, but instead in their usual meeting place a grave, complete with granite head stone and R.I.P!

But that's doing it the hard way, in my opinion. After all, I wouldn't be so fascinated by this whole domain if I thought that you have to stop eating chocolate in order to lose weight.

Another lady, Theresa, also found her future self to be a sad and twisted creature. She, on the other hand, chose to make her future self happier, **to change and heal the future self**, as it were; and duly and as if by magic, changes manifested for her in real life.

Like Rupert Sheldrake's Morphogenic Fields, the future self can thus be used to create the present, when it is more normally held that only the present creates the future.

This is like writing a murder mystery - you start with the solution and then the rest of the story will have to appear and all the events before will have to organise themselves in such a way that the solution can be reached.

When dealing with time in the Sanctuary, do remember that you are dealing with Quantum or Cyber Time - the past and the future have already been and gone, time is as one.

Lastly on the subject of Future Selves, (or Future's Elves, as one of my people remarked!), on the odd occasion someone feels very intimidated when meeting someone who they cannot begin to imagine will be them one day. It must be said that this was my personal experience when first we met. My future self seemed to be so - how can I put this? - together, so quietly powerful that at first I hardly dared talk to her and felt highly uncomfortable in her presence.

As I got to know her better, our communications and my self esteem improved, and she has been a great source of comfort and inspiration to me ever since.

Whether you just sit and talk, take walks around the Sanctuary, or engage in some form of activity together, this is a learning experience you should make sure you don't miss out on. I highly recommend it!

There is one last aspect of the future self that some find very difficult, yet others profoundly rewarding. This is to visit the furthest of your current future selves, i.e. You just before you die.

Those who have dared do this have reported deep changes in their perceptions about what life is all about, and what is and isn't important, or rather, what was and what wasn't important with the wisdom of hindsight.

Taking such a perspective on one's entire life is not for everyone. But you never know, one day you might just like to do it. I must warn you however, life will never seem quite the same after that.

9/3/5 - Parties Of Selves

Now I don't even remember how this came to be, but in the context of a MindMillion project there all of a sudden materialised the idea of groups of selves, learning something new in a whole new way and one that would work for all of them, as a group or entity - thus revealing some kind of global learning preference for the entirety of a self that stretched over a person's entire lifetime.

MindMillion is a prosperity-directed mastermind network and one of the most fascinating experiences in human endeavour, thought and learning you could imagine. The focus is very much on physical, practical change - members photocopy their bank statements and send them to each other so there is direct proof of change and not just talk, or feeling a bit better although you're still sitting in the exact same hole in the ground you started out in.

The idea was to have all the past selves who have any bearing on the topic of earning money come together and engage in a learning activity, with or without a teacher, doing exactly what they needed to do to make the requisite changes - whatever they might be, we did not know at that point.

We had expected that this would be a kind of school class setting with Einstein the teacher or something like that, but that was not at all what really took place.

Not for a single individual who ran this experiment was there a school room. One person really tried but all the selves just walked out immediately!

My own selves gathered in a fairly pleasant, warm country setting and then they declared the desire to sing together. I was completely astonished by this but even if I had wanted to, I could not have stopped them because as soon as the idea had been expressed, they stood or sat and started to sing, from a little 3 year old past self via a teenager with streaked hair and purposefully torn blue jeans.

Another member of the group reported that as soon as his selves had gathered, they conferred for a moment and then took off at high speed, to get on an airplane and do a lot of travelling to exotic places.

One gentlemen found his guys playing football with each other; a lady reported that her people all lay down together in a forest grove and began to sleep and dream together.

It was really extraordinary how this just happened so freely and spontaneously - and bear in mind the context had been **to learn something new** about prosperity of all things!

This really shows, in my opinion, how in the realm of metaphorical interfaces and problem solving, we have no idea of what would be for the best and usually, our conscious mind cannot even conceptualise the necessary solutions. We thought school rooms and what was really needed was singing, dreaming, playing football and travelling, amongst other and equally highly individual solutions.

What was also really amazing and fascinating about this particular example was the fact that the groups of selves completely **agreed** on the right way forward - there was no dissent at all, they **all** needed this activity, no matter how different all these other things about them had become. I have the notion that during the prosperity exercises we discovered a core need for those individuals who took part that had remained the same throughout all their life's many changes, and that is a very, very valuable thing to find out about indeed, not to mention having an opportunity to do something about it and finally fill it to their heart's content.

One night, before you drift off to sleep, or when you are contemplating a problem, question or issue, make a space and call in such a 'group of your selves' from across time. Check out what they do if left to their own devices to make them happy - and be prepared for a surprise.

9/3/6 - Selves From Past Lives

Whether past lives are really past lives, or just a metaphorical representation of a concern from this life, the fact is that hundreds of thousands of people all over the world have successfully used Reincarnation Therapy and Past Life Regression (PLR) to make deep, lasting and profound changes in their lives.

For those of you who have done PLR already, you might like to make use of resources, learnings and experiences represented by the various people that you were at one point or the other.

I have a Jesuit priest amongst mine who comes to visit my Sanctuary every so often, and who can provide very enlightening insights on some spiritual matters - in fact, when once faced with a client who manifested a whole bunch of medieval demons, you could say his experience in this field and in depth knowledge of exorcism ritual was absolutely invaluable to me!

Another tremendous resource is a woman who had a smallholding and worked as a midwife in the Middle Ages. Her knowledge of medicinal plants and all matters relating to birthing and rearing children is second to none, and she has been of great help when we were stuck with neglected younger selves, including pre-birth younger selves, and healing matters.

Particularly nasty or unresolved past lives are also tackled much more safely and easily in the tranquillity of the Sanctuary, with the help and guidance of all those we've mentioned so far and others beside, because by taking the main characters out of their own past life scenario and transplanting them and the issues they represent into this familiar and other setting, it is much harder to become emotionally overwhelmed or freaked out. (A technical term, by the way, denoting an instantaneous loss of belief in the ability to cope.)

If you have never done any PLR, it could just be possible (especially after reading this!) that a past life concern might turn up in your Sanctuary.

Heather found at one time, upon taking a walk in hers, a badly injured middle-aged man. He had what appeared to be appalling torture wounds all over his body, had been blinded, and was very close to death. She told me how shocked she had been at first, but then decided to make his last few hours as comfortable as possible, so created a shelter with a soft bed, put soothing lotion on his wounds, and just sat with him, talking to him gently until he died quite peacefully as the sun began to rise. He transformed into the ghost of a young and powerful warrior from some past age, and he thanked her most graciously and sincerely. Then he disappeared and hasn't been heard of since.

What did it mean? I don't know. I don't even care on some level. There was a man who needed help, she gave it, lots of good feelings all around were had - that's all we can know. Whether he was from a past life, a metaphorical representation of an injured part of Heather's self, or just someone floating out there who spotted Heather's Sanctuary and thought it was a good place to get help, who knows? In the end, that's what global metaphor therapy is all about. To trust the process and not to ask too many intellectual questions, because that will get you nowhere in the enchanted realms of symbolism.

On the subject of 'many lives', if you're so inclined, you could also try a spot of 'Future Life Progression'. I've done this in the past because I'm a bit of a Sci-Fi fan and just for fun, but it can be seriously useful if someone feels that there's something they should be doing in this lifetime, but can't figure out just what it's supposed to be. If the Future Self doesn't know either, looking at a future lifetime may provide the clues to what kind of Karma they're supposed to be working on in this life time. Major spiritual concerns can also be addressed in that way, especially if you choose a very far out into the Future Self and then turn around and look at the progression of the interim lives in total.

Future Life Selves may also have resources that are different, unique or simply not to be had anywhere else.

A middle aged lady called Kath who had been scared to death by the computerisation of her work place gained a sympathetic rapport with the machines literally overnight when she called in a Future Life Self, who had grown up with technology far ahead of what her boss had perched on her desk.

"It was completely bizarre," she reported. "It seemed that I instinctively knew what buttons to press and how everything worked, I just learned it so easily. I still can't believe it on some level. The other people in the office now come to me for help when something goes wrong, can you believe that!"

9/3/7 - The Higher Self

Many approaches and religions hold the idea that there is a part of us that is eternal and lives in the light. That this part remains unchanged through all incarnations, is our core, our soul, who we really are.

From a practical viewpoint, you can call upon your Higher Self at any point when you feel you should be doing something or other, but you're just simply not enlightened enough yet to do it - forgiving someone who abused you as a child, for example, or healing a particularly bitter and destructive relationship.

OK, so you just can't forgive just yet - but the part of you that is your Higher Self, which IS love, can and will most gladly do so on your behalf. As you have a Higher Self, so do all the other people in your life. If you have injured and hurt someone and they won't forgive you, turn to their Higher Self instead.

Their Higher Self IS love and will gladly forgive you - or rather, you will realise that you have already been forgiven when you tune into it. Any Higher Self can and will send unconditional love, healing, and light when called upon to do so, gladly and readily, but for the asking.

Another interesting aspect is to more fully integrate with the Higher Self. If there's any time in your life you feel you need extra resources in the way of forgiveness, patience, strength, love, what have you, step into your Higher Self in your Sanctuary and feel its power within you. Of course, we already have this power fully within us. By doing the 'stepping in', you're just simply allowing yourself to access it more fully than before.

9/3/8 - Lower Selves & Demonic Selves

Remember our good friend Nick who found an evil twin in his Sanctuary? Oh yes, there are demons and the like to be had as well. Evil twins are actually not as rare as I thought they were when Nick came to see me; I've met the theme in variations a number of times since.

Unpleasant characters that won't let themselves be talked to in a civilised manner, behave in a less than enlightened fashion, and devils, monsters of all kinds, goblins, gremlins, fauns, demons and witches, you name it - it seems, most people have 'em in some form or the other, and once the communication links between the conscious and unconscious get better and more open, previously repressed and incarcerated 'unwanted' aspects will turn up and present themselves to you for resolution.

Firstly, **remain calm** if this should happen. I have found that when working in the Sanctuary realm these guys do not turn up until such time as you are actually ready to deal with them. And, you see, with all the help, magic and resources you've already realised by getting this far, of course you've got more than enough resources to banish even the most grizzly of demons.

Here's a story to this end: Susan found, to her horror, that an ugly, demonic witch woman had appeared and had started to shrivel plants, make birds drop from the sky, just the usual kind of evil stuff you'd rightfully expect such a character to perpetrate. This, however, completely freaked Susan out, because she was really heavily into the what I call "dancing bunny rabbit" scene of personal development - where angels are fluffy pink things, everyone floats about in a enlightened fashion all day long, and the sky is a consistent and never changing powder puff blue. You can imagine that a giant evil black witch would sit rather awkwardly in such a representation! She was on the phone to me, nearly hysterical, but I calmed her and asked her to do something to stabilise the situation for the time being. (Because a state of advanced hysteria is not the best state from which to make good decisions, I thought.) She brought out a host of angelic beings, incarcerating the witch in a cage of energy, and heaved a big sigh of relief.

"I can take it from here," she said, and I thought that would be the end of it. But not so. Apparently, she had instructed the angelic host to destroy the witch, using the energy beams like lasers, but what had happened instead was that the witch had fed on it and grown to ten times the size she had been before. Now, in spite of calling in reinforcements in the form of just about every self she could lay her hands on and every single guide, and all her friends and their guides, the witch was about to break free from the energy cage.

Help!

At the time, and thus put on the spot, I was a bit at a loss at what to advise, at which point I then go inside and seek guidance from my own metaphorical friends. After all, it's their domain, and they would know what to do.

The resolution proved to be very simple indeed. The witch was a creature of negativity. It fed on and thrived on negativity. **The only way to overcome the problem was through unconditional love**. Pretty obvious, really. Love is much stronger than negativity, it's just a bit of a human reflex to want to fight fire with fire instead.

And so, the assembled forces were instructed to find whatever love they had within them and to send it to the witch - which proved to be a lot easier for the angelic host and the guides than for the humans present, but still, they did what they could. And, lo and behold, the witch shrunk, and shrunk, until it was just a sad and pathetic old woman, and then changed from black to white and simply dissolved in a rainbow shower of light. Mission accomplished! Apparently, there was much celebrating amongst the assembled crew and a party was enjoyed by all - especially by Susan.

This particular crisis and its resolution had a remarkable real life side effect on Susan - she used to suffer from migraines ever since she'd been a child, and in spite of having any known form of treatment under the sun, nothing had shifted it. But since the witch dissolved, she hasn't even had a mild headache - and as I write this, it's been over 2 years. Oh well. So much for those who think that this kind of thing is nothing more than a weird little mind game.

This brings us to a very core principle of dealing with any creatures and manifestations born out of darkness or negativity - **you simply cannot overcome them by fighting back**.

Well, let me re-phrase that.

You can overcome them **temporarily** by fighting back, but it doesn't allow for full and complete resolution of the problem in my opinion.

Let's go back to Nick the advertising man for a moment. After his fight and triumph over the evil twin, he experienced what can only be called an 'unwanted side effect'. Yes, he felt much happier all around. Yes, he had hardly any temper tantrums and the ones he had had were very mild in comparison. Yes, he got on with the people at work a lot better, so much so that there was a rumour going around that I had put him on drugs. But, and here it comes, he found it virtually impossible to come up with the bright ideas and flashes of brilliance which had been the very core and foundation of his work and his life. It was, he said, as though there was just a fog where his inspiration used to be. It had become so bad that he found himself turning to work he had done previously and dressing it up as new in order to get by.

I nodded sagely - I must admit, I'd kind of expected something like that to happen. Often, the very creative parts of the self are the ones most in conflict with the world around us, and when Nick was growing up, being a boy as well, being creative was simply not something that was even tolerated to any great degree. So the kind of division between 'Good Nick' - meek and mild, reliable and constant, does as he's told, works hard at boring tasks, is nice to everyone; and 'Bad Nick' powerful, dangerous, creative, temperamental and immoral, is one that's fairly standard, if not always as dramatically played out as with this guy who was now very concerned that he'd have to choose just one, or the other, either of which didn't really make his life seem like worth living.

I told him that the only way out was that the two must be re-integrated and become one 'Human Nick' - someone who can't be either good or bad all of the time, but someone who does their best to grow and enrich themselves and those around them.

He very nearly cried at that point, never really having considered himself as a member of the human race before; however, he certainly understood and was more than willing to co-operate - even if it meant communicating with 'Evil Nick'. As 'Evil Nick' had been slain some weeks ago, time travel was in order. So we went to the point in time where the two come face to face, and before the fight begins.

Now, in the medieval landscape with the lightning flashing all around and the skies a deep blood red, there's three of him and one of me - talk about getting complicated! But, as an aside, this is really fascinating stuff - like co-authoring a block busting million dollar movie. God, I love this work! Anyhow, eventually we managed to get the two to communicate. (Although it involved a wild spot of wrestling and having both of them tied up side by side to start with.)

What followed was an intensely emotional experience that had all four of us in tears at some stage and culminated in the two opposing Nicks coming to a mutual agreement, hugging, and then melding into one, at which point the lightning stopped, and rain began to fall on the stony ground in the Sanctuary.

We were both pretty knackered after this. By the way, I never, ever send a client away like that, as has happened to me on more than one unfortunate occasion. I prescribed some coffee and something to eat for both of us and then waited with baited breath - metaphorically speaking, of course! - for the outcome.

I must bow to him - he really did get behind himself. He called me a week later to say that it was nearly like being back to his old self, only that he found it a lot easier to 'suffer fools gladly'.

He had had one major temper tantrum with the production manager, but, as he put it, "It was different from before. To everyone else, it might have looked the same, but there were parts of me that were kind of watching myself with amusement as I was yelling at him. It felt as though I could have stopped if I'd really wanted to. I've never, ever had that experience or hope of any kind of control before." His work was now back on schedule, and most importantly, he wanted to do more inner work as he now believed he could "do a lot better all the way round".

Well, to come back to the point of the story; positivity, regard, and unconditional love will melt the gremlins and demons like warm water melts an ice cube. **Light always triumphs over darkness.**

This is the basic, underlying and unchanging rule.

You can break it for a time, but it'll come back threefold, as the old magic saying goes.

Smashing things, destroying them, cutting them up, ripping them out, blowing them up, or any suchlike representations have inherently 'negative' or 'non-growth' aspects about them, and if you can find a way to avoid ever using something like that, so much the better. Leave the battles to the fundamentalist. Resolution, flow, evolutionary change, healing and good ol' plain universal love are, in the end, the only truly enlightened answers and not only that, will work a treat for you and will help you to really get things right.

Whilst we're on that subject, banishment and incarceration are at the very best only temporary options. How many horror films have you seen where something or other broke free after centuries of incarceration via a powerful binding spell and was ten times worse for its time spent in solitary? Yet people do lock up their demons under stone slabs or in their darkest dungeons; quite a few people reported having sent parts of them 'into the wilderness' because they wanted no part of them, if you'll excuse that expression.

The incarceration thing is a really bad long-term option for many reasons, and it's just like the prison systems in the modern world. It takes enormous amounts of resources to keep the dark ones in there, by the way of life energy - I've known people who expended so much energy of keeping their demons from breaking free, as it were, that there was hardly any left over for leading any kind of life, never mind a happy one. Further, just like in the prison system, it isn't a solution - the dark ones don't get any better whilst they're in there, and there's a good possibility that they'll end up ten times worse. Also, and here is where it's the same story with banishment and exile, these dark parts are still parts of you, meaning that **you are not whole until they've been re-integrated** in some way, until *they have been allowed to come home*.

I'm not saying that you should never resort to banishment or incarceration; sometimes it is a useful short term containment exercise to help you gain a breather, more perspective, and give you time to call in help or gather further information on how to deal with this situation properly.

I would urge you, however, to make such a situation a top priority for resolution, should it occur; and I would also suggest that you might start a repatriation programme and a rehabilitation programme for your dark part offenders that were locked away in the past as soon as you feel ready to do so.

9/4 - Genealogical Relationships

9/4/1 - Blood Is Thicker ...

Blood relatives are God's gift to therapists. I swear, if they didn't exist we'd be out of a job, or wandering the streets, hoping someone might be traumatised by a log falling on them unexpectedly from above. Whether they were aunties, grandpas, evil brothers, dreadful sisters or, later on, horrendous children and their respective families, I reckon you could amuse yourself forever healing the scars left over from such loving family relationships.

But look on the bright side. In your Sanctuary, you're in charge. You can turn them all into frogs, if you feel so inclined, or as one woman did, into tiny little copies of themselves, and then sat and watched them all running around, squeaking high-pitched and waving tiny fists at each other. Of course, in the end you'll have to love them, forgive them, and make peace with them to avoid ending up all bitter and twisted, but that doesn't mean you can't have a bit of fun first.

Those amongst you who don't know who your blood relatives are, don't fret. Just allow representations to materialise regardless and go ahead and resolve and heal any conflicts with these representations instead. I've had quite a few clients who were adopted or abandoned and it works very well.

So let's take a deep breath and turn to those who had the major hand in creating the person we are today.

9/4/2 - Mother & Father

Can you bring your mother and or your father into your Sanctuary? Don't worry if your toes curl at the thought - you are by no means alone. If the very idea of having them or any representation of them in there with you freaks you out, just relax. As you gain in strength, purpose and compassion, there will come a time when you'll be able to tackle this - and believe me, that's a part of you that really will need sorting out and healing, if the last 100 years or so of therapy experience with millions of people are anything to go by.

There is an interesting school of thought that holds that any changes you make to the past in such a realm as that of your Sanctuary reverberate through time and creates changes in the now and future in turn. This might help as a starting point. If you can't deal with your parents as you remember them, perhaps you can start by getting in touch with younger versions of them first, even child selves of your parents. Many well known healers and speakers have variations on this exercise, because it's really hard to stay bitter when you see what a mess of a childhood they had to suffer - ten to one, it was probably even worse than your own and it shows up how much they struggled and how hard they tried to do better than that, even if they fell far short of anything approaching being good parents themselves.

By the way, you might have noticed that I don't seem to be very bothered about whether your parents are alive or dead. In many ways, it doesn't matter, because it **isn't your parents that are the problem, but the representations you hold of them inside your own head**.

After embarking on Sanctuary work in this area, many people whose parents are still alive experience a profound change in the nature of their relationships in practical terms, and that's very nice but really quite beside the point.

Like it or not, there are parts of you that are your parents, and, yes you know, the nicer you can find it in yourself to be to them, the nicer you'll be to yourself in fact, and the more of a peaceful, powerful and integrated personality you can become. As Milton Erickson said, "It's never too late to have had a good childhood," and I would add to that, "and it's never to late to have had decent, loving and understanding parents."

Often, I prefer to work with the parent parts directly rather than with injured child selves, because if the parenting was dreadful, there are of course bound to be hundreds of these injured children as a direct result. Sort the parents, and the time line will have changed and the inner children will have grown up to be healthy and integrated.

You can give parents resources they were lacking in the form of metaphorical gifts; you can heal them, you can introduce them to their own guides and guardian angels and let those do the healing for you, or you can simply bypass your human parents altogether and communicate with their Higher Selves directly - any which way you choose to deal with it is just fine.

Joan, a retired headmistress, reported that she had thought about 'making peace' with her long dead parents for many years. After having her Sanctuary up and running, she eventually decided to invite her parents for a brief visit, making sure that a couple of dozen assorted friends, literary figures, selves and guides were right beside her 'just in case'. (I had to hide a little smile, because I certainly wouldn't want mess with Joan and couldn't begin to imagine what kind of monsters her parents must have been, but that kind of overkill in the spiritual protection department is perfectly OK to do if it'll give you the courage to proceed.)

Well, as her parents arrived via the recently installed interdimensional gate, she was amazed to see that they were just people, quite small too, and that they were absolutely delighted to have received the invitation. They went on a guided tour around the Sanctuary, greatly admired the wonderful landscaping and exotic flowers and features, had tea on the terrace and talked freely. The parents expressed regret, amongst other things, that they hadn't known how to be more loving, and apologised for being far to strict with her at times. When the tea was finished, they got up, thanked her warmly for a wonderful afternoon and then went back to wherever they had come from.

Joan said that after they'd gone she'd just cried and cried and cried and wished she'd done it so much sooner, as it had "lifted a great weight from my heart". Following this experience, she made a little pilgrimage to her parents' graves in the North country, which she had never seen, laid some flowers and felt that she had really finally laid important ghosts to rest.

For both men and women it can be very important to address the parents individually, as well as in the couples context. People who have problems that are sexual in nature, or gender related, can often find much relief in dealing in some shape or form with the metaphorical aspects of maleness and femaleness regarding their mother and father.

Something I should also mention at this point is that it might also be time at some point or the other to give credit where credit is due. Because most therapy is about solving problems, we get used to sifting through our memories for all the bad stuff that was perpetrated upon us, and fail to ever **sort for the good**.

Here's an example of such a case.

Sharon was full of bitterness about her mother, who was still alive. Their relationship was cold, hard and strained, and as Sharon had all kinds of problems and had had much therapy of one kind or the other, she was now at a point where, if here mother was mentioned, she would nearly spit, and this in spite of much meditation and a firmly declared belief that she "could see the light within".

I kind of just fished around a bit, following my intuition, and the following was revealed:

108

That Sharon's mother had always tried to protect her from her volatile father, as best she could.

That mother had, when Sharon was a sickly baby with deformed legs, ferried buckets of seawater from the coast 12 miles away by bicycle every day to bath and massage her legs, with the result that they were now completely normal.

That mother had, when Sharon had experienced severe headaches all through her teenage years, done the only thing that would relieve them - put her on the back of her little motorbike and drive around in wind, rain or snowstorm until Sharon felt better.

Now, does that sound like a candidate for the 'Worst Mother In The Entire Universe' award?

Yes, let's be honest, Sharon's mother certainly helped 'fuck her up'. No doubt she treated her cruelly at times, badly at others, insensitively at many others, hurt her, frightened her, squashed her, distorted her, took irreplaceable futures away from her. Yes, she did all those things, knowingly or unknowingly.

But, always remember, mum's a big part of you, and if you go and blanket-hate entire huge parts of yourself, you just end up damaging yourself even more.

Further, there's also huge parts who 'love mummy unconditionally' and so the conflict just gets worse - and the only one to suffer, once again, is your current and future selves.

The other point is that when one buries or denies a part, one ends up denying oneself access to the good qualities, resources, experiences and learnings tied up in that part.

Joshua's unconscious mind presented him with the following idea for dealing with the problem of parents; to my amazement, he imagined his father as a junkyard. There were toxic waste containers there, poisons of all kinds, destructive machinery that could shred and squash, and of course, old cars and airplanes too. Joshua drove in with a big pick up truck and found all manner of items that were of interest and of use, such as tool sets, certain spare parts that he felt were needed elsewhere, and things that could be repaired and would be very useful indeed.

Eventually, and quite some time later, he send in a clearing crew to turn the place into a park-like landscape complete with playground areas for children, skating rings, and BMX track - for some reason or other, he was very insistent on the BMX track! The duck pond was optional, but he thumped his fist on the coffee table to make me understand how vital that BMX track was. Oh, the wonderful world of people's internal representations! Even later still, a younger version of his father appeared and they began to open tentative lines of conversation.

What was especially interesting about this was not so much the changes that occurred in Joshua's own life as a result, but the intriguing co-incidence that his father was reported to have visited a detox unit to get his alcoholism under control - at age 62, for the very first time ever, and after a life time of drinking, violent relationships and petty crime.

What I also particularly like about what Joshua did was that it was easy, logical and circumvented, because of its quite extreme encryption, all the various prejudices, walls and blockages that existed between him and his father.

He took the resources that he needed and then healed the rest. Gentle, profound, easy - in other words, excellent.

That's the way it can be if you let it.

9/4/3 - Other Relatives

When I was working as a hypnotherapist, I used the Pin Point approach for preference. This is the idea that whatever the problem - psychological, bad luck, health related etc. - today, if there was a time when it had not yet been, that must mean by definition that there was some kind of turning point experience that caused the problem to come into existence in the first place.

When the person remembers what the experience was, changes the experience and in doing so lays the ghost to rest, so to speak, the problem may then resolve or simply dissolve.

During the time I used to do this virtually every day, it struck me how many of these significant experiences involved some kind of relative - probably more incidents pro rata than with the parents directly.

A few that readily spring to mind were; an aunt who thought it a good idea to take along her three year old niece to visit her husband in a good old fashioned lunatic asylum way back in the 1920's, and then told the shaking child on the way out that "This is where you end up if you don't do as you're told"; a grandfather who wanted to toughen up a two year old boy by throwing him into a freezing river; a grandmother who, every time she was supposed to be looking after the child, committed the most abysmal acts of sadistic sexual abuse under the guise of personal hygiene; an uncle who completely traumatised a small five year old boy by having lengthy "man to man" talks whilst under the influence; an older sister who would perpetrate the most sadistic acts imaginable upon her small brother when the parent's back was turned; an older brother who used a small boy as a handy prostitute for himself and his friends every night for at least 10 years starting at age 18 months and so on and so on and so on.

Even when there are no such traumatic incidents that stand out as defining events of someone's childhood, such family relationships are intensely complicated and are often not taken into consideration when someone quests to find the truth about themselves and their current problems.

As a part of a general pro-active approach, it can be quite useful to go through the relatives one by one, invite them down to the old sanctuary, and just have a little chat.

You might find amazing - and possibly healing - revelations.

9/4/4 - Family Burdens

In many ways, the sins of the parents are indeed re-visited upon the children.

Whether you believe it's Karma, or a past life thing, or genetic, or simply that the children learned the underlying patterns from the adults around them, it is rare to find families that do not have some kind of repeating theme played out over and over again down through the generations.

The Kennedy Clan in America might like to have a go at a spot of global metaphor therapy to find out what they've done to deserve their repeating themes! This is, of course, a bit of a dramatic example, but even that is not as unusual as you might think.

You might also think that your family doesn't have such an issue (or two, or three), but it is my experience that the same theme can be played out in many different ways and still remain the same theme.

For example, in Charles' family, you struggle and struggle and just when you think you're getting somewhere, there arrives this awful disaster out of the blue and knocks you right back to square one. Now, Charles, from being a tiny child, decided that he wasn't going to be like that, and he's got millions to his name now and is only 38. But wait a minute - what is he seeing a counsellor for? Because in his personal life, he struggles and struggles and just when he thought it was going to be alright, some awful and unexpected disaster occurs right out of the blue and he's back to square one again.

He imagined himself walking out of his Sanctuary and into the surrounding twilight wasteland. Eventually, after he had covered a considerable distance, he came across a village of people who looked vaguely familiar. As he arrived, there was much commotion - a baby was about to be born.

He joined the circle of villagers waiting for the outcome, and then noticed that each one had attached to their neck and shoulder a black entity, vaguely reminiscent of a slimy black spider but much larger.

The baby was born and brought out, and to his horror, an elder had a junior version of the spider entity in a dish and it was attached to the baby whilst everyone cheered.

"Now, you're really one of us. Welcome!", the elder said.

A neat and very obvious representation of the 'family burden'. Charles was horrified, I was excited. "Don't you see? This is nice and clear. What are you going to do about it?"

He considered this for a while, and then it occurred to him that, with these people apparently living in perpetual twilight, the spider things might be sensitive to light. So he got a torch from his pocket, turned it on, and shone clear white light onto the baby's spider. It screamed horribly, shrivelled up and fell off at once. But the villagers were outraged. They wept and shouted at him that the spiders were defining them as a group, were setting them off from the rest of the world, were, in fact, a gift from God.

An interesting dilemma. As I'm not into destroying or shrivelling anything as you know by now, I asked him to consider alternatives which might also be acceptable to the villagers.

He could not think of anything that the villagers would accept; they wanted no change at all to their spider controlled, twilight existence.

It had been like this forever, and this is the way it had to stay.

Time Travel looked to be a good option at this point, and so we set out to go back to the time when the very first spider had appeared.

When we arrived in the past, Charles couldn't believe the difference in the landscape. Pre-Spider, the climate had been bright and temperate, the vegetation had been lush, and the village had been a thriving agricultural community.

As we're standing on the hilltop watching, a trader is approaching the community, pushing a hand cart. Charles says, "Oh my God, that's where they came from. The first few were bought as a kind of trendy adornment. Look, he's showing them. Let's go and break this up." So he walked to the trader and the small crowd of villagers that had gathered and in effect told them that he'd had a spider, and that they were a complete waste of money. So the transaction did not take place, and when we returned to the "now", the change had rippled through the time line, taken effect and the previously ever-dark wasteland had turned into a mature farming community with not a spider infested person in sight.

What does it mean? I've no idea.

But I do know that Charles got married last year and a baby is on the way.

Further, his sister who had been struggling for years on low income had quite miraculously found someone who liked the tapestries she was making and had found a 'new lease of life' expressing her creativity and earning extra money for the family.

Did any of this happen because the spiders were gone?

I've no idea!

I've told you before - in this realm it doesn't do to speculate and hypothesize.

It's just a waste of time. Instead, go back and see what else you can find and do to make your life even more elegant, attractive, fulfilled, delightful, magical and prosperous.

9/5 - Friendships

Friendships are something that are often taken for granted, sort of like an absence of pain, until such time as something goes wrong and you don't have them anymore. As they are usually not as intensely exciting or as intensely painful as romantic or family relationships, they take second seat - but I think people are coming round more and more to the idea of how important long term friendships are in someone's life and overall development as a person.

Friendships that have 'gone bad' in the past are something that might well require healing; and friendships that were practically terminated because someone died, or moved away, or became so involved with something or someone that there was no room left for the other, all might want to find resolution as well.

Lastly, current working friendships can receive a quite magical boost by calling the friend as a representation over to your Sanctuary for a meeting and telling them all the things you would like them to know - but without the embarrassment of having to do it face to face.

Friends are, of course, an amazing resource to call upon when you need help. Here are a few general pointers on the "Do's and Don'ts" of using friends in the Sanctuary.

   If you call for general assistance, anyone who turns up is willing by definition. Just remember to thank them sincerely before dismissing them.

   If you're calling specific people to help, you should ask them first if they are happy about doing it. I personally had a really funny experience with a friend. I rang him up and asked him how he was doing. "Not so good, I've been having this funny recurrent nightmare. I'm digging in some kind of swamp and it's exhausting and I hate it and it goes on and on and I wake up the next morning completely knackered." Oops. Perhaps just a weird co-incidence, but at that time I had a marshland that needed clearing and he was amongst the people I had roped in for this very endeavour - without asking their permission first. I apologised profusely, relieved him of his astral obligations and he hasn't had that nightmare since!

   Whatever you do, please don't be tempted to sort other people's problems out for them if they haven't specifically asked for your help. This is a serious 'no-no', both in spiritual as well as in magical terms. Another person's problems are none of your business. You might be seriously endangering their karmic lessons as well as your own if you go and busybody in their affairs. This is different from the changes that happen to them as a side effect of a change you have done with their aid for your own benefit - so, for example, it's ok to change your parents so a younger self can grow up better, but it isn't ok to drag your old dad in to remove the cancer growing in his body if he hasn't asked you to do so, or at least given informed consent.

   Be careful of approaches that are designed to 'cut' relationships in order to end them. In real terms, relationships never end - unless you develop sweeping amnesia. It's also a bit like saying during the divorce proceedings, "Which half of the piano do you want? The black keys or the white ones?", whilst standing over it with an axe. It doesn't serve either of the combatants, nor the piano, and the chance of further music ever being created from that particular instrument has been destroyed.

It is better to leave such relationships alone and ask for them to be 'frozen' in some shape or form for a while until the time comes when a mutually acceptable arrangement between the two can be reached; this might involve returning certain aspects that were originally traded between the two parties, and other aspects that might have been held hostage, in order for the relationship to be truly and permanently healed.

A very safe and ecological way to deal with such relationships may also be to ask for guidance as to what exactly to do in each specific case. (See also resources - Problem Solving)

9/6 - Romantic Relationships

(Imagine me heaving a heavy sigh.)

Now, shall we begin to open this can of worms, or, shall we lift the lid on this tremendously exciting treasure chest to reveal its breathtaking sparkling beauty? Which one is it for you?

I'm just joking, really.

To start with, there's two areas of topic which need to be addressed here - the real romantic relationships you have, have had or wish you will have in the real world, and your own beliefs, attitudes and general outlook on the topic in general.

These, of course, are interlinked and interlaced but it sometimes helps to view them separately.

9/6/1 - True Love

I don't know, of course, if you've ever really been in love. The Romeo & Juliet kind, Beauty & the Beast, immortal (well, at least at the time!), overwhelming, intelligence destroying, completely-swept-away kind of love you hear about in poetry and popular song, read about in novels and see in movies.

It's one of the most overwhelming human emotions, it can overcome every limitation you ever thought possible, and if you've never experienced it, I do hope you'll do so before you die so you can fully join the human race.

It's hardly surprising therefore that, as far as significant emotional experiences go, here's a top candidate to really transform someone's character for good - or to permanently scar them, if it goes wrong, as it so often does for a multiplicity of reasons.

Now unfortunately many spiritually-based personal development approaches hold that this kind of experience is 'just a delusion', that it doesn't mean anything, that it isn't really love at all, that, in fact, if you feel it coming on, you should hurry into your monastic cell and put on the hair shirt for fear of losing any chance of enlightenment.

Many 'scientific' approaches too, chime in and come up with even more reasons why this kind of emotional outburst is immature, stupid, hormone induced, irrational, and how one should hurry into the ivory tower and put on the pure white lab jacket for fear of losing any chance of scientific respectability!

Frankly, I don't give a damn about either enlightenment or scientific respectability.

I've been there, know what it's like first hand, and when someone sits on my couch suffering from the side effects of this kind of major head-, heart-, mind-, and soul trip, I know that they're not deluding themselves - this is as real as it can get.

What often breaks my heart is that people will berate themselves for having felt like that about another human being, call themselves fools, idiots, stupid, and wish it had never happened at all because it was pain beyond imagination if it went wrong.

If you have any kind of heavy duty, unresolved romantic relationship clogging up your past and stopping you from allowing yourself to fully partake in this mind bogglingly amazing arena of human existence, here's a few suggestions that might be of help.

Remember, firstly and fore mostly, that **the more you loved that person, the bigger a part of you they most likely became.** Hating them now is hating a part of yourself, and it also involves turning your back on another part of yourself, namely that past self that really and truly felt that way.

Hating is obvious, but pretending it never happened, detaching yourself from it or disclaiming the whole experience in some other way, is in many ways just as bad.

Michelle was very dissatisfied with her current relationship. It was cold, unemotional and unsupportive - it was like living with a robot, she complained. Yet, she had chosen this guy, had chosen to be with him. Why? Well, her first marriage was to an instable man who had beaten her often, had drunk, adulterated and never provided for the family properly. She didn't want to talk about him, **didn't even want to tell me the first name of the father of her three children.**

"Was there ever a time when you loved this man?", I asked her.

Coldly, she replied, "No. I was just stupid."

Do you really think that Michelle had any hope whatsoever of a decent relationship in the future with a man she can deeply love? Now I suppose a miracle may happen - there's always the chance of that - but that's what it would take, in my opinion. Further, and as an aside, what kind of effect does it have on the children, half of each being an inheritance from some nameless monster placed right next to Satan in the popularity stakes?

I agree that this is an extreme example of denying the past.

I understand also how traumatic the whole thing must have been, how Michelle used the only strategy that she knew about at the time to keep herself from falling apart completely, and I don't blame her for it in the slightest. She did the best with what she had at the time.

This is so for all of us.

If you were born in my body, with my genetic heritage and my upbringing, and I was born in yours, you would have made my mistakes and I would have made yours. It's as simple as that.

No-one can do any better than what they can do, given all the ins and outs of who and what they are, and the who, how and what of the external circumstances they find themselves in.

I put this thought to Michelle, and she agreed. Then, I said, "Well if that is true for us, is it not also true for your ex-husband?"

She said nothing for a very, very long time.

I did not, and would not ever, ask Michelle to even begin to forgive him for the pain she suffered.

I did not, and would not ever, ask Michelle to go ahead and make peace with that nameless man.

What I did suggest, however, was for her to honestly re-visit the girl she used to be when she first saw him, first decided that he was worth being with. In fact, I asked her to begin to unseal the tomb of a love that had been buried so many years ago, and to slowly and steadily, and no sooner than she was able and ready to cope, to look at all that had been left for dead down there.

And there was so much, and so much beside just pain and suffering. His name had been Martin, and he had a charm, silky black hair and sparkling blue eyes. When he touched her, she felt as though she was going to melt, and when they made love, it was like going to heaven.

He'd been quite good natured with the babies, and in the beginning he could always make her laugh. He had sincerely tried, all through the relationship, to keep his problems under control, but simply hadn't been able to cope.

In the end, not even the very real connection that existed between the two of them had been enough to offset the pain of the fights, the arguments, the never ending frictions and frustrations, nor the guilt Michelle felt at having somehow failed in her quest to make them be happy.

"God, I loved that guy", said Michelle, and then she started to cry and cry and couldn't stop. It was nearly 6 months later that she finally got herself to the point where she could meet with him in the Sanctuary space and talk with him. Both of them agreed that they would be forever part of each other in a way, and that they both needed to begin to allow themselves to heal now and to get on with life.

A short while after that, the oldest of Michelle's children had one of his particularly bad temper tantrums. Michelle talked to him and then found herself telling him that he had his father's beautiful blue eyes, which was what had attracted her to him the first time they met. The boy fell silent and thoughtful, and the two of them had their first ever conscious communication about Martin. "I have the feeling, for the first time since I can remember, that things are really going to be alright," said Michelle.

How and when you will choose to address your own 'ghosts of Valentines past' is entirely up to you. If you don't want to just yet, you don't have to. When you're ready, please be kind to yourself and remember the little slogan I'm planning to have engraved on my headstone:

"It seemed a good idea - at the time ..."

9/6/2 - A Dream Lover

Let's now turn to some of the internal issues impacting external romantic relationships.

A neat way to begin to explore such issues is by creating what I would call a 'practise partner' - an imaginary lover who can help you understand yourself better, and with whom you may practise at any time, any thing, in complete safety and confidence.

You may wonder at this point whether you've not been doing this for the last few decades already anyway - but a Sanctuary relationship is very unlike your average outrageous sexual fantasy, because your imaginary partner is very much more than just an obedient, pre-programmed hologram. Although you remain completely in charge of all that transpires - as you can stop it, change it, improve on it at any time - your Sanctuary partner can interact with you fully in every way, and may take on a life all of his or her own.

They can speak with you, listen to you, try things out with you and advise you on all manner of very private things. Also, unlike in the sexual fantasies many have, you are supposed to be you - your current self - in your Sanctuary - and not some 16 year old anorexic super model Barbie Girl, or faultless plastic action man with a 20 inch penis.

Louise found out, when it came to the time to take her clothes off in her imaginary bedroom in the Sanctuary and with her willing practise partner rubbing his hands in happy anticipation, that she could not reveal her body to him.

Now just let's back up here for a moment.

I mean, if you go ahead and create someone who is obviously both totally attractive and totally attracted to you, in your own imagination, and you can't get yourself to get your gear off in front of him - do you really think there's a snowflake's chance in hell that it's going to happen with a real man, in a real life situation?

Well, I suppose with the aid of a great deal of alcohol or other suchlike substance it could be achievable - but then again, you might as well just have a general anaesthetic and get it over with that way!

Louise discussed the matter with her partner, and he suggested they get into the swimming pool together, him first, and then, when his back was turned, she could quickly slide in as well. That way, they could be naked together in daylight hours, and she would become accustomed to him being around her. Apparently, this worked a treat - I didn't dig for further details, but Louise's body posture told a thing or two regardless...

Dream lovers are a most amazing resource that really, most people never explore or use to their full potential at all.

One middle-aged gentleman had recently been married and had grave problems with making love to his wife. Eventually it turned out that for nigh on 25 years he had always masturbated in the same position, lying on his back, and always using the exact same fantasy to achieve orgasm. This is some serious entrainment! Little wonder that when he was trying to do it with a real woman who "made noises which put him off" he could not really perform as he had 'practised' all those years, many times a week.

It is true, I had never really considered personal sexual fantasies in this way before I met this gentleman but as a result I've always suggested trying something new, trying something different in order to not get stuck in a particular groove ever since the topic arose.

Change the body type, the age of the practise partner. Try some very different kinds of people - just try it out, you might never know, you might like it. If a strong change completely puts you off your stride, make small variations at first and in that way, **extend your range** to encompass more of the possibilities of humanity in your choices.

Also, inviting lovers in and not stipulating what they might look like, appear as, **be like** and leaving this to actually become a 'blind date with your own unconscious mind' can be absolutely fascinating and teach you so much about yourself, your own preferences and even how they might have come to be.

This is an area where you can really, really play to your heart's and body's content and get experimenting in absolute safety. And, just as an aside, why confine yourself to humans? Have you considered what it might be like to be loved by an angel... ?

9/6/3 - Sex In The Sanctuary

More than one person, when faced with the possibility of sex in the Sanctuary, began to feel very uncomfortable with the entire idea. They had no problem with eating there, or exercising there, or swimming, wrestling with demons or having long and meaningful conversations with the world and his wife, but sex? Oh my God! "I thought this sanctuary was supposed to be safe, and an enjoyable place to be in!"

One lady, who shall remain nameless, told me in worried whispers that she had made love with her spirit guide, who then exploded and hadn't been seen of or heard of since. This had led to her feeling very guilty; now, she had acquired a new one and - oh no! - was beginning to find him very attractive as well.

"This time, I'm going to keep that sex thing right out of it. It always screws up any relationship that's worth anything," she said.

I suggested she discuss this properly with the guide in question, before taking such unilateral decisions. I also suggested she call back the previous guide, to find out what had really happened there.

As it turned out, the first guide was mortified that she had sent him away in a lightning storm and had never called on him again. He didn't know what he'd done wrong and was very upset indeed.

The second guide duly pointed out that the only thing that screwed up their relationship was her very own belief that "sex screws up relationships" - he felt it to be a perfectly normal expression of their gradually deepening understanding and rapport and esteem for each other in a more physical form, rather than a total sacrilege. The lady in question admitted that this particular belief had led to a life of celibacy in spite of having many close male friends and was, as she put it, "Probably the corner stone of my dissatisfaction with life in general."

If you're not comfortable with the idea of making love to your spiritual advisors, then by all means don't do anything that would make you feel any less than entirely happy. If it's only a question of guilt, as in the case before, it might be an idea to discuss what's going on with all the parties concerned.

If the whole subject makes you recoil, but parts of you are wanting for some forward movement in the general direction of increased joy of life and happiness, you might like to consider translating the issues into something along the lines of, "My sex life is like ...." and then check out where that might lead.

Do forgive me if I spend a bit more time at this point on sexual hang-ups. If your sex life is fine and dandy, you probably will be romping about in the grounds of your Sanctuary with anyone who you're really attracted to, to your heart's and body's content anyway and you won't need this section. If, on the other hand, you really feel that this is a major problem area, and you can't seem to get anywhere, it's probably time to turn to the past with a view to resolving the blocking issues.

With some people, there is so much in the way of issues, it might be worth considering having a big clearing event of some kind, else they would be going through it a memory at a time, and by the time they were through, they'd probably be sitting in an old people's home, now finally ready to really get going!

You could consider having a parts party. This is an idea from Virginia Satir, and it's a good option when there's more than a just few parts involved in a major issue.

One gentleman, when he called in everyone who might be having a bearing on this issue, ended up with a whole clearing full of ex lovers, relatives of all shapes, sizes and ages, figures from past lives, fictitious characters from countless novels, movies and sex magazines, and an assortment of authority and clerical figures to boot. I was, at the time, deeply intrigued how he would choose to go about persuading this motley crew that he should be allowed to have a decent sex life, and his resolution was really imaginative.

He served them all a dinner, and part of the dinner was a special cake, glowing pink. As each of them ate a piece, they softened visibly and began to admit that they too had desires and longings, and that they wished they had found a better way to deal with it all. He reached an agreement in the end with their spokesman, which involved taking notice of sensible precautions and safety measures, promised not to break up any marriages or have hoards of illegitimate children, and in return they agreed to ease up on him and let him start to find out more about himself and his sexuality.

"It's not been easy," he said some weeks later. "After all, there's 25 wasted years to make up for. But I'm learning and I'm gaining in confidence all the time. That pink cake thing was the major turning point, just when I'd about given up hope altogether."

You could also;

- make a full and entire representation of everything to do with your sexuality and then roll up your sleeves, call in the handymen and get ready for some major re-modelling. In some cases, this process involved not just a single landscape, but an entire world, complete with Babylonian style sin cities, swamps, roads leading to nowhere, ruined watch towers, roaming bands of marauders and fire eating dragons.

- if the two above sound far too radical, you could also ask for the main issues to be brought to your attention one at a time in metaphorical or symbolic form, in such an order that it would be gentle, safe and ecological for you to deal with, and with a time limit of your choosing on the entire process being completed to your satisfaction. Don't doubt and trust in your mind - it can handle these kind of complex instructions quite easily once you've had a little experience in the matter.

- if you still feel that's beyond you, pass on the job to an internal sex counsellor and have them sort it out for you - and then you can just sit back and feel the changes manifest in the form of new thoughts, new behaviours and new situations in real life.

Lastly on the subject of romantic relationships, let me just briefly remind you that you can call your current partner also into the safety of your Sanctuary and discuss any kinds of issues that you might not be able to resolve in real time yet. I've been told over and over that after such a discussion, changes in the other's behaviour and attitude did occur 'as if by magic'.

10 - THE ANIMAL KINGDOMS

10/1 - Mythical Beasts & Fabulous Creatures

I've hardly met anyone who didn't have a dragon or two somewhere tucked away on a rocky hill top or sleeping in a lake. Mythical animals are intriguing things and, once again, I would strongly warn you about consulting dream dictionaries or the like for any advice on how to 'unravel' their inherent symbolism.

In the Sanctuary, we will not demean these wondrous creatures with unfounded prejudices and we will take them entirely at face value.

Unicorns, mermaids, phoenixes, centaurs, the aforementioned dragons in all different shapes, sizes and appearances, all have their parts to play in this internal world and, once again, I would suggest you look for options to resolve conflicts that appear through them or with them in some form other than violence.

It's been standard practise for millennia for knights to slay dragons, for example; however, it's also been standard practise to have wars, and famines, and all other manners of miserable-ness in human history for millennia as well, so perhaps it doesn't do sometimes to be too conservative or traditional. It's your own business what you do with your internal dragons; I would play it safe and find a more ecological solution to deal with the problem, one that **allows the dragon to find his or her own place within the system.**

An interesting and intriguing solution someone once found to the problem of a herd of marauding dragons was to reduce them in size to a flock of birds, and to find an alternative food supply for them (they were basically eating anything that stuck its head out into the clearing). Changed thus, the dragons became a very beautiful, and vital, addition to the landscape; and it certainly saved many internal knights from dying needlessly.

Another person whose dragon also behaved in a less than desirable fashion created a wild life reservation for him, after consulting with the dragon in question as to what his requirements were. This reservation was, in the end, the size of an entire continent; the owner of this particular world would journey there every so often and found the dragon to be a powerful ally in moments of need.

Mythical creatures and animals are pure magic. They hold the key to the most amazing revelations and to treasures beyond belief; when they appear, take notice and show the utmost respect.

10/2 - Spirit Animals

There is an essence or a vibration, if you will, of each particular animal species that is unlike any other; there is a quality that makes each and every kind of animal special. Within this general quality, of course, each individual animal is subtly different again, and thus the animal kingdom, from the lowliest of worms to the most magnificent of African elephants, has within itself a tremendous spectrum of - what?

I don't know what it is, either. I just know that many people find themselves drawn to one or more particular species very strongly. They either live this out for real by having representatives of these species about, or they may like to collect figures, or decorate their house with pictures representing the species.

These people gain something from their connection, calling the essence of that species into their lives.

Pre-technological societies know a lot about this kind of thing; in our society, connecting to the animal kingdom on any level is usually done quite unconsciously, and mostly driven by a real need which the conscious mind can not explain.

Once your Sanctuary is underway, the animal kingdom will move in with you in some shape or form. When, and how, this happens, is highly idiosyncratic.

One lady, we will call her Ellen, had a most beautifully designed Sanctuary, which she had worked on for some months. It took a long time for her to realise that it was extremely quiet; then she sat up with a start and exclaimed, "This is so sterile!"

There were no fish in the rivers, no birds in the trees, no deer moving amidst her luscious forests; in short, the animal kingdom was highly conspicuous by its absence. Even after having recognised this, she was extremely reluctant to invite any animals into her Sanctuary; in the end, and just because it began to nag her and to prove that she could, she put a single goldfish into one of the many ornamental water features. Still, it worried her that the fish would 'mess up the clean water' and it wasn't until she installed an elaborate filtration system that she could manage to relax. Do we think there's an issue here ...?

But anyway, whether it's whales you love, or elephants, or penguins or whatever, when the time comes, move them in. You can have conversations with them which provide most interesting view points; and animal guardians and advisors of all kinds are a very common feature. It is traditional for witches to have a 'familiar', a spirit in animal form which complements their own nature and helps them in their magic.

Totem animals which provide their specific essence as a resource are also a popular option, and one specific 'spirit animal' which you turn to on a regular basis can be very helpful.

In many personal development approaches and in shamanic soul journeys, when there's a problem that needs advice, a space is created for a representative of the animal kingdom to manifest that can help with the particular issue. This is an open invitation; the animal thus called can be of any species, and if you choose to approach a problem in this way, make sure you accept whatever animal spirit manifests in good grace, even if it's not one of your favourite species.

Whilst we're there, animals you particularly dislike or even have a phobia of may be made peace with in the sanctuary setting, for the good of all concerned.

One lady who was very scared of dogs made contact with a 'dog spirit' which manifested as a white wolf named Timo. This ancestral dog spirit explained to her many of the ways of his people, and although she had no desire following their conversations to acquire a real life canine companion, she was not afraid of dogs any longer, having gained, as she put it, "a kind of resonance", and, more interestingly, was no longer a target for every neighbourhood dog to have a go at.

10/3 - Companion Animals

If you are someone who simply cannot comprehend why anyone would want to go through the dirt, restrictions, expense, heartbreak and general hassle related to owning a pet, I invite you to skip this section, for here I want to talk in private only with those who develop relationships with companion animals that are in many ways as profound as those they develop with humans, and sometimes even a great deal more meaningful.

The whole area of how a companion animal and their owner interact with each other, and shape each other over time, is one that has fascinated me for many years. I am also fully aware of the extent of the bereavement that can exist when a particularly beloved companion dies. Unlike with a human based bereavement, the guilt feelings involved are often magnified intensely, because the companion and their entire life was totally the owner's responsibility; often, old and suffering companions are euthanised at the owner's request and signing the form at the veterinary surgeon's office is just like signing an official death warrant for a beloved friend; lastly, pet bereavements can stack up in a way human bereavements rarely do throughout someone's life time.

One way or another, for someone who has loved their past companions dearly and has shared a deep, 24 hour a day, no pretence required, no holds barred intimacy with someone who loved them unconditionally and without question or fail for ten or fifteen years, through ups and downs, marriage break-ups and job changes, let downs by friends and relatives - losing such a companion is a major league, very significant and deeply emotional experience.

Bringing these companions home to live in the Sanctuary is an experience that defies words; having a chance to express to them what their lives meant and possibly discuss how it ended is tremendously healing.

Konrad Lorenz, the famous animal behaviourist, wrote in one of his books that as he walked, he often felt the presence of his beloved friends right behind him, following in his footsteps, just as they did when they were with him in the flesh.

I leave you with that thought.

11 - Relationships With Places

It's not so very long ago that I didn't know that people can have immense and long standing relationships with places - with towns they lived in, with landscapes, and with houses they left behind.

I once had a lady called Kay come to see me whose friend had moved away and who felt a bereavement akin to this friend's having actually died in real life. Although we cleared up the issue thoroughly, some of the symptoms did not disappear as had been expected. The clue finally came when she revealed that she could not drive anywhere near where her friend's house had been, in spite of being in regular telephone contact with her and having visited her since a number of times, and in spite of having a full social calendar and being otherwise happy in her many other relationships.

I took her out of the office and we drove to the house. It struck me forcibly how much the house itself was tied up in Kay's bereavement problems - she had had so many good memories of being there, had so often raced up the drive in happy expectation of what was to come, that the place itself had become a meaningful and powerful part of that friendship - perhaps even a potent symbol of what existed between them then, which was certainly different from what was the reality now.

This was a long time before Sanctuary, and the only thing I could think of was to use an old witchcraft ritual, whereby you go and collect your memories in a jar, seal it tightly, and then bury it in a special place in nature. I'm not really sure what the estate agent made of the whole thing - Kay was crying most of the time, laughing through her tears at others, and in the end, with some very nervous glances towards the empty Nescafe Gold jar, he retreated to wait for us outside!

Well, it worked for her and "really set her free", as she put it. And since, I've come across many other people who have such open wounds about places in one shape or another. If you think about it, it's obvious really. Our homes represent ourselves, our families, our lives at the time; with very many people, moving house is a traumatic experience and denotes a definite 'goodbye' to a prior self as they move on in life.

There are many ways in which to heal relationships with places. Nowadays, I wouldn't dream of advising anyone to bury their happy memories in a jar - rather, I would have them bring these back inside, to have and to hold, and to be able to re-visit any time this should prove to be desirable, or even necessary.

Whether you choose to give any such place a place in your Sanctuary, or whether you would like to make a representation thereof instead and bring that home instead; whether you would like to conduct a 'farewell and thank you' ceremony inside your mind that you never knew would be necessary way back then, or whether you would like to simply keep it 'as is' and visit once in a while, do whatever you want if there's such a relationship within you that requires healing.

12 - Relationships With Things

Can you have relationships with things? Well, of course I can't know if **you** can have relationships with things, but I well remember completely identifying one year with the Christmas tree who had served its purpose and now, brownish and needles drooping, stripped of all its finery, was unceremoniously thrown from the upstairs sitting room window to lie in the snow below.

At age three, I **WAS** the Christmas tree and I went from having grown happily and strong in a sunlit forest to the shock of being in a house, the joy of being admired, to being discarded carelessly and without a thought, to lying broken and unloved in the snow, in a deep and complete identification flash-through that was all of a heartbeat long.

My parents used to tell the story of how I was in hysterics for nearly a week and had nightmares for many months afterwards - and from that year on, kindly bought Christmas trees with roots in pots and planted them in the garden to avoid a re-occurrence.

A hypnosis client once had developed a long lasting phobia of extreme proportions as a result of his mother having ripped up the favourite teddy bear right before his eyes - and frankly, if my Christmas tree experience was anything to go by, she might as well have ripped this man's intestines out for real, so deep can this identification become in imaginative children.

Relationships with things, however, need not be confined to childhood toys and objects, although there is often tremendous emotion tied up with such things.

Quite a number of people have brought old toys of theirs into the Sanctuary in some form or other - one was absolutely delighted to have discovered an old handmade patchwork quilt which he had spent hours looking at, imagining about and dreaming over, for years as a child, and which his mother had carelessly thrown away one day when he was at school.

Natalie mentioned, with some embarrassment, that she was obsessed with a ring she had lost as a teenager - it had been her very first gemstone and gold ring, and she had been so very proud of it until one day she'd carelessly lost it at the beach. She didn't like the way she kept thinking and dreaming about it, especially since she was now living a subsistence-style New Age Traveller life and had decided that earthly possessions were basically evil and would stop one from being a truly spiritual person.

There's two things I have to say to that.

Firstly, if everything in the Universe has been created by God, Goddess, All There Is, The Universe, that means by definition that Natalie's gold ring was also created by the same, and carrying with it in every atom, every electron, and every quantum particle of its very being the essence of spirit. From that point of view, it's ok to have a relationship with it anyway, and in fact it could be said that if one were truly enlightened, one should have **a relationship with every aspect of creation, including golden rings**.

The other thing that springs to mind is the old story of the two monks who met a beautiful young woman by the side of a river. The older monk picked her up, carried her across, set her down and graciously received her thanks. Some miles down the road, the younger monk said, "Why did you do that back there? You know we're not supposed to touch women," upon which the other replied, "I put her down an hour ago. Why are you still carrying her?"

'Carrying' any kind of issue, be it a golden ring, an old patchwork quilt, or a disembowelled teddy bear in the form of thinking about it, worrying about, dreaming about it, grieving for it, debating with yourself about it, means that the issue is an issue that is crying out for some sort of resolution. And, if it comes to that, what do these objects truly represent? That's a rhetorical question, so don't worry about hallucinating whether Natalie might have lost her virginity that same night on that same beach where she lost her precious ring - although, in fact, she did. Simply accept the fact that there's something that needs to be resolved, and go ahead and resolve it now, easily, practically and once and for all.

How?

The simple answer is to bring these and any object you have a relationship with, **home to you**.

Let them come home and be with you and provide for you whatever it is that they provide; and the beauty of it is that it doesn't matter whether they were destroyed many years ago in real life, or stolen from you, or damaged or simply lost in the river of time; in your Sanctuary they can come to life, be with you until such time as you are ready to let go of them, if you should ever want to.

Natalie found her treasured gemstone ring in a little jewellery box in one of the subterranean levels below her house. She put it on her finger, it's been with her in thought ever since, and I'm glad for her.

12/1 - The Red Bicycle

Here we come to a very important principle of relationship with things - namely, that when you have wanted and desired something at some point in your life most intensely but did not get it then, that this sets up a form of injury that can haunt someone a lifetime.

We call this the Red Bicycle principle, named after the gentleman who, in his seventies, bought a red bicycle for his granddaughter for Christmas. The little girl wanted no such thing and was very disappointed as she had hoped for a computer game; he watched her reluctantly riding it around outside on the drive for a bit to please him and felt a huge wave of sadness descend upon him 'from nowhere'.

The fact was of course that he had once wanted a red bicycle, wanted it so much that it nearly became an obsession, but he never received it then.

We all have our own red bicycles and the tragedy is that no matter how many of them we buy when we're 25, 35, 55, 85; no matter if we buy whole warehouses full of them and sleep there, bury ourselves beneath them, dedicate our lives to them, we **can never fulfil that original need** because that moment, that time is gone irretrievably - it's too late now for red bicycles.

Well, let me re-phrase that. It is too late for **real** red bicycles - but it isn't too late to go back in time and give that boy he once was and who stood for hour upon hour outside the bike shop, staring in through the window at the shiny, expensive red boys' bicycle with the white handles and saddle and the cat's eyes in the spokes, his hearts desire at last.

We can appear, and we can take him by the hand into that shop, and buy it for him, and help him take it outside, and watch him cycle off down the road, that one true and honest heart's desire filled at last.

For some of us, there is such a momentous 'unfulfilled needs reservoir' that it feels like the size of an ocean and if we even began to make a breach in the dam, it would wash us clean away.

As you have been reading this, I am sure you have already began to think of some things of your own you wanted with that extraordinary intensity of a child and it might well be that you recognise some resonance purchases of this in your life right now which still fail to fill the old need.

When next you go shopping, and you find yourself attracted to some object that common sense tells you you shouldn't be wanting or needing, stop and consider just what that resonance is and where it came from.

I had an experience of this not too long ago. I saw a shiny plastic sword and shield set in a toy shop whilst looking for a birthday present for a niece. I very nearly bought it because I was completely drawn to it and fascinated by it but then found enough wherewithal to have a brief Sanctuary moment and ask the part of me who **needed** this toy to step forward. I was not surprised to see it was a tomboy me of about 6 years old who fought mock battles with the boys in the neighbourhood and to whom this shiny silver sword and shield would have been just about all the birthdays, Christmases and general festivities wrapped up in one.

I made the transfer from the real object in my hands to the Sanctuary space and the little girl was as delighted as delighted can possibly be, snatched it from me and ran off at high speed. At the same time, the object in my hand turned from a fantastic magical thing to a simple, quite well produced toy that I no longer needed to purchase under the guise of giving it to a girl who was nothing like I used to be, for a strange and most likely highly unwanted present.

The Red Bicycle principle extends to many other circumstances and not really just objects; and make no mistake, even today there are things that are the current Red Bicycle in your life and you need these 'energies' NOW - not in 30 years from now, because by then their time in your life has long passed and they are no longer appropriate.

Whether it's a jaguar or a swimming pool; a corner office or a swing in the garden; a garden of your own or a bed with valances; a summer house in the mountains or a luxury yacht, a recording studio or a nature reserve of your very own - go right ahead and have this now. Have it, live in it and take from it what you need as fully and completely as you ever will, because chances are it isn't the bricks, mortar, metal or actual physical reality that is what is important about it, but a state of being, an experience or an energy represented by those 'hard metaphors' instead.

It is a very important process and one that can not only save you a lot of money on unnecessary and, in the end, unsatisfactory purchases; but also something that can contribute significantly to your happiness in the here-and-now, and entirely achievable immediately, regardless of your financial situation or any other circumstance.

Now here's the last of the relationships that I want to discuss, and some hold it's the most profound of them all.

13 - RELATIONSHIP WITH GOD

I'm sure you've heard it said that even atheists have a relationship with God - so I'm afraid, we all have one then, and there's no getting away from it.

I had a right old laugh the other day - this person told me he was brought up a strict Catholic and had "lost his faith". Now I thought that was extremely careless of him - but then it struck me with horror that, if no-one else had found it, the faith could still be lurking out there, waiting to launch itself on an unsuspecting passer by. My God! You go out for a nice little walk, and boom! You find yourself a strict Catholic!

But all jokes aside for a moment, I think it's really nice that people once more turn to more spiritual considerations and allow themselves to find time for the question "What am I doing here?" once more, rather than sticking strictly to discussing the price of tomatoes.

Now I'm sure you have your own representation of "god/goddess/all that is" (I borrow that term from Mr Lazarus, it rather covers the bases, doesn't it), but if you feel your relationship with God could be closer, more intense, more generally supportive than it is at present, you will find that the Sanctuary environment makes it easy to open new lines of communications in many ways.

Some years ago, I experienced what you might call a spiritual crisis. It occurred to me to invite the parish priest over for a cup of tea to discuss the matter, reasoning that if you're physically sick, you call out a doctor; if you got problems in the mind department you go to a psychologist and if it's spiritual, you call a priest.

The poor man nearly had a heart attack as this is not the kind of thing, it seems, Church Of England vicars deal with a lot in their current job description, but still, he was brave and he came. I found the good man to be very sweet, very helpful, and spectacularly unenlightened.

He didn't have a clue about mystical experiences, didn't actually believe in God and found the whole subject rather distressing, as though this kind of thing had gone out of fashion with the martyr saints a few hundred years ago.

Since then, I've learned that the particular experience that caused me to seek his help is very common indeed, well described as far back as ancient Sanskrit texts and as far forward as a recent publication on enlightenment experiences by a couple of bona fide professors of psychiatry; and that it represents nothing more than a quite ordinary step in normal human development.

Boy, what I wouldn't have given if someone had told me that at the time, rather than gently suggesting that I was probably turning psychotic, should consider voluntary hospitalisation and start on the medication immediately!

Luckily, I knew myself enough even then to **trust the processes** that I was engaged in, and now can happily say from personal experience that when the unseen realms open themselves to you, although it may be frightening at first, it certainly makes life a much better place, and a much more **realistic** one.

We've already talked a lot already about spiritual mediators, in the form of guides, angels and higher selves, to mention just a few.

These are a great way of beginning to make contact and to consciously re-connect, as it were, to the 'all there is', safely and easily. However, as most of the really enlightened folk (such as Jesus and Buddha) rightfully point out, the relationship with God in the end has to be a personal thing, a true one-on-one.

There's the theory that a lot of people prefer to go through mediators such as priests or gurus, then saints, then angels, then aspects of the 'all there is' rather than going directly to the top level, is because they don't think they're worthy of the personal attention of The Source and therefore feel more comfortable with the mediators. However, and I could quote reams of passages from the Bible at this point - although, don't worry, I won't - the smallest sheep in the flock is just as important as the fattest, and you are a child of the Universe, no less than the trees and the stars, and that you have a right to address the source directly - just as much right as everyone and everything else.

I think you should seriously consider a one-on-one romance with the all-there-is if you haven't already done so. The resources on offer, if nothing else, are absolutely breathtaking.

I mean, could you imagine what it would take to have yourself burned at the stake, suffer immense torture, be thrown to lions, or die slowly and excruciatingly over an extended period of time on the cross **voluntarily, deliberately and unfaltering in the strength you have found through your connection with the source?**

Could you imagine having your deepest love affair multiplied by a factor of a hundred thousand -

- and then to experience it with everything there is, with equal intensity of return, with God itself?

That's pretty mind boggling stuff, and I'm sure there's even more to it than that - these examples are only some of the benefits I've heard about, I'm not an expert on the subject. If you think how much effort we put into getting to live in a better house, wouldn't it make sense in this light to put a little more effort into gaining more access to such a relationship?

Anyway, how do you view the source? How would you go about connecting with it more fully? How would you go ahead and enhance your relationship with 'All There Is'?

I'd love to hear how you are going to approach this, and I know you will make great gains. You already have all the resources you need to start today.

From the highest, let's now turn the most basic, and that's found in the general topic of ...

14 - REALITY CREATION

14/1 - Who Chooses Your Wallpaper?

It's common knowledge these days that we each create our own reality, right down to choosing to stand in that particular spot where a part of us knew the lightning was going to strike.

I've sometimes mentioned this subject to groups of people one might call sincerely unenlightened, and when they responded with consternation, I would ask, **"Well who chooses the colour of the carpets in your house?"**

At the very lowest level of reality creation are the material things we choose to have in our worlds.

You'll probably find this hard to believe, but there are people out there who live in houses they don't like, with furniture they don't care for, surrounded by ornaments they hate; who wear shoes that hurt and bras that pinch, work in dreary jobs they abhor and have relationships that make them physically ill.

Some people don't even like their own friends; yet they either feel powerless to do something about it, or worse, don't even know that they have a say in these matters at all.

Physical, practical reality creation seems to be one thing, and the kind of reality creation that is in the realm of magic seems another.

Yet they are both part of **one and the same system** - there's consciousness at work that makes choices and plans, and then they manifest in the form of practical objects, situations or people.

In my experience, the physical and the magical are not opposites as is so often held, but they are at the end of a sliding scale of a truer representation of what the world is really like in the classic 'dimmer switch' scenario. The world is physical and magical both, at the same time, always interwoven somewhere along a scale with infinite subdivisions.

For some of the people I've met, creating a Sanctuary within was the very first time where they got in touch with reality creation at any kind of level. Ok, creating a safe, supporting and beautiful world inside for yourself to enjoy is not exactly the same as being able to snap your fingers and manifest a pot of gold in your living room - but it's certainly a start towards that end.

Now I cannot know how many books, lectures and workshops on the subject of reality creation you have ingested already - these might have been said to be about abundance, or how to have better relationships, or how to overcome weight problems, or how to be a Reiki practitioner; in the end, all these are about creating a better reality for yourself.

Perhaps you've done none of these things and don't intent to - it doesn't matter. Whether you are already a reality creating wizard, or you've just begun to prick up your ears at the possibilities for a better life inherent in the concept, Sanctuary building will be good practise for when you're ready to carve your own "heaven on earth" out there from the good ol' rock hard reality.

Sanctuary building, decision making about what you want from it, repairing, re-decorating, finding and building new resources, and expanding it, provides an ideal and super safe setting for learning some very basic lessons about the whole business of reality creation.

14/2 - Reality Creation 101

Here are some of the things that you will learn in the process of creating realities in the Sanctuary realms, entirely free in every way to do, have and be what you choose exactly:

14/2/1 - What Is Possible For YOU?

Faced with unlimited choice, and unlimited possibility, you will learn one heck of a lot about your limitations of belief of what's possible FOR YOU, what's necessary FOR YOU, and in the end, what *you actually believe you deserve* to have and not to have.

I've had people who could not surround themselves with pleasure and beauty, try as they might, and in the end had to come to the conclusion that it was because they didn't believe they deserved it. Well I'm glad they discovered this inside their heads whilst stuck in a traffic jam, whilst lying on the couch or washing the dishes - rather than after a lifetime of wasted struggle and unhappiness, on their deathbeds!

This kind of information about yourself is absolutely invaluable in order to sort something out that is blocking real happiness and positivity from EVER manifesting in your real life - **because you can't have on the outside what you're not ready to accept on the inside.**

What you actually believe you deserve to have and not to have, is what you will get. One gentleman who shall remain nameless had a most enchanting Sanctuary with great relationships but couldn't contemplate "dirtying" it with any kind of sexual activity. Strangely, in his own life he was successful in just about every aspect - but had not had sex with anyone in years.

So, doesn't it make sense to address your views on relationships first before spending the money on a dating agency?

Sanctuary building also nicely exposes what you think you're good at, and what you think you need help with. Just read that last sentence again, and in case you're not yet listening fully and completely, I'll repeat it for you: Sanctuary building also nicely exposes what **you think** you're good at, and what **you think** you need help with. People think all kinds of weird and limiting things about their own skills and abilities 'as are', never mind about their own potentialities 'as could be'.

You wouldn't believe the stuff I hear - "I can't draw to save my life." (Oh yeah? Let me just go and get the kitchen knife and we'll test that assumption!), "I'm useless with numbers" (How come you're sitting in my house instead of with a very confused neighbour across the road?), "I'm a terrible driver" (So how many people have you killed this last two weeks?), "I'm just not physical enough" (OK you stand there and I try and walk through you); and stuff even more ludicrous than that.

Not all of these people are fishing for compliments, either. Some of them really believe this kind of nonsense about themselves!

In the Sanctuary project, the time comes when even the most worm-like of people finally begin to realise where these 'inner advisors' and 'wise helpers' they rely on so heavily actually come from. Do you remember the lady who felt so inadequate in the decorating department that she called in an interior designer to do this work for her? Well, she rang me up a few months after the session, to tell me that she had just moved into a new house and astonished everyone with the decorating ideas, but no-one knew "that she had cheated by using her inner designer instead". As she said the words to me, she all of a sudden started to laugh uncontrollably and simply couldn't stop. I was also laughing and we just set each other off again and again until we were both exhausted. Last I heard, she was advising others on the subject and had even gotten paid for a job she did for the firm her husband worked for.

"I am the designer," she said.

In your own explorations and creations, of course you call in help as and when you feel you need it. You can use the information thus revealed about your lack of self belief in these areas in a conscious manner, or just let it go and use the marvellous resources you've discovered thus, like our decorating lady did and allow these things to integrate smoothly and joyfully over time.

14/2/2 - How Do You Make Decisions?

An ability rather highly priced by the army and the business world, decision making involves taking risks and overcoming fear of failure. It's a way of thinking, or you might call it a strategy on how to approach such situations in general. When people are faced with difficult decisions, the issues themselves often overwhelm this underlying process and strategy, but it's in the strategy that the power lies.

In your Sanctuary, you can make decisions in perfect safety, because you can **undo anything again** and try something else if your first decision failed to deliver to your expectations.

What you will find out, if you don't already know, is that whether you took a right or a wrong decision is really rather impossible to judge, especially in the long term, and even more especially in the very, very long term.

Every decision sets into motion a whole series of connected events, or ripples, if you like, that will influence in ever widening circles more and more people, situations and events the longer it goes on. I've made some dreadful decisions in my time, yet they have led me to places that I wouldn't have missed for the world; I'm sure you've got some similar examples in your own life.

The thing is, these interconnected events don't get to manifest in the future if no decision is taken, and either nothing happens at all or, and that's much worse, you get swept up in someone else's reality creation by default and this very possibly might not be to your liking and very often not in your best interest! Therefore, finding out how you make decisions, how you deal with the consequences, and all the ins and outs of your own particular way of coping with this aspect of reality creation, brought to an elegant solution, is going to be a gift of tremendous value to yourself in everything you'll ever do in the real world.

14/2/3 - The Nothing Principle

One of the very core concepts of reality creating is the 'nothing principle'. This simply states that nothing is nothing and must always remain nothing, because you can't improve, develop, grow, streamline or adjust a nothing.

Nothing is nothing.

Something, on the other hand, and regardless of how miserable, small, pathetic, simple, or useless it might appear at first glance, is something.

And something **can be improved** when attention is given to it - it can be developed, morphed, even erased if necessary. (Which is not something you can do with a nothing!)

To understand this clearly is a major task for artists, for example, who seek perfection in form and function and have the unfortunate habit of tearing up their beginning 'something' efforts because they are displeased with them and turn them into a 'nothing' instead, from which, as we've observed our principle states, then nothing further can grow.

Similarly, for Sanctuary builders and reality creators, **any** effort - and no matter how haphazard or childish it might appear - should be treasured and hailed as a great accomplishment - you've actually done **something**! That is a starting point and now we can go on and make it better, make it brighter, make it other, make it more and make it become something amazing as time goes by.

If you want to build a castle, you can start with a single mud brick in the middle of an otherwise empty field and guess what? That is already more than 99% of the population ever achieve - they never get that far! You add another and then some more, and the foundations are starting to take shape. After a while, the first little castle stands in the middle of the field. For sure, it's not very impressive but you have something there that 99 out of 100 people will **never** have at all - and now you can improve it and make it better with the wisdom of hindsight, the bricklaying experience you have gathered and should you at some point pick up and make a second version somewhere else, you can already bet it's going to be even better than your first effort.

So, the important lesson in the Nothing Principle is that things get better with time and effort and it expects you to start with a small something somewhere - that is the very core of reality creation and something you can practise to your heart's content in Sanctuary so that when the time comes, you will be able to replicate this principle in the Hard as well, not allowing negative comments from yourself or others to dissuade you from your creations and keeping firmly in mind that you are dealing with a developing system in which you, the creator, are learning the whole time with every little thing you do, with every little decision you make, and it doesn't really matter at all if an individual decision results in this or that - it's feedback and **ALWAYS AND ONLY** a learning process and a step on your way as you develop your abilities and powers over the time of your life.

14/2/4 - Accepting Responsibility

I used to think of responsibility as this terribly heavy grey thing you lug around on your bent and aching tired shoulders. I realise now that's just what the 'powers that be' wanted me to believe so I would be ready and willing to hand this supposed burden over when they came asking for it - like the conquistadors 'relieving' the natives of their gold.

This delusion of mine lasted until the day someone pointed out that the word is actually made up from two words that define a very different meaning: response - ability, i.e. the ability to respond.

When you're looking after a baby in a room by yourself, and it starts to cry, it's your response ability to deal with this. It means nothing more and nothing less than that you are the only one in this situation who has the ability to respond - and then it's your decision whether you are going to go ahead and accept this and say, "Yes, that's correct, the kid's too little and also he's the one who's saying that there's something that needs to be dealt with, there's no-one else here who could respond, I'm the only one who has the ability to respond in this situation."

This "acceptance of responsibility" doesn't mean, however, that you now need to go and do something about it, nor for that matter, **that there's only one way to respond**. Whether you're going to do something about it, or what precisely you're going to do, is entirely **your choice**. You could respond (because you have that ability!) by simply walking out of the room and closing the door behind you.

A long time ago I was speaking to a young woman who was bitterly angry about the way a couple in her street mistreated their pet animals. She had called the RSPCA and they had done nothing about it, and she "couldn't get to sleep at night for thinking about the suffering of these poor creatures; and I there's nothing I can do."

I pointed out to her that she could simply cut a hole in the fence when the couple went out and steal the animals in question, if she felt that strongly. She was completely taken aback by that suggestion and spluttered and stuttered for a while and in the end cried out, "But I'd be arrested!"

At this point, and being somewhat tired of the conversation, I leant forward, looked her in the eye, and said, "If it's that bloody important to you, then stop whining, do something about it, and accept the consequences."

One of these side effects of responsibility are the consequences of your actions. Whether it's the external 'laws of the land' as in the example with the mistreated animals, or your own internal law, or even a combination of the two as in the example of leaving a crying baby in a locked room - response ability also includes that you are willing to respond to the outcome of your choices. If you can't do the time, don't do the crime, as it were.

For many people, the idea of taking response ability for their entire lives is about as shocking a suggestion as the idea of sticking their head in a blender. It would mean accepting that the mess that is their lives is of their own making, of their own creation. Don't get me wrong. I don't blame them for it. It is of course based on low self esteem and a society that teaches you anything other than that you are a free individual with the ability to respond according to your own beliefs, values and attitudes, that you are the absolute owner of your own body, your thoughts and feelings, the master of your own destiny, the creator of your own reality, the lord of your own domain.

The idea of taking responsibility for your entire life is also a bit of a big chunk - like eating the proverbial elephant. You can only get through the whole damn thing a piece at a time.

So, starting to take responsibility for an imaginary inner realm, with perhaps just a little walled garden or even a small prison cell, that certainly is a first step towards the whole elephant-devouring business of stepping up to the knowledge that you have the ability to choose to respond, no matter what the situation - even if you choose to respond by doing absolutely nothing about it.

Also, as people experience this in action, they will also become much more aware of the benefits response ability has for the person who wishes to claim it as their very own right by birth.

See, it's a major way towards freedom. Without it, you remain a sad little whinger, forever reliant on counsellors, help lines, pressure groups and ever more restrictive legislation designed to 'protect you'.

Without it, you'll be like these sheep who just trustingly put themselves in the hands of whoever promises to relieve them of this response ability 'burden', and then bleat horribly when they found they've been led to slaughter instead - like the people I heard about on the radio just this morning, who chose a plastic surgeon from an advertisement they spotted in the paper and because he was cheaper than everyone else, failed to research his practise, ended up with horribly deformed features and now demand more legislation to protect others just as irresponsible as themselves, and just as unwilling to admit their part in the tragedy, from having to take responsibility for their own stupidity in the future.

The amazing turn-around from being a victim to being the master of your own destiny has been expressed most beautifully by Virginia Satir, who wrote this truly beautiful piece called 'My declaration of self' I recommend highly that you copy this into your journal or attach it to a wall so you keep it in mind. It's easy to forget amidst our busy lives but truly, this encompasses the truth about response ability and our lives here in the Hard.

14/2/5 - Help, Gifts, Assistance & Miracles

In between the whinging, "I can't do anything - won't you do it for me please 'cause I'm so stupid and useless?", and the arrogant, "I don't need anybody, I can do anything myself and at least it's going to get done properly" there lies somewhere a place, where calling for help doesn't mean you're an idiot but quite on the contrary, that you acknowledge realistically that there's some things you could use some help with!

I've met very few people who found it easy to ask for and accept help **from a position of strength**. Yeah sure there's lots who manipulate, hint, point, cough discreetly or blackmail you emotionally, but very few who can ask without embarrassment or aggression.

The whole area of giving and receiving in general is one of these weird places where human interaction in the Western world seems to have gone awry in a bad way; and it's one of these things you can practise and explore in complete safety and total confidence in the Sanctuary.

Many metaphysical teachers hold that the reason more people don't experience more miracles more often is that they block themselves off and won't allow it to happen. Here's an interesting fact for you. Do you know the experiment when you throw a coin fifty times and try to predict which side it'll land on? As there's statistically a 50/50 chance you guess it right, one would normally expect, if it was chance alone at play, that you'd be right half the time - about 25 times in all.

In the '60s and '70s, thousands upon thousands of such kinds of experiments were performed in Universities up and down the globe - either to prove the existence of ESP, or to disprove it. A very small proportion of people predicted the right outcome way beyond the bounds of chance, and that is really what most of us have come to expect in life.

However, recently someone re-checked those studies and found that there were just as many people who predicted it wrongly so many times that it couldn't have been chance either! As these "never ever get it right" guys were previously lost in the statistics, having being lumped in with the 50/50 crowd, all of it had to be re-calculated and now the results prove, scientifically and statistically, that ESP must exist.

The moral of the story? It is just as unlikely to **never** have any good luck as it is to **always** have good luck - in both cases, there's reality creation at work, only in the first case, it's the negative, denying, and blocking kind.

Statistically, you should be able to expect some good fortune some of the time - half of the time, in fact. Statistically, and if you don't do anything to block it, you have a 50/50 chance of receiving miracles in your life. Miracles are invaluable gifts that you did **nothing** to deserve - a scary concept for many of us who have been brought up to believe that the only way to getting **anything** in life is by 'working your fingers to the bone'.

In the context of reality creation, miracles are just one of the ways in which the Universe can help you if you let it.

A teenage girl called Allie who had been Sanctuarising for a while told me that one of her main pleasures was to go back and check out what new gifts had turned up - she giggled and said it was like an Easter egg hunt - a diamond bracelet on the branch of a tree, a pretty little statue sitting on a lily leaf in the pond, on one occasion she found a book of poetry. This rather intrigued me for many reasons, but mainly because no one else I'd ever talked to had considered the idea of somehow creating little surprise gifts for themselves.

It's such a thoroughly nice thing; one would have thought it to be more common!

See, I don't see reality creation as something you do all by yourself, grimly planning, laboriously creating, studiously affirming, spell casting, symbol empowering and deadly seriously acting in accord. I think of reality creating more like a dance that weaves together your desires and abilities, resources and opportunities, with co-incidences, synchronicities, as well as a little help from other people, situations and the Universe at large, all held together and given form and shape **by the intention of your mind.**

14/3 - Reality Creation - Step By Step

Just by building a new house in your Sanctuary, does that mean you will automatically get a new house in real life?

I don't know - why don't you find out?

This kind of thing certainly happens an awful lot in some form or the other as the result of internal planning and re-structuring - like in one case, a lady had lived in a place for twenty years and then "somehow" got the desire to become involved in home improvements - with the result that the house ended up "as though it was a different house altogether". No-one who knew her could get their heads around the depth of transformation - new extension, new windows, walls knocked out, loft extension, totally different interior decoration, the lot.

Certainly I have found in the past that there is truth in the metaphysical principle of "where attention goes, energy flows".

14/3/1 - What Your Heart Desires

The one thing that saddens me about the author/reader relationship is that I won't get to hear what you decide will be your first reality creation target. It's just amazing what people want, and how they go about getting it!

So, whether it's something very big like wanting to own the equivalent of the Microsoft Corporation, or something very little, like a stranger giving you flowers, that in itself can be a gauge for you as to how much you believe you can do this, and how much disappointment you're willing to let yourself in for!

No, I'm just joking. Let's be serious here - **you can have whatever your heart desires.**

If you've got an enormous shopping list, you can chunk up a bit - sorting things into categories and finding the underlying resource. So, if you want a new house, and a new stereo, and a new car, they can all be bought with money and so you might save a lot of time by manifesting more money instead of each item one by one. If you're miserable and lonely, you might go straight for "more love" than doing friends, casual acquaintances and lovers separately.

If that's too overwhelming, start smaller. Always remember, you're calling the shots. And please, please trust your intuition. If the thought of trying to create something massive worries you in the slightest, don't try to convince yourself to attempt it just because "you should be able to by now, after 25 years of Transcendental Meditation".

There's no-one in your Sanctuary to judge you, you've got all the time in the world, and ice skating judges give higher marks for a single jump that was executed to perfection than an ambitious triple toeloop that landed the skater on his ass.

John had dreamed of owning a fishing boat all his life. Not a little rowing boat, mind, he already had one of those, but a real ocean going sea fishing vessel that could take passengers and which required a boatman's license. These things are not only extremely expensive to buy (in the range of a super luxury motor car, I was amazed to find out), but also need a lot of money to maintain, to buy petrol for, and for berthing fees, and so John had more or less resigned himself to never being able to afford one.

Still, he kept dreaming.

I met him on the beach whilst taking my dogs for a walk and we just got talking. He made the serious mistake of asking what I do for a living, and about twenty minutes later, he had told me that his internal Sanctuary was nowhere near the sea and only contained a little lake just big enough for a small rowing boat.

By the time I went home, the lake had acquired a river connection with the Big Blue and a gorgeous mariner with a fishing boat with John's wife's name on it.

I met him again recently, using a massive winch to drag his ocean going vessel up the beach. It had his wife's name on it. I waved and he came running to tell me what had happened - and the interconnections of various bizarre circumstances that had led to him acquiring this boat were so unbelievable, I kept laughing and shaking my head.

There's still parts of me, it seems, that in spite of all the things I've seen and done still won't believe that miracles do happen, each and every day, some big and some small ones as well. But in a way, that's alright too. It means that you don't have to congruently believe to be able to manifest. John didn't, and I still don't, and yet we both do it. There's hope for all of us.

Not everyone, however, has such a clear and long standing and, let's face it, simple dream as just owning a fishing boat. John was lucky there, I thought. For many of us, it's hard to say what would make us completely happy, what would complete us, in a way. What is it specifically that would make all the difference?

A lot of people just sigh at that point and say, "If only I knew. If only I KNEW! Then I could go out and get it!"

If that sounds like you, find the section on 'Mythical Quests'. For now, I would suggest as a practise matter, to choose something you'd quite like to have in your life.

I mean, if you had just started out as an architect's apprentice, you probably wouldn't be looking to re-build the Great Pyramid Of Giza as your very first project. A project of such magnitude is too awe inspiring, with too many possibilities of your own inexperience to lead you to make mistakes; plus, the pressure would be such that you'd probably make some where it wasn't even strictly necessary. So choose something now, take it easy and let's look at the next step.

14/3/2 - Inner Feng Shui

Just in case you haven't heard about it, Feng Shui is a Chinese system for allowing energies to flow harmoniously in and around your home, to make living easier, more abundant and more joyful.

This is achieved by firstly finding out what kind of energy there is, and then working with this energy to create maximum benefit. There are all kinds of different energies - fast, rushing ones, negative and disturbing ones, tranquil gentle ones, and old stuck energies that assemble especially in corners. There are the basic energies inherent in the earth, that of the building itself in context of its environment, and the energies that are brought in by people and objects.

In the system, there are all kinds of ways to channel, re-direct, harness and clear these different kinds of energies, using natural materials, shapes, mirrors, plants, water features etc. and their placements to create balance and harmony.

I am by no means an expert on the subject, which I can highly recommend to you as being very positive, powerful and good fun to boot; however one specific Feng Shui idea has benefited both me and many of my clients most tremendously.

See, before you go ahead and manifest something new, there's got to be a space for it, else you just clutter up your life with many negative effects. Also, the very existence of a welcoming space makes it certainly easier for something new to turn up that wishes to occupy it - if you've ever had a brand new cupboard in your house and rejoiced in the potentiality of its emptiness, you'll know how quickly stuff appears that wishes to move in and in no time at all it'll be just as full as your older cupboards.

So, I suggest the first step on the way to creating something you require or desire is to sort out the old first. Sometimes this might involve clearing something out or throwing away old unwanted clutter.

In the real world, this doesn't always work so well on all levels. It's ok for closets and drawers, but not so easy on the major manifestations. After all, if you had to sleep in a ditch for six months before you were allowed a new house, or get rid of all your money before you can manifest more of it, practical problems of all sorts would arise.

In Sanctuary space, this is of course not a problem, and so we can go ahead and sort this inner space deeply and completely for 'maximum pull' in metaphorical - and metaphysical! - terms.

This step often gets somewhat overlooked and is in my opinion a major stumbling block to flawless reality creation on the inner plane.

A neat example was a client of mine called Jake who wanted desperately to own a nice car. He didn't have much money, and this, by the way, wasn't the problem he came to see me about, just something that cropped up during the conversation. In spite of his desires in this direction, Jake had driven old and worn out cars all his life; once, someone had given him a really nice car but within a couple of months, he'd had a couple of accidents and the car had been vandalised by a gang of youths and it had turned into a knackered old wreck yet again.

It occurred to me to ask what had happened to all these old cars he'd previously owned in Sanctuary terms, and duly, he manifested a car park for me as a response to that question. Ok, so I'm guilty of installing it in the first place simply by asking about it I presume, but sometimes this has its uses, as you will see.

In this internal car park, not only did he find his own old jalopies, but also some that his parents had owned as far back as he could remember. He was quite emotional at looking at all these dusty and sun bleached old cars, as they were tied to all kinds of fond memories. He had, he said, always had a hard time taking them to the scrap yard or selling them on in the real world, because he had grown fond of each one, in spite of their various problems. He would have told me each one's little quirks and foibles, if I'd let him, along the lines of, "Oh, this one never ever started in the wet, God, all the times I had to bump her to get home!"

I really felt that these poor old cars needed to be let go of in some shape or form, so that they might move on to wherever it is that beloved old family cars go, and he wholeheartedly agreed with me.

"You know," he said reflectively, "I never realised how much I appreciated their individuality."

As cars were not the point of the session, and I felt that he had understood fully how to take it from there, we said goodbye and he promised me to let me know what happened. I must confess that with this kind of work, I'm like someone who has started to read a really interesting novel and can't wait for the next instalment. God, I love this job!

He duly rang and told me that he had realised a couple of things. Firstly, that his relationship with each car was a personal relationship and had nothing inherently do to with them being faulty; that was just something that got tied in to the whole thing by mistake because of the first few jalopies he had owned. Secondly, he had found out that it all had started when he was about three and his dad's car was taken to the scrap yard, where the whole family watched it being lifted by a crane, dropped into a hole and then crushed, and he remembered crying bitterly and desperately begging to try and make them stop it.

Jake did not want to get rid of the old cars in his mind; he'd tried and it had felt awful. Instead, he had made the decision to enlarge his internal car park to provide space for any new car he would own in the future; further, he'd found an inner mechanic for whom he manifested a fully equipped work shop and unlimited spares department who would repair and restore each one of the old cars already there to full shiny glory, and also look after the new ones that he would acquire in the future.

I thought that this solution was really neat, and congratulated him on his discoveries and choices. When I saw him again a few weeks later, he came in grinning like a Cheshire cat, "I've got something to show to you!" Yes, you've probably guessed it. Outside stood a shiny classic car - a Triumph Stag, as he told me proudly. He'd got it really cheap and a friend had helped him do it up; his father had given him the money for the re-spray. He's still got that car, it's been about ten months now, and it still looks as good as new.

The moral of the story is four-fold.

> Firstly, it illustrates nicely the principle that if there are recurrent problems in any department you have chosen for your first attempt of direct reality creation, there's some clearing, tidying and 'making room' for the new to be done first.

Secondly, you don't have to chuck things away in the Sanctuary space as you would do in real life if you don't want to - as long as it's all neat and organised to your satisfaction, there's no limit on how much you can have. Your internal world is not a closet that can only hold 4 shirts, 6 pairs of socks and 3 drab suits.

Thirdly, as Jake's example shows, when you go ahead and suit yourself, taking all your own feelings and motivations into consideration, you can end up satisfying all parts of yourself in a way you never contemplated as a possibility.

He had always thought of a "really nice car" as being something that costs hundreds of thousands and not only being completely out of his league in financial terms, but also being out of his league in self identity terms. He's got a car now that cost him next to nothing, that's both old and quirky as well as gorgeous, flash and shiny, and it fits the bill of a "really nice car" to the degree that he can't help but smile proudly every time he sees it.

Lastly, Jake's car problem, how he overcame it and how he came to own his Stag, was, please remember, accomplished entirely by himself, in his own world, in his own way, in his own time, to his own satisfaction. And that, as far as I am concerned, is the most encouraging thing of all. If Jake can do it, so can I - and without having to find me a Guru first.

So, to back up, with anything you would like to have a go at manifesting for yourself, go inside and visit the place where it will be represented when it comes to move in with you. Clearing may be in order. Like in gardening, a weed-free, nicely dug border of rich soil will help any kind of plant to grow.

So, now that we've tidied up our treasure rooms, enlarged the jewellery boxes and released all the monsters from the attic of the old house, we can begin creating what we want in the Sanctuary.

14/3/3 - The Desire In Context

There are loads of inner journeys available in books, tapes and workshops that let you manifest desires in metaphysical terms by working on the non physical planes and with symbols and metaphorical representations.

Sanctuary work is different, because here we are faced with an interactive, ecological system where every part affects every other - just as is the case in nature in general and in your neurology in particular.

Something that you might like to consider therefore is: Where does it fit in?

Sally wanted more 'Personal Power' (yes, of course you can have attributes or resources as well as material objects!). She represented this by a huge, magical mountain with a castle on the top.

Unfortunately, it kind of squashed the rest of the Sanctuary and cast shadow on most of it; and I shudder to think what would have come out of this in practical terms if she'd just let it stay like that. As it was, the mountain didn't 'fit in' anywhere with the rest of the landscape; some major re-structuring work was in order to create a pleasing and functional whole.

Another example of the same nature was a lady who wanted more money and thus created an empty ready-to-receive strong room in her Sanctuary house. Once again, it didn't really fit in very well with the existing oldie worldie cottage with roses round the door - and the solution lay in finding a harmonious combination that would enhance both instead.

I have much trust in the fact that humans are absolutely capable of figuring out the underlying harmonic principles of the Universe - a bit like how the temple designed by Leonardo Da Vinci is universally pleasant to the eye, and when you change the proportions even ever so slightly, it looks unbalanced and becomes uncomfortable to behold.

This, by the way, is an important safety check not just for your new structures and manifestations, but also for existing ones. If it's pleasing and harmonious, then it's probably right. If it isn't, consider how it can be arranged differently, or better; **an interlacement of function and form, which may serve you outstandingly in the overall context of the whole.**

14/3/4 - Roadblocks To Desire

It is very possible that, like in Jake's case with the cars, once you've started clearing up and creating the space, the new manifests itself automatically and without any further help or planning.

Sometimes, however, there are further stumbling blocks to overcome first.

Gill, a teacher, wanted a romantic relationship and to this end had cleared a part of her garden and planted a potentially beautiful red rose just as you would get from a gardening centre; the idea being, that as the plant grew and developed, so would a new love arise and when the rose started to bring forth her first flowers, love would be there, growing stronger and becoming more full and complete as the years go by - in theory, a good idea and a gentle, natural unfolding process which was much more suited to Gill than being "swept of her feet by violent flood waves of emotions", as she put it.

However, the damn thing refused to grow. She'd plant it, water it, feed it, and every time she came back to check on it, it just lay there again, floppy and dead. Rightfully, she recognised that there was obviously something very wrong, a major stumbling block within the system that would not have this rose thing happening. So she began trying all kinds of things - changing the soil, changing the place, trying a different species and colour of rose, trying it in a planter, in a greenhouse - nothing worked. No matter how healthy and well cared for the plant was when she left it, every time she got back, it was dead yet again. As there was no help forthcoming from inner guides or advisors on how to deal with this, Gill started to read books about how to care for roses, and in the end, went to a real gardening centre in the real world and asked advice from a lady who worked there! (Now that's what I call acting in accord - I must confess that I wouldn't have thought of doing that.)

Any rate, the lady listened to the story, Gill obviously pretending they were talking about a real garden and real roses. In the end, the lady shook her head and said, "I don't know, but it surely reminds me of something that happened a long time ago, on my father's allotment. He had leek plants dying mysteriously like that, and it turned out it was another man from the allotment society poisoning them at night because he wanted to get rid of a competitor for the annual prize giving."

Gill told me later that she virtually ran back to her car, locked herself in, closed her eyes and planted another red rose on the spot.

This time, she found herself a watchman in the form of an old owl and asked the owl to keep an eye on the rose until she came back. And right on, the owl reported that from the surrounding trees, a black shape had emerged as soon as Gill's back had been turned, and stomped viciously around on the plant until it had died.

Now here's neither the time nor the place to go into the ins and outs of how Gill first entrapped, then sorted out the black shape; the point is, in

the very idea of a problem there lies the pre-supposition that there must exist a corresponding solution, as surely as the idea of night can only make sense in the context of there being also a day.

No matter what obstacles you encounter to your creation, no matter what goes wrong or what weird things happen, it's all a part of the overall process and it just means that there's a puzzle to be solved, or a detective novel to be written, if you will. The interesting co-incidence - if that's what it was - that the particular woman Gill asked for advice had had a father whose experiences led to Gill solving the puzzle, is a common theme.

Sometimes, it's a question of hearing a song on the radio, flicking across the television channel, or even a chance remark overheard in passing, that holds the key to a particularly bugging problem and triggers an instant revelation.

I love learning. I love all of it. From the excitement of first hearing about something, to the first tenuous contacts with the subject, then rolling up your mental sleeves and really getting stuck in; to the plateau of frustration that tells you the good stuff is j-j-just round the corner; to the marvellous feeling of "Oh my God! I understand!", to the maturing of the subject and the realisation that you are able to do it yourself, right to full integration and being able to use what you've learned with elegance and ease, I just love the whole process and every single step within it. I don't know if you feel the same, but even if you don't as yet, I'm pretty sure you must be catching some of the excitement of the chase that exists when a really good puzzle or problem presents itself.

Also, of one thing you can be sure, once you've thoroughly dealt with your equivalents of Gill's black stomping shadowy thing, you're certain to share her feelings of relief, joy, pride in having overcome it, and the unfolding of future possibilities.

I've done it myself and I can tell you, it feels great - and that's quite apart from the practical repercussions for your self and your projects, dreams and plans.

14/3/5 - Acting In Accord

Once you've figured out what you want, cleared the space for it, manifested it to your satisfaction and sorted any possible problems, you might like to do a bit of 'acting in accord'. We have mentioned it before quite a few times, but I'd still like to take this opportunity to remind you that **the inner world and the outer world are really part of the same interdependent system,** and the more you are aware of it and **learn to transfer resources** and communications freely around the entirety of this system, the better both of them have the opportunity to become.

I do my 'acting in accord' in many sneaky ways that by-pass people who don't know me very well completely. If I had been Gill the romantic rose lady, I would have either painted a corresponding picture of the rose and hung it in a prominent place, or actually gone out and planted a real one in my garden. I might have bought a T-Shirt with a rose on it or, even sneakier still, might have acquired rose scented perfume or worn a bit of rose quartz jewellery.

Does that begin to sound like good old kitchen magic?

Yes, I suppose that's exactly what it is! And that's ok, because it's a pretty ancient tradition, energised by billions who have gone before us, and honoured by everyone excluding the Western society in the last five hundred years or so.

Which ever way you want to look at it, bringing a symbol out of your unconscious mind and having it be real in your daily life, certainly works as a reminder and an affirmation of what you want, every time you look at it, and every time you think about it.

It's a proof to your unconscious mind that you're finally taking it seriously; and it's simply got to help bring about the desired changes - where your attention goes, energy flows.

14/3/6 - The Result Materialises

Metaphorical change work is not like hitting someone over the head with a hammer.

It's more complex than that, and has the added intriguing dimension that the observer and the observed are one and the same. In order to make any kind of rational evaluation on how you're doing and on how you've done (which, by the way, is amusing and encouraging to start with and then becomes less necessary as you learn to trust in the process), you've got to freeze the current you in some shape or form in order to be able to make the comparison at a later date.

It's like living with someone every day - you kind of don't notice that they're growing, or getting fatter, or getting greyer, because it's such a gradual process; only, when we're dealing with ourselves, this 'not noticing' is even more pronounced.

Making a quick written testimony on how you currently feel, your plans, your problems and your views in the form of diary entries or, even better, letters to your future self, is one possibility. Being of a somewhat artistic persuasion, I use poems I wrote and pictures I painted as such reference points to show me what I've gained in the interim.

What happens to many of the people who have done Sanctuary work, as has happened to myself, is that reality starts to shift gear on you and things start to happen really quickly, taking your attention away from the inside because there's so much going on the outside.

At one point, after a major breakthrough type of puzzle solving and 'ghost laying', I found myself putting together a CD, getting my paintings ready for an exhibition, re-writing some old books for publication and, on top of that, finding the time to fit a gorgeous new man into my life! Ok so it might be said that that wasn't quite what I'd had in mind - but I can tell you honestly and from personal experience, people can find they've unleashed a whirlwind of opportunities once a particular underlying problem has been resolved.

So, if you're in the internal planning stages at present, moping about your abode and whilst you still have the time, write down who you are, so you can pick it up in six months' time and amaze yourself at what you used to be, and what has come about since then.

To round up this short treatise on learning the basics of reality creation in the safety of Sanctuary, a few words about a commonly asked question.

14/3/7 - The Dream Weaver

If, so the questions goes, my thoughts do indeed create reality, do all my thoughts go out and create something? What happens to my negative thoughts? Does this mean I can never contemplate something bad happening for the fear of creating that bad thing instead?

Now I'm not an enlightened Zen master or a major metaphysical teacher, but I see it like this.

Imagine, once more if you will, that there's this little man in your mind, whose task it is to weave tapestries out of the thoughts you think. But his job is very frustrating - as you think about one thing, he weaves that, and then as you think about another, he has to stop the first one, run across the room, and then start weaving the other instead. A new thought is a brand new tapestry just started, an old, recurring idea a tapestry in advanced stages.

Over a period of time, the ones he's allowed to spend the most time on will become complete, and when they do, the reality manifests.

A distant relative of mine told me long, long ago and before I ever got to hear about metaphor therapies, that they had this recurrent idea of themselves sitting lonely and friendless on a battered old suitcase on a railway station in the middle of nowhere in the rain.

This idea haunted them and so they worked like a mad person all their adult lives often twenty hours a day or more, backed up by hoarding and scrimping and saving.

Somehow or other, and this is hard to believe, they managed to accrue hundreds of thousands and then managed to get rid of it all in the most amazing ways you could begin to imagine so that by the time they died, they were poverty struck, friendless, and their possessions would have easily fitted into a small and battered suitcase.

This person has been dead a good long time, but if anything could convince me about the 'real life' value of internal metaphorical representations and pre-teach the whole subject many years before I came to consciously meet it, that was it.

If those are the kinds of instructions you give to your dream weaver, over a period of forty years or more, then he will manifest just that outcome for you. He doesn't know any better. And fleeting dreams and fancies that only cross your mind every so often won't be enough to offset the end result or even influence it greatly, they might just slow down the inevitability of it all to a minor degree.

Then, one day a client came my way, we shall call him Garth, who was a very 'witchy' person, a talented Tarot reader and local healer of some renown. His problem was that he had a long, long history of 'predicting' all kinds of disasters, which, no matter how mundane or bizarre, would come true in the end.

He could buy the most reliable of washing machines, then one day look at it, think to himself, "Oh dear, this is going to flood the entire kitchen," and, surprise surprise, so it would come to pass.

What amazed me was that it had never occurred to him that rather than *predicting* these disasters, **he might be creating them instead!**

When I pointed this possibility out, Garth had what I call "the goldfish moment" - that's when the look in the eyes goes vacant, and the mouth opens and closes involuntarily.

"Oh my God!", he said. "Just this morning on my way out here I was driving behind this truck piled up high with bits of fire wood. I was looking at it and had this really strong picture of the binding breaking loose and all the wood bouncing down on the bonnet of my car! As I was thinking that, the whole load started to vibrate weirdly, and I slowed right down to give him more room, and then the logs really started falling off the back! Do you really think I could have made that happen?"

You know what I'm going to say - I've no idea!

But, let's face it - predicting the wood falling is ESP (Extra Sensory Perception) just as much as causing the wood to fall without touching it. Even if there's only a ten percent chance that it was telekinesis rather than precognition, I should think it might be wise to get a hold of what you're so vividly imagining - just in case!

I suppose the more talented you are in the field of reality creation, the more important it is to open some lines of direct communication to the Dream Weaver - at least to let him know what you want creating, and what you're just kind of idly thinking about.

We do need to think of unpleasant outcomes sometimes in our lives; it's one of the great advantages of being a human that we are able to play out an imaginary scenario, thus testing it for hidden dangers or side effects before we go ahead and act. It's a warning mechanism and can be very useful in its proper place.

So, Garth had a little communication with his Dream Weavers (he had many more than just one), and came up with a kind of code to allow him to contemplate problems without compounding the problem or creating it; as he dealt mostly with pictorial representations, he would frame the ones he wanted to come true in green, and the ones he didn't want in red; the red framed ones were just put down some kind of astral rubbish chute and bypassed the weavers entirely. He said that it was a bit of an effort at first, but became quite easy and automatic after a few days; further, he now realised that his negative thoughts out-numbered his positive ones by at least one hundred to one, and that he was glad to be made aware of it and to be able to start to change that. Last thing I heard, his previously continuous and unbroken string of disasters had noticeably declined in severity as well as in frequency, and "he seemed a lot happier in himself, too."

If this approach sounds far too complicated to you, another client of mine, who was also a member of the British Union for Disaster Creating Specialists, chose to instruct her dream materialisation team to give preference to instructions which were written down and repeated three times, over all others.

Yet another had an even better idea - a fully trained and highly enlightened liaison manager who would decide what was to be created and what was just a passing fancy, thus sorting out the work for the dream weavers to get on with, for the good of all and harm of none.

15 - HEALING

For starters, a disclaimer: should you be suffering from a life threatening illness, I would suggest you seek specialist advice on what visualisations are the most appropriate to overcome that particular malfunction.

Amongst the holistic practitioners' community, there's by now a vast body of knowledge and experience in the field of which you should take full advantage. Any such advice can, of course, easily be integrated into the Sanctuary setting for overall harmony and ecology.

But now, let's consider DIY healing and health related problem-solving in the Sanctuary environment.

15/1 - Rest And Relaxation

My favourite all round healing and soothing tool in my own Sanctuary is the healing pool you might recall from the 'Water' section. I slip into it when I'm stressed out, have aches and pains, and I also use it for healing the various selves and parts that are injured and need such services. I am, however, generally very healthy anyway and so have no need for more specific healing tools and installations at this point.

What I do suffer from however is exhaustion and stress, overwhelm and tiredness because I work like a lunatic and always juggle with more balls in the air than an ace circus performer. Apart from the aforementioned healing pool I use Sanctuary spaces to re-charge me, soothe me and slow down my hyperactive mind so I can get some sleep at night.

Very useful and very helpful to me is to simply go to sleep in various different kinds of locations around my inner worlds. Sometimes I feel the need for sleeping in a hot place, in the shadow of some high cliffs, soft sand, near a slow waterfall. At other times, I seek a nest in a cold world, fine furs warming and absolutely snug whilst just outside, snowstorms are raging. I have gone to sleep in a birch grove on dry autumn leaves, in a forest grove by a beautiful sunlit pool and in many other locations and I do believe that these choices of places provide some form of very unique and balancing energy for my depleted systems that is most specific and 'just what the doctor ordered'.

Apart from these very specific locations, I sometimes have sleeping companions too and this is regardless of whether I am alone in bed in the Hard. These may be various beings that keep guard or simply happen to be there, and sometimes animals are either around or lie down close to me - once again, this is quite specific and a response to my real energetic needs at the moment.

Using Sanctuary in this very non-active fashion to simply soak up rest and relaxation is a very helpful thing in most circumstances. For actual illness, there are as many different ways of going about finding a healing solution as there are stars in the sky. In the following sections, there are some ideas on the subject.

15/2 - Healing Solutions

15/2/1 - Metaphorising The Body

Metaphorising the area of your body which seeks treatment is one of the oldest and simplest ways of beginning to find a healing solution. You could, for example, ask yourself to manifest a representation of your body - as a garden, a landscape, a plant, a house, a machine, whatever your mind will respond to.

I once dealt with a lady who had been told she was diabetic. As she wasn't really old enough for 'old age diabetes' and far too old for it to have been hereditary, I asked a few questions and it turned out that it had started after a massive trauma which involved a number of bereavements and a complete 'systems failure' type breakdown in her health - and that ever since then, she'd been on high prescription doses of insulin.

I told her the following story, "Well, imagine there's this worker in charge of blood sugar levels. He's had a nervous breakdown and couldn't work for a while. Now, he's beginning to recover, but as he's trying to get back to work, he finds they've hired some machine in his absence to take his job away."

She listened to that with interest and remarked that that was not unlike herself, that she had taken quite some time to be able to do things again, and if she didn't have to take care of her cat, she probably would have laid down and died altogether.

A little while later, she collapsed in a supermarket. It seemed that, quite miraculously, her pancreas had taken to functioning again and this, in combination with the pills she was taking, had caused her to faint. The hospital immediately withdrew the insulin prescriptions, and she has now learned to eat more carefully when she's very stressed, as "I don't want my little man to get too upset, I'm trying to help him out as much as I can."

This story is from way back when I had not yet understood that it's much more helpful to work with people's own metaphorical representations.

Luckily for the lady above, I had picked something intuitively that she could relate to - but you can imagine that this process is so very much more powerful when you use your own ideas instead.

Once you start deciding on how you would like to think of your body, as in: "My body is like a ....", it becomes very easy to spot just where the troubles lie and mostly it becomes just a matter of a bit of ingenuity of how to go about solving the puzzle.

Angela saw her body as a swamp, complete with toxic gases, crocodiles and long dead bodies in the murky darkness. Ouch!

You've probably heard the expression, "My body is a temple", often pronounced by those who try via plastic surgery to create an immortal marble facade.

Dean viewed his body as a cityscape, like Greater London from above, with obvious problems such as motorway congestion and inner city slum areas.

Wyn, on the other hand, saw a mostly natural landscape with few problems - he was fit and healthy at the time I asked.

Gene saw her body as a tree, blossoming out of season in winter and felt a strong sense of foreboding about the whole thing.

And each one of these, and many others beside, found their own various ways of dealing with the issues that presented themselves thus, just as you can deal with your own issues in this way should you choose to do so.

15/2/2 - Sanctuary Therapies

Another way of dealing with health related issues is to turn to internal therapists, healers and medicines.

As energy healing of one kind or the other is becoming more and more popular, and more and more people are attending workshops on the various healing arts, it's also becoming more popular for people to have a specific healing guide or to 'channel' some amazing astral healer for their insight, knowledge and resources on the subject.

Although your general guides and helpers most certainly are of great benefit in this area, you might consider getting yourself the equivalent of a personal Chinese physician - over there, you don't go the doctor when you're ill, but pay a doctor a fee all through your life in order so he can advise you on how to remain healthy instead. Whether it's a Native American Indian medicine woman, a Celtic shaman, an Atlantean energy healer or one of the top consultants from Chicago Hope Hospital, having an internal advisor on health related issues can be very beneficial indeed. But it's not just good advice that you can thus acquire.

166

I once attended a particularly dreary workshop. As the day progressed, I became more and more uncomfortable in the horrid plastic chair and by 3pm I had developed a stiff neck, sore shoulders, aching back and the beginnings of a headache. As the speaker waffled and mumbled on, and the rest of the group either sagged into themselves more and more, or shuffled around uncomfortably in their chairs, I called out my guide and asked him if he could massage my aching shoulders. It was great! I instantly begun to feel better, and after a few minutes I was virtually purring and stretching in my seat with a blissful expression on my face. If there'd been anyone around that day able to see auras, they would have noted in the next break that amidst 50 deflated people in grey, there was me, shining bright and chirpy - I think I was the only one who couldn't wait to get back to my seat ...

Was it all in my mind? Yes, I guess it was. I'm sure if the lecture had been more entertaining, I would have never experienced all these symptoms in the first place, because many's the day I've spent in identical plastic chairs and never even noticed because I'd been so riveted by what was going on up front.

I've come to the conclusion over the years that just about everything is "all in my mind". So if it is, then it makes a great deal of sense to me to cure it by using something else that's all in my mind - such as an extremely sensuous massage from my handsome spirit guide!

But all jokes apart - mind over matter really works. It really can reverse every single disease in the book and lessen the discomfort in many more cases. Here's some more ideas on how you could use Sanctuary resources and therapies.

15/2/3 - Colour Therapy

This is one of my favourite therapies, because no-one sticks you with needles or tries to break your bones. I'm also a painter, and I love to look at colours in all their many splendoured manifestations both in nature and in artificial creations, so I admit I'm biased on that one. As I'm sure you know, there is a massive amount of scientific evidence to back up the fact that colour has a major impact on immune system functioning, well being and general states of mind.

Anyhow, bathing in light, shining a light on a particular problem spot, dressing in sheets of pure light, surrounding oneself with light, using shining crystals or flowers or foods of a particular colour, and any possible permutation on the subject you might care to imagine are amongst my favourite recreational Sanctuary activities.

Having used colour therapy approaches in the past to back up other kinds of techniques in my professional work, I would suggest that, whatever other kinds of healing you wish to engage in, do a little of that as well. Let go of any preconceived notions of what a colour 'might mean' and allow yourself to follow your intuition - if everything in you screams out to wallow in puce, so be it!

This is a moment to also mention the wider realms of Project Sanctuary for the first time.

In the beginning stages, everything is much like you'd expect from the Hard - not too different really from what we are used to experiencing and what we already know, with animals and mountains, sunsets and houses, plants and so forth.

When you have a little more experience with Project Sanctuary and those realms where thought becomes manifest, this tends to loosen up and now we have manifestations which would be impossible in the Hard, they simply cannot exist or be conceived of as existing here.

A lightfall, for example, is an example of such a thing.

Light travels straight here in the Hard, but in the Sanctuary realms you can have rivers of light that flow upward as well as fall just like a waterfall and in the context of colour therapy, you can imagine the benefits of such a thing, I'm sure, as well as a sense of its sheer beauty and the fact that standing beneath a lightfall might present an experience to you that you simply never expected to have had.

15/2/4 - Medicines and Medications

In the garden section, we've already met the lady who grew all manner of beneficial plants in a greenhouse for her various ailments; in the treasure rooms chapter, someone had a whole pharmacy full of pills, potions and healing herbs. There are umpteen different ways of creating that which will help balance the system in your mind.

I once felt unhappy and out of sorts for no apparent reason, and asked for a remedy for this. Duly, on the entrance table of my Sanctuary dwelling there appeared a pretty blue glass bottle with 3 large, shining golden pills inside, and instructions to take one each week. I took the first one and felt better immediately, then forgot all about it. But just before going to sleep about a week later, the picture of the bottle appeared before my mind's eye - I was being reminded that there were still two doses to go. Well, I took them, and although it's interesting to idly speculate what it might have been that I never got in the end, it doesn't get us anywhere, as usual, and so I simply thanked my unconscious mind and decided to use this again if necessary.

All the Sanctuary resources can also be employed to help you pick out a relevant remedy in a shop or from a catalogue. Homeopathy, Flower Essences, Gemstones or their essences, Aromatherapy and all such like complimentary healing aids have a lot of use, and work on very subtle levels - and as you cannot make mistakes with these remedies, seeing as the wrong one will simply fail to work, rather than kill you as can often be the case for allopathic or herbal medicines, it's a safe way to involve your unconscious mind in a healing process.

15/2/5 - Contacting The Body Mind

Perhaps you are already familiar with Dr Deepak Chopra and his views on healing - if you are not, and you are at all interested in healing approaches, I would recommend you look up his bestseller "Quantum Healing". He basically suggests that the nervous system contains a 'body mind', a part of the overall neurology that remembers a blueprint for how to be healthy. Further, as the body is constantly re-cycling itself - we take in food, water, air and light and convert it into new blood, bones and tissues - there is, in truth, not a single atom left after a few years of the you that existed at that time.

This idea throws the possibility of reversing absolutely any disease wide open, and explains how, for example, people with massive cancerous tumours can simply make them disappear just like magic, and how the various medical miracles we've all heard about in our time could ever happen.

From this view point, it just becomes a question of how to contact the body mind, and how to assist it in its task of following the basic blue print to health that existed at one time. If you were to start talking with your own body mind, what do you think it would look like/be like?

Some see it as a person, others a system, a symbol, a machine or a city - it matters not what you choose to represent the body mind to you.

You may like to explore the following issues:

- Has something gone wrong with the basic blueprint at some time in the past? This could be a single significant emotional experience of a traumatic nature, a nice post hypnotic suggestion by a well meaning family doctor such as, "Well in your family, no-one ever lived past 55." or simply many little stacked beliefs over time along the lines of, "Of course, once you're over 25, you're over the hill."

- What can you do in real terms to help the current functioning of the body mind, to relieve some of the stresses in some areas so that it may function more smoothly throughout? This, by the way, is a very interesting thing. One lady who asked the question fully expected her body mind to tell her off about her excessive coffee consumption, but that, apparently, wasn't a problem. Instead, her body mind wanted her desperately to stop eating fish! She tried it for a fortnight and couldn't believe how much better she felt.

Another lady had a much harder time with her body mind's request - it wanted animal based protein and she was a vegan. After some lengthy negotiations, they agreed on a few free range eggs here and there, and the odd piece of free range chicken cunningly disguised in a broth, and once again, the lady in question found herself to be more energetic, and more resistant to the many colds and coughs which had plagued her previously, and with a much more sympathetic attitude to her body in general.

- Is there any kind of gift or metaphorical resource the body mind would like to make it feel happier or more comfortable? Most body mind representations, whatever form they took in the first place, responded to this question with the same degree of enthusiasm a parching man in the desert exhibits when asked if he'd like a drink. I've known them to ask for a colour, a plant, a gemstone, a new source of water, all kinds of things; I think that's a particularly nice gesture to make whether you're ill or healthy, because it shows for once how much we appreciate what the body mind does for us, all through our lives, 24 hours a day.

15/2/6 - Chakra And Energy Healing

Just in case there's still anyone left out there who doesn't know the basic chakra system, here goes:

'Chakras' is the name given to energy vortices which exist within the overall force field that is the human body. There are very many of them, but the main big eight are as follows:

Base Chakra	- Tail Bone	-	Red
Second Chakra	- Lower Abdomen	-	Orange
Third Chakra	- Solar Plexus	-	Yellow
Fourth Chakra	- Heart Centre	-	Green Or Pink
Fifth Chakra	- Throat	-	Blue
Sixth Chakra	- Third Eye	-	Purple
Seventh Chakra -	- Crown Of Head	-	Indigo
Eight Chakra	- Above The Crown	-	White

In a healthy, fully realised, spiritually, emotionally, mentally and physically present person all these are drawing in and distributing energy not just through the physical body but also through the astral bodies. When they all come on line together and connect, one is said to experience a tremendous rush of energy and instant enlightenment.

In chakra visualisations, usually one or more are not functioning properly in some way - this may be expressed as a dimness of colour, an absence of the spinning movement that would be natural to a vortex, or damage, blockage, or deficiency of any other kind.

There are some who feel that dealing with these vortices is not just repair work for the actual body, but works to re-balance the astral bodies as well, thus leading to long lasting and very profound healing in all areas and not just the physical.

I'm sure you must have seen an acupuncture chart somewhere, with all the lines drawn on the human body to represent the meridians, i.e. the channels through which life energy flows around the body. You can make a representation of yourself made of glass, if you will, and this makes all these meridians clearly visible.

Then, you might like to do whatever feels right to you to balance them out, harmonise them, and get all flowing freely and efficiently.

If you felt like it, you could also work with the various astral bodies, which form what is generally called 'The Aura'. Practitioners who can see auras can see disturbances, black spots, low energy fields etc which will eventually cause physical disease to manifest. In your Sanctuary, you too can see auras - all of them, if you wish! - and use whatever means come to mind to make them more to your liking. Just a quick general note on such work: look for balance and harmony in whatever you're looking at. If it's pleasing to the eye, it's probably right; if it's uncomfortable to look at, it's probably not right and could do with some help.

Healing energy work in more general terms, whatever the way you would like to visualise or experience it, can all take place and, apart from the very real physical repercussions on your illness, most definitely will help your immune system by reducing stress, relaxing you, giving you something practical to do in between visiting real world physicians, and generally speaking keeping your mind alert and occupied, whilst all the while your self learns how to communicate more successfully with its self in all its different forms and guises.

EFT and Meridian Energy Therapies

Meridian Therapies are the state of the art choice for mind body healing amongst professional healers right now. Extraordinarily effective yet simple to apply, meridian energy therapies such as EFT (Emotional Freedom Techniques) are sweeping the globe.

I cannot recommend this therapy highly enough; it is a superb healing and change technique.   In the context of Sanctuary interventions, EFT can unstick you if you are stuck like nothing else I've ever learned and can also tremendously improve your general visualisation / lucid dreaming / conscious-unconscious communication and intuitive skills.

You can use EFT on aspects of the self and others in the Sanctuary. This is known as surrogate or proxy EFT, and is the most effective distant healing method known to mankind.

You can also use it to change entire mindscapes; I have personally used it to ecologically resolve a problem I had with towering mountains that cut off access to an ocean and a whole realm beyond. During the EFT treatment, I could see the mountains melting away as thought by magic. If you are not familiar with the new Meridian Therapies yet, go ahead and find out about it now at http://www.theamt.com

EmoTrance & Sanctuary Approaches

My own energy healing system, EmoTrance, has a great deal to do with Sanctuary realms and spaces, because it was here that I learned the things I needed to know in order to understand the energy body on a whole new level and open my mind to both new observations and new thoughts on how things might be working.

EmoTrance recognises that emotions are nothing but the pain system of the energy body; emotions become apparent when the normal energy flow in the energy body changes.

In order to target healing interventions, ET simply asks, "Where in your body do you feel this (problem, sickness, bereavement, emotion, pain, unhappiness, stress etc)?" Wherever it is felt physically, that is where the energy body has a problem even though we can't see it with our eyes. It may be a blockage, or an old unhealed injury of some kind; once it has been localised, we treat this with healing energy and the intention to restore the 'Even Flow' in that part of the systems of the energy body (which extends way beyond the skin barrier of a person).

Project Sanctuary deals absolutely with energy - with energy disturbances, energetic occurrences and a person's energy matrices of memory, body, future and past in the quantum spaces - and it does so by creating a custom made **interface device** between these energy patterns and our own conscious understanding by coding the metaphorical languages, pictures and happenings as the bridge to these other realms where there are no symbols, no language and too much information for simple linear speech. The lesson from EmoTrance applied to Project Sanctuary is this, namely to know that the mountain or the monster in your Sanctuaries are not mountains or monsters, but forms of energy and, as such, are under your control, under your command and at your disposal in every way. To remember when faced with a ruined landscape or a towering demon that 'It is JUST an ENERGY' and find the correct leverage to deal with this so the Even Flow is restored in this area takes a great deal of uncertainty and fear from all the processes; and to channel the energies raised in Sanctuary work cleanly and clearly is a huge contribution from EmoTrance.

As with the EFT protocol, you can use EmoTrance as the problem solving tool and Project Sanctuary as the device which shows you what is wrong where, and to give you feedback on the success of your treatments and changes to be sure you are going in the right direction towards restoring health, potentiality and happiness.

16 - PROBLEM SOLVING

I think it was Einstein who said, "You cannot solve a problem from the same space where it was created".

Makes a lot of sense to me, and this is one of the many reasons why I like metaphor therapy so very much.

I wonder if you remember Joshua, the young man who could not deal with his anger towards his father, and represented the father as a scrap yard instead. The resolution - keep the best resources and heal the rest - was easy and only presented itself in that other space, because in the real life relationship Joshua and his father were like two people wrestling in a muddy swamp. That's all they could do in that place where their problems had been created.

Any kind of problem can be addressed thus - all it takes is to allow for a representation of the problem. "My fear of failure is (like standing alone on a battlefield, facing a massive army of foes about to attack me) - (like trying to walk on a frozen pond but the ice is about to crack and I can't move) - (like drowning in a dark sea) - (like a broken vase) etc, etc, etc.

You then take the representation into the Sanctuary, forget what it was supposed to be about in the first place, and deal with it 'as is', finding solutions that satisfy you completely and that **make sense in the context of the story**. This is dead easy, good fun, and if nothing else, will certainly take your mind off the problem for a while! No, jokes apart, using such representations in good faith and trust will allow you to find solutions that you wouldn't have come up with in a month of Sundays, if you'd just applied your usual thought patterns to the problem.

One lady who expressed a fear of close intimate relationships said it was like "Being scared of being washed away, swamped somehow, so I can't breathe anymore and I must die." I asked her to consider allowing herself to make a mental movie of what she thought was going to happen, and she described standing on a sea shore, looking out at the blue tranquil ocean and being quite happy.

Then, however, she would notice the horizon lifting and coming towards her, like a giant flood wave, ready to swallow her up and smash her to pieces. I suggested she pause the movie at that point and consider something other than just running away in a panic. She thought about it for quite a while, and then said, "If I was more than a tiny little person, I could merge with that wave somehow. Then its power would be mine as well and I would not have to be afraid of it anymore - in fact, that would be quite an amazing experience." We both smiled at each other then, and she allowed her body to dissolve in the wave, whilst her mind and spirit remained intact, alert and sentient, and I admit I was a little jealous of the intensity of that experience for her.

More often than not, however, it isn't so easy to determine that, for example, 'fear of failure' is the key issue in the first place.

Half the time we do things and we don't know what causes us to think, feel and act the way we do - or we delude ourselves that we do when in fact we're a million miles off the mark.

One elegant way to find solutions to such underlying, yet totally unconscious, key problems is to look at your ...

16/1 - Interests, Fascinations and Obsessions

The only difference between an interest, a fascination and an obsession is the severity of the manifestation - these three are just random names for a range of points on a sliding scale, yet again. Half the time if there's a problem, whether you're aware of it or not, you will probably find that it is reflected very well in your interests and obsessions.

A friend of mine went virtually mad over Disney's version of Beauty & The Beast. She loved the movie intensely, bought the video, watched it repeatedly and went around humming the theme tune when she wasn't watching herself.

It was blatantly obvious to everyone but herself that the reason she was so obsessed with the movie was her own internal wrestlings about a relationship she had recently entered into, and whatever the metaphorical goings on in the movie, they were striking a deeply resonant chord within her own mind. This went on for six months; then the relationship dissolved and so did her interest in the movie.

A teenager I was working with recently had a similar - if more long standing - obsession; namely, with vampire movies, vampire TV series and vampire novels.

This time, however, I showed him how to create a complete Sanctuary, and, when it was ready, to be able to play out some of the central themes that had particularly fascinated him about some of these films he'd seen. The ins and outs of what went on are enough to write an entire book in their own right; the subjects and ideas he addressed were incredibly profound, deep and serious for someone so young and seemingly uneducated.

When it was all over, a deep change had taken place that was immediately observable both within and without; the most obvious one was that once the vampires had been laid to rest, he changed his hair colour, redecorated his room and changed his wardrobe from black only to a more fashionable and laid back selection; and when his mother painfully enthused, "We've got our little darling baby boy back", he responded not by throwing furniture at her as he had previously done, but by raising an eyebrow, shaking his head and smiling tiredly instead.

Frankly, without the help of his obsession to guide us in the correct direction, I don't think we would have ever figured out the depth and power of what was troubling him, nor how to resolve it so successfully.

The point of these stories is to take any kind of interest, fascination or obsession, be it your own or someone else's, **very seriously indeed**. Whether it's stamp collecting, S&M, football or archaeology - here are the signposts to what aches to be addressed and resolved. The stronger the obsession, the stronger the warning - sort it out, now, if you would rather be free.

"Now why would I want to be free of my interest in collecting ceramic frogs?" you might ask. "It's harmless enough and has given me much pleasure over the years; ok so I've got 786 of them now and it takes a week to dust them all, and my husband and children have stopped bringing their friends round, but it's not a problem, is it?"

Well, nothing is ever a problem unless you decide that it is. I personally have for a long while considered various ideas from Zen Buddhism, one of these revolving around 'unhealthy attachments' which are said to seriously impede your spiritual path. If I meet a Zen master, I'll ask him if a collection of 786 ceramic frogs falls into that category ...

16/2 - Recurring Resonant Themes

Works of fiction in general, but movies in particular, are a superb tool for exploring underlying conflicts that hold you back.

The kinds of movies you like, and within that category, the kinds of scenarios that **strike the deep, resonant chord** with you, are ready made set ups to resolve problems of all kinds - the situations are there, the circumstances, locations and the characters, all ready and standing by for you to find out what's going on, and then to resolve it successfully.

I was loosely working with an acquaintance called Thom in a practise group who was aware of this idea. One evening, he called me up to tell me that 'it' had happened to him during the movie 'Braveheart'.

The main character in the movie, the leader of an army of freedom fighters, had just lost a battle and had been captured. As he is led away, he encounters a knight. When this knight removes his helmet, he realises that he has been betrayed by a trusted friend.

At this point, Thom described "feeling so horrified I had painful tears in my eyes instantly. I was nearly physically sick, breathless and it was as though this had happened to me in some way - losing the battle for the kingdom was nothing in comparison to the pain of betrayal."

Following this striking of the deep, resonant chord, Thom chose to investigate the matter and found an unresolved past life where he had also been betrayed. The whole thing and its eventual successful resolution led to a complete turnaround in the way he viewed not only friendships but relationships in general, a virtual spring cleaning of his personal life, and tremendously wide ranging changes in other areas.

Thom said, "The strange thing is that I wasn't even aware that there was a problem on any level. Sure, I had a hard time trusting people, but I never questioned it, it never occurred to me to do so, and on a conscious level I would never have considered investigating that area or even beginning to suspect that there may be a problem there. It sometimes frightens me to think how long I would have gone along like that - perhaps to my dying day? - if I hadn't seen that particular movie and realised the connection. I'd like to give Mel Gibson yet another Oscar, and to the 'resonance theory', my sincere gratitude."

16/3 - Practical Problems

If you want to stop smoking, lose weight or give up a cocaine addiction, Sanctuary work might not be your first option. In many ways, that's not really what it's about, anyway.

You see, I'm looking for an evolutionary system that will heal underlying issues of all sorts, so that eventually, self destructive behaviours like the ones mentioned above become redundant so they will either drop away all by themselves, or the person in question wakes up one morning with this "Right, that's it, I don't need this anymore" attitude that will make any therapy, no matter what, a fine candidate to help resolve the problem once and for all.

The changes made in the Sanctuary at the metaphorical level are gentle, holistic, complex and involved; for this reason, urgent practical problems such as phobias and addictions that make your life a misery might well benefit from other and faster first aid techniques such as Hypnosis or NLP for 'on the spot' relief, or any of the other problem orientated therapies such as TimeLine Therapy or Past Life Regression, for example. A superb energy technique for such purposes is EFT (Emotional Freedom Technique) which I cannot recommend highly enough, and then of course there is the sheer power of transformation with EmoTrance.

If you choose to engage in such resolution approaches, and I would encourage you to do so if you have an overriding practical concern that haunts all your daylight hours, you will find that the Sanctuary you have built with all its resources is a superb back up system to the therapy, and also a superb long term check back system that truly supports all your other efforts in the personal development department.

This is not to say, however, that direct practical issues such as impotence and co-dependency cannot be addressed in metaphorical form to full conclusion and to very satisfactory outcomes; indeed I have used Sanctuary therapy with the kinds of clients who "have tried everything" and failed to get the desired gains, to great effect.

One particular client who had failed to stop smoking his average of 40 cigarettes a day for the last 30 years after every conceivable treatment under the sun - and these included electro shock aversion therapy! - imagined himself standing on the edge of a cliff, mesmerised in an updraft from the sea which both energised and incarcerated him. A guide helped him to break free and fly away. Following this, he actually smoked more for a time because he had completely stopped worrying about giving up altogether, until one day he became aware that his consumption had dropped without his even noticing. He's now down to about 5 a day and doesn't even give it a second thought anymore, when before the stop smoking issue had been a quest of his life and a source of never ending internal conflict, harassment and misery. One day this guy will wake up and realise that he's forgotten to buy cigarettes for the last 6 weeks and never even noticed!

I'm not suggesting that this is exactly what will happen to you if you choose to go ahead and manifest your bugging practical problems in a metaphorical form; but this is certainly an example of how I like to resolve such things - elegantly, easily, stress free, naturally, ecologically, holistically, and once and for all.

After all, always remember that I wouldn't be in this business if I thought you had to stop eating chocolate in order to lose weight!

16/4 - Problems With People

No matter how enlightened you are, I reckon there's not a person alive who doesn't on occasion experience problems with people. I'm a member of an Internet NLP group where someone recently stated unequivocally that they never get annoyed with anyone.

Sorry, I don't believe it. Even Jesus was said to have lost his temper on quite a few occasions; and I personally think that it's just human to respond in a less than entirely enlightened way once in a while.

We're not supposed to be angels yet. There's more than enough time for that when we're dead. Whilst we're still here I think we're supposed to learn *how to live successfully as a human* - and that includes firstly allowing oneself to experience emotions, and then to deal with them in a civilised manner.

Unfortunately, I was never really taught as a child how to deal with emotions - I was just told to keep them inside, and, whatever I did, never to express them. I misunderstood and took it to mean that I wasn't supposed to have them at all - and so I went ahead and tried very hard for many years to be as emotionless as a robot, thinking that that was the idea and the grand aim towards which to work.

When it didn't work, and I'd burst out into tears, throw objects around, scream with rage or throw a temper tantrum, I'd take myself to task and berate myself and generally beat up on myself and vow to do better in future; when it did work, it led to a glass screen or ivory tower detachment from the world around and a feeling of disconnectedness, and of loneliness. Either way, I could never seem to win.

In the last few years, I tried a different way of dealing with emotions. The first thing was to even recognise it was happening - a simple task, but I'd trained myself well. It took quite some time until I had dismantled the various barriers within to even allowing myself to spot disappointment, anger, fear etc. when it first appeared; then even longer until I allowed myself the right to feel that way, and finally took the dramatic step of just letting it happen.

What happened was that the emotion would come, wash over me, and be gone - just like that. An internal sensation that passed within a split second. I could not believe it could be that easy.

So why am I telling you that?

Well, firstly, to make you understand that it's ok to be angry at people, to get annoyed, to be jealous, or even to experience moments of murderous rage, because it's my belief that if you block off your negative emotions, you'll end up blocking the good ones as well. Love, compassion, joy, ecstasy, and so on run along the same channels in my opinion.

Further, I don't believe that you can 'exhaust' emotions.

Some psychotherapy approaches hold that if you've got 'repressed anger' (like a compressed bail of hay, I suppose), you can get rid of it by being very, very angry for lots and lots of times and then it'll go away.

I have the theory that emotions are not kept in buckets that you can just empty out, but that in fact there exists something akin to an emotion generator or even an emotion muscle if you will - the more you practise, the better you get at it; the more you practise being angry, as in the example before, the easier it becomes to get deeply angry very quickly and stay that way for longer.

There are a lot of dead rock stars out there for that reason. They experience a peak moment of angst or depression, then bottle that emotion in a song - which they then go and perform seven nights a week for the next ten years, thus re-entering that peak state of depression and re-accessing all the pain involved, over and over again. Little wonder that their lives are less than happy and that they turn to drugs and suicides of all kinds! On the other hand, the 'sunny side of the street' crowd amongst the popsters seem to go on and on, and on, ... and on, remaining youthful and chirpy way after their sell by date has long since faded into oblivion.

The point is that to experience emotions is to be alive. That to repress or deny emotions just makes them fight harder and find other ways of drawing your attention to their existence. That repeatedly re-accessing peak states of negative emotion can be damaging to your health. And finally, that you have a right as a human being to experience the whole, amazing range of emotions - but you don't necessarily have to act them out.

That's also your right of choice as a human being.

A teenage girl called Stella had been sent to me because of her 'rages'. Listening to her and her life, I agreed that I would probably rage as well if I'd been treated as she was - with a lack of understanding, sympathy, rapport and intelligence that left me at a loss for words at the time, by her loving parents who were ever so happy to pay the bill so I would 'fix' her.

"I don't want to lose it all the time," she told me with tears. "I'd give anything if I could just be a nice person, and be good, and fit in, anything. I hate being like this. And no-one gives me any credit because they don't know how hard I try."

It took me a while to explain to her that it wasn't fair she should hate herself for responding, having being repeatedly provoked without ever having being taught how to respond differently. It finally sank in when I pointed out that if I was in a relationship with someone, and did or said something that caused him to freak out completely, I'd have the sense to understand that I could have probably approached the subject in a different way, and that I'd also have the sense to not then go ahead and do the very same thing again, day in, day out, day in, day out.

She then said, "But what about the guy? Has he no responsibility at all?"

"No." I said with a little grin. "He's just like a TV - you push the button, and boom! Light, Sound, Music!"

Stella laughed as well at that point, and wondered what the imaginary man might be able to do to be a little less predictable.

One of the strategies she had used before to try and stop herself from going berserk with her parents was to run from the room when it got towards the outer edges of her tenuous control. Unfortunately, her parents didn't approve of this kind of behaviour and would follow her into her room, to continue the exact same conversation where it had been disrupted by Stella's flight, and with highly predictable results.

Over the next couple of weeks, I let her in on a few tricks of my trade - like pattern interrupts, how to use the meta model to drive anyone absolutely insane in a conversation, a few mind-warping hypnotic language patterns and some other effective little bits and pieces, and then introduced her to Sanctuary work.

Her parents looked a little pale and fraught when they brought her back for her next session, but Stella was much improved in attitude and demeanour.

"That meta model thing," she said as soon as they'd left. "What a weapon! That should have a government health warning on it!" Apparently, it was the parents who were now running from the room instead.

Stella had regained some self confidence and personal power, and in the preceding two days, neither her mother or her father had had the nerve to start on a major diatribe in that household at all.

The playing field now being a little more level, and the imminent danger of Stella being put on psychoactive drugs having been thus removed, we could go ahead and now resolve the problem in a cohesive and ecological manner.

Stella informed me that she'd set up a screaming room in her Sanctuary dwelling - "as it was less strenuous that doing it for real". As soon as she felt threatened, she'd go there and say what she really wanted to say in the most ferocious terms, and that "sort of made it go away", as she put it. At school too, she'd use this kind of 'time out' to remove herself from imminent danger of losing control, and she found that thinking about her Sanctuary was a great diversion during the more boring lessons. It had developed and grown nicely, and her favourite resource was a guide in the form of a large, black dog; he did not only advise her, but served as a protector, too.

You might think that this is an unusual approach, and you might be right. I personally have a leaning towards the idea that the most outrageously behaved youngsters have probably the most potential; that any kind of seriously anti-social behaviour is rooted in a belief that one has no personal power and no worth; and that when these issues even only begin to be tackled in such a way that the person in question begins to feel more in control of their lives, positive changes can't help but happen.

After just 4 months, Stella was a different person. The last three of these four months, we basically just had coffee together, discussed Sanctuary resources, how to resolve conflicts and whether Liam Gallagher was sexually attractive or not. All the gains she made in being less out of control when challenged, being less fearful in her dealings with others at school, finding it much easier to speak up for herself rather than letting it brew and then exploding over the littlest things, and greater tolerance for her parents, were essentially of her own making, her own design, and her own direction. Further, the basic skills and tools she acquired, and the resources she found within herself, will remain with her, wherever she goes from now on. Her parents consider her 'fixed' now, but she comes by after school every so often anyway, and I'm always pleased to see her.

Looking at her, you'd never guess the mind-blowing landscapes that now exist within her mind.

16/5 - Difficult People

Stella's parents were, to all intents and purposes, 'difficult people'. Well, at least according to Stella they were. If you'd asked them if they considered themselves to be 'difficult', they'd probably be quite aghast at the suggestion. In the Sanctuary with all its marvellous resources at your disposal, you can do quite a lot of 'voodoo without the dolls' to your heart's content. I do feel, however, I have to give you a few words of warning on the subject.

Jim had acquired a new boss at work - when he'd expected he was going to be given the promotion and the job after his previous boss retired. "To make matters worse" - his words! - the new boss was ... a woman twenty years his junior, and with a university degree to boot.

He shuffled very uncomfortably around, wrung his hands and then admitted that he'd had "thoughts" about what he would do to her whenever his mind wandered - I refuse to hallucinate what other people's thoughts might be in general, but in this particular case I was rather grateful that I make that a habit.

Apparently, his relationship with his new boss had deteriorated into trench warfare, the other staff members were siding with her, work and the thought of going to work was becoming unbearable to the point where he experienced momentary paralysis in the mornings - he couldn't get his legs to move for a few minutes on waking and had to sit on the side of his bed for a time, willing them to take the first step of the day. His GP had referred him, wisely, to me.

"Do you believe in magic?" I asked him.

He was completely blown away by this, but at least it stopped him shuffling around and twiddling his hands.

"No, it's all a lot of mumbo jumbo," he then stated categorically.

"I wonder if we could, for a moment, believe that it's all true. That somehow the things you do in your mind with another person really influence them in real life. That whatever you send out, returns to you threefold. What if that were true?"

He laughed a little. "Then, my dear, I would be in very deep shit indeed." he said.

I put it to Jim that his legs were just trying to protect him from having to walk yet again into a situation that was so hateful and damaging to him. He was very surprised by that notion; I was surprised yet again how elusive the elusive obvious can sometimes appear. It made sense with hindsight to him, however, and so we went on to discuss his various options.

Although Jim in his pinstripe suit, greying hair and 'mumbo jumbo' attitude might not at first glance appear to be a good candidate for the kind of things I have people do with their minds, I nevertheless went ahead and had him create a safe place where he was fully in control; and as he told me about the stronghold with the huge metal doors that only he could open, tension began to fade a little.

I then told him to get his boss in for a chat. That's fast and drastic, but Jim was a strong and experienced man, very used to doing things he abhorred, and had trained all his life to perform no matter what his state of mind; unlike a tender, far more 'enlightened' gentle soul on the spiritual path, these hard won resources allowed me to go straight for the jugular in this case.

He didn't like the idea one bit, but then imagined her tied up and fully muzzled (!!) in a titanium cage on the far side of a large metal room. To make it even better, the cage stood on a trap door which could make it and its contents disappear the instant a big red panic button close by his right hand was activated.

That seemed to be enough for him to feel reasonably safe in her presence; and he began to make tentative contact with her.

To make a long and complex story short, he learned that she was as desperately unhappy as he was, this situation being her worst nightmare as a first introduction to directing a team of people; was afraid of him on a physical level; felt intimidated by him personally as well as by his professional experience; that he reminded her of her overbearing father, and finally, that she was also under a lot of pressure from her own superiors to resolve the situation of which they were completely aware.

At this point, I offered Jim the chance to get out of this relationship altogether by finding alternative solutions that would satisfy 'his legs' - such as another job, early retirement, a different position within the company etc. etc. He, however, expressed a preference for sorting out his problems with the woman in question.

"How would you go about it, seeing that you've already done many negative things to her in your mind so far and it hasn't worked?" I asked.

"You're not really suggesting that if I did NICE things in my mind to her, it would?"

"No, not necessarily. But wouldn't it be worth a try?"

He considered that for a while, and eventually agreed that there was no harm in trying - after all, it couldn't get any worse and he was tired of the energy it took hating her and wishing her dead.

"But what nice things could I possibly do to her?" he asked, shaking his head.

"I don't know - remember, we're playing at magic here. You could wave a magic wand, just like Tinkerbell."

He laughed at that a bit, but still couldn't get himself to think of anything nice for his nemesis.

"What do you enjoy having? If it comes back threefold, you might as well pick something you like in the first place!"

That did the trick. All of a sudden, there was this great big long shopping list of 'nice' things - peace of mind, better self esteem, pride in the work, a sense of importance, being respected, being a worthwhile person, having money, having good health, being popular ... the list grew longer and longer as I wrote each item onto the big white board in my office (I prefer my clients to see what I write down rather than muttering to myself and scribbling ominously on a clip-boarded pad when they've said something particularly profound).

"Right," I said. "Now here's the list. Your mission, should you choose to accept it, is to go back and give her each one of these as a gift in any form or shape you would like, even if it's just saying the words."

He swallowed a couple of times, folded his hands, went back to the metal room with the caged woman, cleared his throat and began "Ruth Smith, I give you the gift of peace of mind."

It was hard for him to start with, you could see how he struggled to say the words, but he was a strong and determined man and he did it, although on more than one occasion his voice faltered and nearly broke. When he was through, he looked as though he had just run a marathon or something - exhausted but proud.

"Now, how does that feel?" I asked. Apparently, just a third of the way into the list, the cage had dropped away and then, the bindings. Towards the end, it was just the woman, sitting on the floor with her head on her knees, crying.

"I don't know how I feel," he said. "Strange. Will this work?"

"I can't know that." I said, trying to hide a little smile. I did instruct him, however, not to change his behaviour in the slightest when he went back to work, to check if there had been a change in her behaviour towards him in the absence of any other intervention.

He rang me the following evening. It seemed that there was something peculiar going on - Ms Smith had been behaving very out of character; she had avoided him, not given him any public dressing downs, and seemed all of a sudden very unsure how to relate to him all of a sudden.

"Honestly, I've done nothing - what's going on?"

Well, I can't tell you that these two got married the week later.

What I can tell you is that Jim's chosen to stay on, the department is relatively at peace and working productively, and 'the legs' now work fine in the mornings. What I am especially happy to report is that following a spot of road building and countryside-scaping in and around Jim's internal stronghold, it occurred to him to sign up with a senior executive job search company - because "You never know where it might lead, and there's no harm in trying, right?"

Note: The case story above is a precursor for the wonderful 'The Gift' pattern which you can find in the Resources Section.

16/6 - Questing

Questing is an activity you can engage in when you don't even know what the problem actually is, as well as when faced with a problem that you have utterly failed to overcome by any means known to you.

You can also do mythical quests of some form or shape to help with future creation and when there's a general lack of direction in life; sometimes, you might find that a quest is required as the natural solution to a problem that has manifested through a revelation, or a dream.

In my opinion, a proper mythical quest involves a journey - but hey, that's just my opinion. You could quest on a map, or do a kind of treasure hunt in your subterranean domains instead; still most people, when the time comes, will prepare for a major journey of some kind.

You can go questing on your own, or you can assemble a group of people and/or creatures, which will be extra resources on your journey; both versions are well documented in story, tale and fable.

Linda dreamed about a mountain in which there lived a single man. Outside the mountain, there was an ice age and a small village nearby, where people were now starving to the degree that they had begun to eat each other. Still, the man would not reveal that inside this mountain there was heat, light and food - he preferred to sit in his mountain all by himself and watch them die.

The dream was very vivid and disturbing, and Linda chose to approach it via a quest. She saddled up her dragon, took a warm cloak and asked to be taken to the place where these events were unfolding.

As the dragon rose above her Sanctuary, she could see that they were heading across the sea towards another continent of her domain; like Antarctica, it was entirely covered in thick ice - yet it wasn't that far North, and the seas around it were temperate and mild.

She soon spotted the mountain of her dream, which was in fact part of a much larger mountain range; she could also see from way up high that the glacier which had covered the entire continent had begun on the highest mountain, where there was a well that created more and more ice instead of water.

This glacier well was guarded by a black shape who told her that it had been enchanted a long time ago and in order to unfreeze it, a particular magic flower was needed to break the spell.

Well, and to make a long and complex story short, after much trial and tribulation as is customary in questing, the flower was found, the spell broken, the villagers saved, the man redeemed and Linda was happy. She also said that, "I can't believe that I've come up with all of that. At school, I couldn't even write a one page composition. Where does it all come from?" Where indeed.

Who knows? Who cares? The point is, here's a really nice example of problem solving via a mythical quest; I like this one because we didn't even know what the problem was that Linda's dream represented. Once you really get down to immersing yourself in the story rather than wondering what it all means, things get underway and a very healing - and exciting - time can be had by all.

Peter, on the other hand, knew exactly what he wanted. He wanted to develop more "trust in the Universe". That might seem a strange request on the surface, but it was central to many issues in his life, from manifesting positive relationships to manifesting abundance and joy. As he'd never had any "trust in the Universe", he didn't know what such a thing might look like; he also didn't want to get this resource through a past life or a higher self but felt he needed to discover it for himself in the here and now.

I suggested a quest.

He set off, the lone figure walking into the sunrise, out of his Sanctuary and into the surrounding badlands. Once again, you could create a top notch fantasy movie out of the events that occurred, the strange creatures and people he met, some of whom aided him in his quest, some of whom tried to stop, side track, or deter him.

In the end, he found it. "Trust in the Universe" was, in fact, a velvet cloak of the darkest purple with all the stars and all the galaxies of all the Universe woven into its very fabric. Not a bad object to have been found by an unmarried 42 year old accountant, what! You should have seen the look on his face when he put that cloak finally around his shoulders. That was really something...

If you think that such mega mental movie world creations are out of your league, **think again**.

I can assure you that it's a simple process that moves along under its own speed, just as a conversation does - something turns up, you respond, the situation changes, you respond, and so on and so on until the conclusion is reached and both conversation partners go home happy.

But going back to the subject of mythical quests, there's one last thing you might like to consider before you move out. The quest is important as an overall process; it's not really about the magic flower or the star spangled cloak.

Quests are the original courses in personal development; right from the decision to go forth and start the journey, in spite of the fact that the outcome is unknown and that the journey might be treacherous, through all the trials and tribulations, to the success at the end. The one at the end of the quest is not the same person who started out on it; the one at the end is wiser, more seasoned, more confident - a true hero, if you will.

A word of advice. It is customary in the fifth act of any quest to experience what is known as 'the hero's darkest hour'. This is the moment when everything seems to have gone wrong, the night is at its darkest, the problems seem truly insurmountable, and the audience thinks, oh dear, he's had it. He's failed. At this moment, the true hero reaches deep inside, and finds the strength for one more attempt, one more effort, one more push. And at this moment, the tide is turned, and, with ever gathering strength and ever growing confidence, the hero completes the task and wins the day.

I wish you good fortune on your quest.

16/7 - Familiarizing With the Unfamiliar

In the more advanced forms of lecturing these days, there exists the concept of 'pre-teaching'. What it means is that before a new subject or concept is presented, it is mentioned in passing a few times, or examples of this subject or concept are given whilst on a different subject. When the 'new' subject is then presented, the student experiences a feeling of familiarity, and this allows the new knowledge to be integrated more smoothly and lessens culture shock, as it were.

When there's a dramatic or frightening transition to be made, you can lessen your culture shock and allow yourself to access this feeling of familiarity by using a representation in your Sanctuary.

Catherine, an A* student, was very worried about going to university. What made it worse was that the university she had chosen was Oxford, and she felt the weight of the name of that centuries old institution bear heavily upon her mind and spirit.

I asked her to represent all the schools she'd ever been to in some form, and she though of a number of towns along a road, from a really small group of farm houses, to a hamlet, a town, and there, on the horizon, lay a huge city of biblical proportions.

"Just looking at it makes my heart sink," she said with a sigh. I suggested she turn her back on it for the moment, and re-visit all the towns along the way, checking around for any possible trouble spots or problems that might be holding her back - I'm a great believer in clearing out the past before you can get on with the future. This she did, and found all manner of minor and major problems, such as a dangerous swamp in one village into which small children would be sucked if they didn't take care and wandered by too closely; a library in one of the towns to which she owed past dues; a nasty witch living in a haunted house, and so on. When her affairs with these towns had been properly settled, she turned her attention back to the biblical city.

Over the next couple of weeks and without any further help from me, she spent time here and there exploring it, finding her way about it, overcoming problems and frightening situations, finding rooms to rent for herself, making new friends, finding a mentor, checking out the night life and acquiring a house keeper and a local guide. As a result, Catherine told me that "I'm no longer afraid of going to Oxford, and I don't have nightmares any more. I won't kid myself and think it's going to be all perfect and easy, but I really feel quite excited about the whole idea and I am sure that I'll be able to cope. Others have done it before me and lived!"

Dealing with a metaphorical biblical city circumvents the scenarios which Catherine must have played out in her mind in order to be able to be afraid in the first place. This is the reason why she could cope with the city in her mind and find solutions to all the problems it presented, and why she could not do so with her - just as unreal - representation of Oxford and herself there, lonely, confused and panic stricken. Also, as a result of her metaphorical exploration, Catherine decided to 'act in accord' and do something practical to help prepare herself - such as studying a town map well in advance, acquiring some student's guides on the resources available, and finding out how to do some basic cooking. Her mother was dumbfounded by the latter!

17 - STRATEGIES FOR CONFLICT RESOLUTION

As I cannot presume that you have had training in various conflict resolving strategies, which does come in handy at times, here are a few ideas to help you out should you get stuck in your dealings with your inner crew.

17/1 - Negotiation Skills - Talking With Your Selves

If you have two or more representations who are in conflict with each other, you will have to negotiate some form of peaceful settlement. If both can talk, you might like to use the following model and find out as the first priority what the end result of their actions and intentions might be. What is it that they are after?

So, a part that keeps nagging and nagging and nagging might well do so because they wish you to become a better person and to be happy. The conflicting part, who hates being nagged at, might want peace and tranquillity, so they can become a better person and be happy.

Once a common aim has been established, all you need to do is to get them to acknowledge that their aim is, in fact, very similar if not exactly the same, and usually an agreement can then be reached. In the example above, once the peace part finds out that the nagging part doesn't hate them at all but just wants them to be happy, they can get to talk about how the nagging part can find a better way to pass on their insights, and the peace part can find a better way to listen and take action when necessary.

Going 'behind' or 'beyond' the actual behaviour in order to establish the behaviour's purpose is a great way to resolve conflicts, because there's always more than one way to skin a cat. Here is an example to get a single part to change its ways; this is from the excellent Core Transformation process by Connirae Andreas.

To discover the intention behind the behaviour, first the part is allowed, perhaps for the first time, to imagine that they could have or be whatever they want, fully and completely.

Then, the question is asked "What would that give you?" which means, "Why bother with the behaviour at all? What's the point?"

As you keep uncovering layer after layer of intentions behind behaviours, eventually you reach a 'core' - the real, deep and underlying reason for the behaviour. This core reason can then be discussed and alternative, easier and/or different routes to the core may become obvious in the process.

For example, I saw a young lady who had an internal representation of a warrior woman, an angry Amazon, who would "take over and wreck all my important relationships". This warrior woman part stated that she was proud to be aggressive, served an important purpose and would not think of changing in the slightest.

Following a technique from the Core Transformation process, I asked, "If you could just imagine what it would be like to be completely and totally aggressive, what would that give you?" The rather unpleasant answer to that was, "I would have killed everyone and be the only person left alive". With a slight shudder, I went on.

"So, imagine you had killed everyone. Allow yourself to experience it fully and completely now. What would that give you?" Answer: "Feeling secure."

Ok. "So, if you had this feeling of security fully and completely now, what would that give you?"

"The ability to have an intimate relationship, to be able to love."

"Oh great. Let's just back up here a minute and look at this - so, in order to be able to love someone, you need to kill everyone first?" at which point, as happens so often in these kinds of conversations, the warrior woman part in question begun to scratch her head, and started to look very sheepish indeed.

This part had never thought any further than security; and, **by opening up the reasons behind the behaviour**, understood finally that what it was trying to achieve was in direct conflict with the means by which it was trying to achieve it.

In many cases, this is all that's required - it's a breakthrough moment, and from then on, negotiations can proceed and normal conversations can be had.

Often, problem parts are a bit stuck in that they haven't got much flexibility of behaviour and not much in the way of choices of different behaviours that might serve the ultimate goal.

Therefore, a great problem resolution strategy is to find out how to go about ...

17/2 - Generating Possibilities

Two options don't constitute a choice - that's a dilemma. A choice is when there's **more than two** different options to choose from. Another point about choice, as BF Skinner points out, is that choices are only really choices when the outcomes are similar and the amount of pain and gain involved in each is similar as well. For example, giving you a choice between a strawberry sundae, a beating with a large stick, and a chalice of 'hemlock on the rocks' isn't really much of a choice, is it!

Before we choose anything, however, we first should go ahead and *generate alternatives and possibilities.*

So, the warrior woman needs to feel secure in order to be able to go ahead and love. In the past, her only option had been to be extremely aggressive. What other ways could one go about securing this security?

By being strong, by being careful, by learning from mistakes, by accepting that the only thing you can ever be sure about is that you can't be sure about anything - well, we haven't got all day, but certainly there's alternatives to being aggressive.

The thing when you're generating alternatives is to not censor them in advance. Get all the possibilities you can think of. If that's not enough, get half a dozen advisors in and get them to tell you their possibilities as well. Then, go ahead and look at each one, no matter how outlandish, and **objectively assess them for what's good, what's bad and what's interesting about each one.**

There's no way you won't end up with a great long list of more or less possible options if you approach it that way. But there is another strategy I would like to point out while we're here.

17/3 - Having Your Cake AND Eating It

The world is not black and white. I used to think it was. I used to think that you could divide the natural world with its incredibly complex patterns of interaction - including human beings - in such a way. Oh, what a fool I have been!

The big, bad, exclusive OR is to blame for this.

You can either have fun OR get married.

You can either have a good time OR you can be healthy.

You can either be stupid OR intelligent.

That's **not** the way the world works.

Firstly, whenever there are what seem to be polar opposites, such as black and white, it isn't so easy to remember that there are quadrillions of shades in between. My computer can generate 32 million colours and is still not getting anywhere near the graduation that exists in an everyday sunset as perceived through my limited eyes. Further, many enlightened folk have argued that such polar opposites are not stuck at the end of a stick, one on each side, but that they're in fact form part of an invisible circle, transmuting into each other - such as in the Ying/Yang symbol, for example.

When exactly is the very moment that day turns into night? When the sun is below the horizon? When the very last bits of pink have faded into purple? When you see the first star? And more, when you take the transition of time into account, simple 'black vs. white' distinctions become even more nonsensical - the sky is black now and it's going to be blue a bit later on. Now there's a mountain, and in a couple of million years, there'll be a lake. Today, I'm nice to you and tomorrow, I might have the flu and bite your head off - am I naughty, or am I nice?

If you take down these nonsensical divisions that only exist in our own minds by virtue of faulty training in childhood, you can begin to generate endless possibilities and permutations of behaviour (amongst other things). So, our warrior woman does not have to choose at all between being EITHER aggressive, OR secure, OR safety conscious, OR strong, OR open-minded - she can become whatever she wants to be by being able to have **ALL** of them together, each one becoming a useful resource in its right place, ready to choose from according to what is going to be the most useful in the context of what's happening around her.

Assertiveness Training has a lot to answer for, in my opinion. Only three choices were presented - aggressive, assertive, and submissive (or non-assertive, if you will); and two of the so-called choices were loaded to the hilt with negative baggage, so that the so called 'assertive' behaviour was all that was left to 'choose from'.

A fully functioning human being, out there in the real world, needs to be able to have all three and at least another two dozen other styles of behaviour beside - and then use each one according to the situation they find themselves in for their maximum benefit. I've personally saved my hide a good few times by weaselling for all I was worth; and have saved it yet again under different circumstances by picking up the power and making unilateral, hard, aggressive decisions. But I suppose that'll be difficult to teach in a one day workshop - or would it?

Lastly, one final tip on resolving conflicts. **What's more important - your relationship,** or that you're right?

I know we can all get terribly entrenched and pig headed at times, and a little give and take can simply work miracles. I remember one lady who had deadlocked herself with an internal guardian by being too righteous and opinionated - they'd just come to complete stalemate and were a point at which the guardian wouldn't even talk to her anymore. I suggested to her to ask the guardian if she'd like a gift. "What's that got to do with anything?" the lady demanded angrily, but then grudgingly went ahead and asked. To her amazement, the guardian expressed joy at this offer and said she'd love a nice piece of antique jewellery! This resolved the stalemate; they got to talking on a very different level and finally came to a mutually satisfactory conclusion.

So, if you want to resolve conflict amongst your crew, let me back up here on the basic tools which will help you get started.

Finding the reason behind the behaviour;

Generating choices including the original behaviour;

Replacing any exclusive "OR"s with "AND"s and watching the Universe expand instantly!

Finding the circle that links what appeared to be polar opposites.

Acknowledging the inherent value of any kind of human behaviour in the right context.

Valuing the relationship above your personal opinions.

17/4 - The Harmony Programme

In all your dealings with the parts of your self, you will encounter a particular set of problems that could be classed as 'attention seeking behaviour'.

Attention seeking behaviour by your body, for example, could be recurrent headaches or pains and illnesses in general - the more severe the symptoms, the more desperate the attempt at diverting your attention to an issue of some kind.

Attention seeking behaviour by your unconscious mind usually manifests in the form of nightmares - once again, the more horrendous and disturbing the nightmare, the more desperate the attempt to gain your attention.

Bad luck in your life, disasters of all kinds and especially repeating themes in any kind of situation or relationship that *seem to escalate*, also fall under that category - these and all the ones before are not sent to make our lives a misery, but to try and **tell us something**.

The golden rule is - the more irritating and debilitating the occurrence, the more important it is to deal with it **as soon as possible**.

As you open up your lines of communication within yourself, you will experience such attention seeking behaviour in all imaginable shapes and forms arriving in your Sanctuary - we've already talked about many, many examples of things that turn up unexpectedly, plans that go wrong unexpectedly, and even demonic selves manifesting right out of the blue.

There's one thing you need to really understand about attention seeking behaviour, and that is that when it gets to a point where it really hurts you, it means that **you've ignored a whole range of much more subtle warning signs that went before**, and now you're paying the price for your negligence.

Attention seeking behaviour is always at work when there's an escalation in the severity of symptoms or repercussions. A dog bite, for example, never happens 'right out of the blue'. There are always warning signs beforehand - a look, a body posture, a growl, a bark, what have you. The reason that so many people get bitten is because:

> They're overconfident (they simply don't believe that such a sweet little Poochie Pooh really has 46 razor sharp teeth);

> They don't know enough about how a dog communicates to detect the earlier warning signs;

> And, even if they do know, that they don't pay enough attention to what's blatantly in front of them in the first place because their attention is elsewhere.

Our whole system of medical care is built upon ignoring, hiding, confounding and pasting over the subtle early warning systems of our bodies - with the result, that in spite of our vastly superior diet, hygiene and living conditions, we have far more disease than a starving African village community, and the only reason we live as long as we do is because we throw all our resources at the problems when they're already in the end stages.

Whether this kind of 'spoiling the ship for a penny's worth of tar' is physical in nature -

- ignoring subtle hints such as tiredness, lack of sex drive, frequent headaches, not rested after sleep for the sake of the oh so much more important A-levels, job or family 'commitments', then taking a bunch of over the counter pills to keep functioning, and then finally crashing down with ME or whatever was decided to manifest for months on end anyway

 or whether it is psychological ...

- being unhappy often, then depressed, sleepless, finding it hard to concentrate, having temper tantrums, ignoring these and many other sign posts completely and pretending 'everything's ok' until the nervous breakdown, the panic attacks or the schizophrenic episodes occur ...

... it's really time we sat down and started **to learn to see the unfolding patterns developing from our past experience**, and re-connect at a much more profound level with all the bits of us that we have been taught are worth nothing and ought to be ignored.

Gina had been coming to see me for a while and was very involved in advanced Sanctuary issues. At one point, an inner concern 'took over' and apparently made it quite hard for her to function in her every day life. She still managed to go to work, do all the housework for her family, tuck in the children at night and all the rest of it, but she felt a bit worried that she had a rising desire to be on her own and get to grips with the issues she was wrestling with. This lasted for about a week, until the conflict was resolved and she returned with added energy and full attention to her real life activities.

"I don't know," she said, "I mean what would happen if I got so involved that I couldn't cook the dinner that night? Do you think I should stop and just be happy with all I've gained so far?"

Upon hearing this, I was quite blown away for quite a while, for I realised that I had thought and done similarly in the past. Now here was a definite piece of mental racism and prejudice at work. It seems it's ok for us to spend 72 years grafting away and directing all our energies into the external world, but it wasn't ok for Gina to take time out and take a walk in order to settle a highly advanced philosophical debate in her mind - after all, cooking dinner is far more important, isn't it? And further, such behaviour could soon lead to being carried off into a lunatic asylum, couldn't it?

I asked Gina (truly really for the both of us): "When real life emergencies take over, it's automatic and instant to stop inner wanderings and to focus on the situation at hand, until such time as it has been resolved. Why can't it be the same with inner emergencies? Are they not also important? Can't they have at least a tiny proportion of our time and energy **as a right** - and without having to feel guilty about it?"

I have always known how utterly slanted the way we conduct our First World civilisation business is towards a non-integrated, non-realistic idea of the world as being some kind of clockwork mechanism. But I must say that I was still shocked beyond belief to discover how deeply prejudiced we all still are when it comes to bringing the forgotten parts of the self back on line.

In the overall scheme of things, is it really more important to have cooked yet another meal or to have come to a personal breakthrough regarding the subject of 'the value of human suffering'? I'm beginning to think it's the latter, and I'm also beginning to think that once Gina doesn't feel the need to see anyone suffer anymore, the quality of her dinners might well improve henceforth as well!

The point is this. Gina's pre-occupation with the subject and its manifestations was classic attention seeking behaviour - here was something that cried out for resolution, begged her for her attention. Thank God she had enough sense to heed the call at this point, before it got any worse, and before it decided to cause a system wide failure.

A long time ago, people used to think that it was good to let babies cry for hours on end rather than to respond to their needs there and then. It was thought that if you rushed and helped them out of their misery right away, they'd grow up to be weak and demanding.

Nowadays, thank the Lord, it has finally been understood that if you feed a baby when it expresses a need, all that'll happen is that the baby will stop crying, its immune system will be less stressed (as will the mother's, by the way), and the baby, rather than growing up being needy, grows up to be self sufficient, because it had its needs met fully and completely and so never needed to develop a complex about the whole subject in the first place.

This kind of negative thinking has waned on the baby front, but is still in evidence all around us in other ways, and turning it on its head and instead of refusing to give, **to give freely until there is no more need**, is a concept so basic, so simple and so profound that it could solve a great deal of problems if only it was understood that extra attention doesn't spoil, but **helps to strengthen and to grow**.

Attention seeking behaviours from your mind, your body, your imaginary companions or those in your real life are nothing more and nothing less than an indication of **a real, existing, urgent need**. The more bugging the behaviours, the more intense the need.

Which leads us to the simple concept that **'a stitch in time saves nine'**. A baby carefully observed and fed when it makes the first nuzzling sounds and does that thing with its lips and tongue that is an obvious communication about hunger, is satisfied with just being fed. A baby that has been screaming for an hour cannot be so simply satisfied, and even after having eventually been fed, usually still cannot settle properly and might well end up having all kinds of health and behaviour problems as a result.

It's therefore not just the spiritually correct thing to do to give attention (or love, or energy, if you will) when someone or something sincerely asks for it, but it's very much in your own best interest - if you want to avoid even greater suffering, that is.

And this holds for attention seeking behaviour by machinery (by the way of strange clunking noises that precede a breakdown), your bank account, animals, children, husbands and friends as well as for your body, your body mind, all your parts and manifestations, as well as your entire unconscious realm.

To sum up this section, here's briefly what I suggest you consider:

1. To accept attention seeking behaviour by any part of you as a plea for help to deal with a deep and often desperate need, and not some kind of a weird power game or an annoying pastime just sent to upset you.

2. To resolve these issues by endeavouring to address the need and to fulfil it, rather than to try and convince the part, person, organ or machine in question that it shouldn't have these needs, or that it should somehow learn to go without.

3. To decide to learn more about the processes involved, and to become more attuned to the needs of your internal community.

4. And finally, to resolve to learn to **pay attention** to the **unfolding process at the earliest possible stage**, thus avoiding the need driven behaviour escalating and becoming a real problem to you.

18 - THE IMMUNE SYSTEMS OF THE MIND

18/1 - Staying Strong Through The Challenges

In some quarters it is now held that just about any kind of physical malfunctioning, bar perhaps a broken bone, is nothing more or nothing less than a break down of the immune system.

The viruses that cause the flu, for example, are always present in the air; but we won't get a cold unless the immune system malfunctions and lets the virus get past the defensive barriers.

This can happen when the immune system is busy elsewhere - such when it is already at full stretch compensating for existing long term stress - or if it has been damaged in some way - by faulty general maintenance, unsuitable or incomplete diet, environmental toxins, to mention but a few.

There may also well be a genetic pre-disposition - please note, just a pre-disposition! - at work, which may have, in conjunction with the above, a bearing on how much any immune system can be reasonably expected to cope with. If it all gets too much, just a tiny little thing can come along and cause immune system failure to occur, just like the flu virus. In effect, the flu virus wasn't all by itself the reason for the flu - it was simply the straw that broke the camel's back.

Understanding this from old, holistic approaches to healing thus go ahead and may not even bother to treat the flu at all, but rather try and work out what other kind of straw there is, how to remove what's unnecessary, how to improve the camel's overall health and how to balance the remaining load so that the immune system can function fully once again and something like a flu virus just ceases to represent a challenge.

When dealing with mind related matters, I've found the system to be very similar.

Two people might suffer a very similar trauma or bereavement - one of them 'shrugs it off' and gets on with life, for others it really turns out to be the straw that broke the camel's back, or caused the nervous breakdown, if you will.

After having given the matter some thought, I would now agree with most of the hundreds and hundreds of experienced specialists that

basic self esteem is, in fact, the immune system of the human mind.

If it isn't functioning at a reasonable level, the littlest insult, injury, slight or other kind of attack will cause a breach and problems manifest; if it is functioning, on the other hand, the most terrible traumas may be endured with some form of composure and a good chance of system survival.

As with the physical immune system, it therefore makes sense to keep a watchful eye on the mental immune system, and to provide it with a general environment in which it can thrive, prosper, and fulfil its essential tasks to the best of its genetic pre-disposition.

When we're talking about the body, the environment required for a fully functioning auto immune system contains water, food, shelter, absence of toxins, and the occasional bit of stress at such a level that it keeps ticking over happily but without over-exerting itself on too many occasions - the difference between keeping fit and training for competition gymnastics, for example.

So what are the environmental requirements to keep the mind's immune systems ready and in first class condition? Here are my personal views on the subject.

18/1/1 - Peace Of Mind

Peace of mind, to me, is when you're looking around yourself, stretching, folding your hands behind your head, wriggle your toes and say, "Aaah, all's well with the world."

How often does that happen in your life? In mine, not so very often. I might think it, but then there's this part that reminds me of an unpaid bill, or something I might have forgotten to deal with, or some unfinished business or other, or even some scary event way out in the future. However, since I've had my Sanctuary, it's gotten a lot better. Now here's a place where I can really relax and experience peace of mind, whenever I want, even in the coffee break when I'm taking a seminar or lecture.

It's nice to know that every time I do this, I'm giving my mental immune system a little 'time out' and a little extra energy to cope with whatever might come its way during the rest of my activities.

An important part of peace of mind is an absence of fear. Fear usually comes about when you find yourself to be powerless in a given situation, or if you simply don't know what the situation is going to be like so there's no way you can plan your response. Here, once again, basic Sanctuary work comes in handy, as all kinds of fears can be addressed in many ways, and there are so many forms of help, magic and resources available to draw upon.

Although I'm not suggesting that any kind of fear can thus be resolved, it certainly helps with many of them, and every time you stop being afraid, you help your mental immune system conserve energy and function better than if you took no such action.

18/1/2 - Happiness

I really think there's not enough happiness in most people's lives. I once read a book that had you make a list of 101 things that make you happy, and then suggested you try to fit as many of them into every day as possible. I highly commend that idea; what it did for me at the time was to make me realise that I wasn't really doing anything at all to make myself more happy more often, rather the contrary - at that time I seemed to be dead set to make my life as hard and miserable as possible, and then bitch on about it endlessly to friends of a similar mindset.

Sanctuary work is about happiness in every shape, form or appearance. There shouldn't be anything at all within your Sanctuary that isn't supportive to that end; if there is, it's high time to address basic issues such as whether you actually believe you deserve to be happy - or in parts terms, whether your internal committee has voted on the matter and whether or not they've come out in your favour.

If you are amongst the not so uncommon percentage of people who really can't say anymore what would make them happy, please re-visit memories to that end, find out what exactly it was that made them classed in your mind and body as 'happy', and then go ahead and create more of it, whatever it was. If you cannot do so in real life, then simply go ahead and do it in your Sanctuary instead.

Your body cannot distinguish between a very vivid internal mental experience and an external physical one; this is why people under hypnosis can manifest blisters from imaginary fires, or start to shiver uncontrollably if you tell them they're stuck in a snowstorm.

Being happy in your Sanctuary, therefore, is a good interim substitute for being happy in a practical setting; every time you can experience pleasure and happiness, your mental immune system will be strengthened and rejuvenated.

Once you've mastered how to give yourself basic happiness, you might like to go on to take the next lessons, in the more advanced subjects such as joy, bliss, and ecstasy ...

18/1/3 - Love

All forms and kinds of love are real energy boosting states (if you think you're loving someone and you end up a nervous wreck, I'd perhaps re-define whatever is going on and give it another name, 'cause it cannot be love by definition), and as such really valuable in boosting the mental immune system.

No matter how much unconditional love already flows from you to others in your real world activities, it is strengthened and supported by sending loving energy through your Sanctuary relationships - and if you remember that section, you need not restrict yourself to loving people; loving relationships with God, minerals, pets, beautiful sculptures and sunsets all count as well. Further, very many of the Sanctuary activities, such as making peace with other selves, dead relatives or past lives, contain a core aspect of learning to love and appreciate the previously unrecognised good in many people and situations, thus increasing the amount of loving that's going on inside of you every time you do such a thing.

18/1/4 - Purpose, Contribution & Direction

One of the key reasons why people in old folks' homes fade away is that they feel useless and no longer needed - a thought which gravely affects the full functioning of the mental immune system.

Sanctuary work can certainly help with that issue. Whether it's in the form of questing for a life's purpose; resolving conflicts with other people, thus setting them free from their obligations at least as far as you are concerned; being more positive and thereby doing your bit to counteract the general negativity in this world; encouraging and discovering talents by which you might serve others better; or in the end, simply by being able to more fully recognise that you are a child of the Universe, no less than the trees and the stars, and that you have a right to be here - if you have your Sanctuary, then you need never feel useless again.

18/1/5 - Mental Stimulation

There's reams of scientific evidence by now that in the absence of mental stimulation, all kinds of problems from low self esteem, via a lowering of general intelligence, to all kinds of psychic malfunctions and behaviour disorders tend to develop (and this is aside from numerous physical symptoms as well).

Now I do sincerely hope that I don't have to go on at this late point in this book as to how mentally stimulating Sanctuary building and exploration is by definition.

Suffice it to say that every single person who has ever started it has experienced a tremendous increase in new ideas, new thoughts, new insights and new ways of perceiving old situations. I haven't tested them, but I'm willing to bet the better part of my salary that they would have scored significantly higher on a basic intelligence test after they've had their Sanctuaries up and running as compared to beforehand.

If it does just one single thing, stimulating the mind is the forte of Sanctuary exploration - and thus a tremendous resource to boost depleted auto immune systems of the mind.

18/1/6 - Increasing Your Intelligence

Contrary to what many people have been told at school, intelligence isn't parroting mountains of facts but to be able to **make connections** between them, develop a sense of perspective and to be able to organise information into useful forms.

At the beginning of this book I've repeated the old myth that we only use 5% of our brains. It is probably a lot less than that in my opinion; in the last section we spoke about intelligence increase when Project Sanctuary and related activities are undertaken.

This is primarily because right from the start, working in the Sanctuary realms entails **multi-dimensional thinking** and problem solving in the context of a complex, unique ecology with innumerable unpredictable factors - when you're doing Project Sanctuary work, you are thinking on your feet the entire time, learning at a rate that is much faster than linear spoken or received information all the while you are doing it, and expanding your understanding of something way, way beyond just knowing a few facts here and there.

When you switch from fact-based, linear thought and speech into the multi-dimensional, time-inclusive, limitless potential movies and developments of the Project Sanctuary realms with their flowing manifestations that are always changing, always developing and always responding to input from your many strata of environments, what happens is that we are dealing with an **exponential increase in data** and information that needs to be processed.

The beautiful discovery is that this isn't something you have to study to do or be a genius to be able to handle; with wonder we begin to understand that we **all already have the structures in our minds** to be able to not just handle this extraordinary flood of information, but to process this information **intelligently** and to do something with it afterwards.

Einstein rode on a beam of light and what he learned there got translated **down** into the much simpler modality of the symbols the physicists and mathematicians use to be able to consciously handle the true complexity of nature.

Einstein knew how to use these symbols to **express his experiences** from the Sanctuary realms; I know how to use linear words, and sometimes music and also paint on canvas to facilitate this translation process.

The true language of metaphor, as we are learning here with the processes I have described and which feel so simple and so **natural** even to a very small child, or an adult who can't even read and write, is the most complex, the most beautiful and probably the most information dense system of learning which exists for humans at this time.

Compared to what goes on when you plant a single little seed in a dusty plain and call upon an underground well to begin the process of making this land come to life again, the most complicated mathematical formula you could begin to imagine is nothing but a child's plaything - simple, brightly coloured and stackable.

Organic metaphors simply are the most information rich messaging device we have to both learn about the universe and to tell others about it.

It is little wonder that the highest traditions of learning were made of story, legend, myth and metaphor and that changing a single deep metaphor can by itself re-shape an entire civilisation over a period of millennia.

If you are seriously interested in developing your human potential and your true human intelligence, working with this realm and its conventions is the most extraordinary gift you can ever give yourself, make no mistake about it.

You might not even notice how much easier and clearer your thinking becomes, how much more you understand (and not just with your head!) and how much more you can relate to all manner of things which seemed always so complicated and incomprehensible.

I, for one, didn't notice this at all. I love Project Sanctuary and have always loved the explorations, quests, surprises and experiences it provided to me, but the truth is that I really didn't appreciate what it had done for my creativity over the past 6 years until I came to write this revision of the material. I didn't appreciate how the lessons from Project Sanctuary had opened my eyes to interactions in the real world, and how this opening up preceded all my other work from that point forward.

Many approaches claim to 'improve your intelligence'. I put forth the proposition that Project Sanctuary teaches what intelligence actually is and what it **can do for you** - and the true wonder is that it's natural, it's right, and it is absolutely what we were always designed to be doing in the first place.

18/1/7 - The Power Of Wisdom

Alright. So what exactly is 'wisdom'? I'm not going to trouble either of us with a dictionary definition of this term but in general, it's held to have something to do with a state beyond raw learning, where knowledge and experience have come together and created a deep understanding of something in a person; when this happens, they are said to be 'wise'.

The very powerful 'wisdom of hindsight', often repeated, creates wisdom.

And herein lies one of the least commonly understood and most incredible resources of the Sanctuary realms.

In the Hard, we can only have so many experiences a day, and what we can get up to in the knowledge and learning department is strictly limited by physical time, but often also by all kinds of other circumstances, including personal set ups, how much money you have or what limiting relationships you're in or what limiting beliefs you are holding at any point.

In Sanctuary, there are **no such limitations**.

I wouldn't know about the dolphins, but chances are we are the only creatures on this planet who can play out a multitude of possible scenarios in our minds to **test the outcomes before they have ever happened**.

People use this incredible ability which is actually way more wonderful than just being able to predict a single simple future (as you are dealing with many, if not entirely unlimited futures!) in general to drive themselves crazy as they lie in bed at night and think of all the things which could possibly go wrong in their near or distant futures.

What is in fact a safety device and the possibility to create unlimited futures and test them out before embarking on any of them turns into a mechanism for insanity with three simple omissions:

The sequence of events is **directed** to show only negative possible outcomes rather than a balanced selection from **all** possible outcomes. Someone who might be afraid of getting onto a plane the next day might thereby be only thinking of ways in which it can all go wrong, from endless waiting for flights that never arrive to various forms of plunging into the sea, the wings of the plane falling off, the pilot's dying of fish poisoning and so forth but NOT the possibility of a comfortable flight where they step out into the exciting new location.

The events don't get played out right to the end but stop at some evil disaster point. For example, someone might just see the plane explode and thatÕs it. Move it on a bit and you could get to ascension from there and sleep most beautifully or even learn something about what happens after death in the process! (See also 'Grovian Metaphor Work' in the Addendum).

They leave the events as a remembered 'hard' event, rather than test them out deliberately in a Sanctuary setting where resources exist that can't be had in the Hard, such as time rewind, replay, stop, make changes, test the changes, check for long term repercussions and ecology effects and of course, magical interventions and possibilities that can't occur when strictly hard thinking is applied to any situation or problem (See also 'How To Make Tesla Machines' in the Addendum).

Setting up scenes and events with people and circumstances, with machinery if necessary and letting them run under various test conditions in fast forward time to be able to 'gain the wisdom of hindsight' is a mindbogglingly useful ability - and what it means is that you can achieve wisdom long before you are white haired and doddering.

You can practise all manner of things and learn from them if you want to do that; you can live **entire lifetimes** as one person or another, in one setting or another and gain incredible understanding about so many things, about so many facets of life in general and your own personality and preferences in particular in the process. The uses of this one Sanctuary technique are absolutely limitless.

All I can say is **try it for yourself**. Take any area of your life in which you think you lack 'experience and practise' and set up the scenarios, let them run and find out for yourself just how much you can learn in this protected space and without ever taking the risk of even stepping outside your own front door.

To conclude this section, I'd like to look back for a moment at what we have discussed here. Love. Happiness. Wisdom. Intelligence. All of this just from a simple little mind game where you make imaginary events happen in this strange space I refer to as 'Project Sanctuary'?

Isn't that a bit over-optimistic, to put it mildly?

Well, here's a story. Somewhere in Africa, there is a lake and in the lake, there lives a species of crab. It's common enough and well documented. One time, some experimenter guy in his lab put the wrong water in the tank where these crab things from the African lake were kept and something very, very strange happened.

The crab things started to **evolve** into a whole new form of being. It seems that there was a stage in their development in becoming adults that no-one had ever observed because the lake was very acidic, had become more and more so over the last few thousand years, and these crabs needed less acidic water to develop into their adult stages. They could mate in their adolescent form and in the environment they were in, but not a single one of them had ever grown up fully to be an adult for at least 10,000 years - and that's why no-one even suspected there could be a third developmental stage for these beings nor what it might have looked like.

After 6 years of Project Sanctuary, I believe that is also true for human beings.

I believe that we have actually **no idea at all** what a real adult human being could be like, what they would think or what they might be able to do.

I further believe that Project Sanctuary is my idea of a special playground for human children who mate just like those African crabs do before they have reached maturity and thus hold the illusion that what they are is all they could be, to help them develop towards an actual adulthood in safety.

A playground where we can learn things about the true fabric of time and space in a sheltered, supportive environment and where we can't hurt ourselves whilst we are learning.

A place where we can play out our challenges of self and others, hone and fine tune our understanding of ourselves and how we work, a place where we can get ready for the transition to true adulthood.

Let's face it.

You give **any** human alive today - and I don't care if they are held to be the most 'enlightened' being on this planet with millions of followers - the power to take the stars from the sky, to truly twitch and ripple the fabric of reality with a single thought, and what would happen?

It is actually a scary thought.

There may very well be good reason that magic is so difficult and elusive - who would give a small child a nuclear bomb to play with? It simply isn't safe for the child, nor for the Universe at large.

If you are willing to entertain the notion, no matter how experienced and wise you hold yourself to be already, that you might actually be nothing more than a small child, beginning to take their first unsteady and tottering steps out into the vastness of the Universe, then Project Sanctuary can actually become your training ground towards something that we can't conceive of as yet.

19 - HOLDING THE LIGHTNING

19/1 - The Fear Of Power

It's a fact that just about all possible human relationship problems and nine out of ten behaviour problems revolve around a **perceived** lack of power.

A really and truly powerful person has simply no need for aggression, domination, exterminating a whole race of people they perceive as threats, throwing their weight around or any of the nasty and highly morally reprehensible behaviours so wrongly connected with the concepts of power - when all of these are simply an admission that whoever is perpetrating said acts is feeling basically powerless, and afraid, and has to resort to such tactics in order to bolster their failing self esteem.

We've already noted that this internal realm we've created might be for some people the first contact with having any, never mind such absolute power - and what they experience is not that absolute power corrupts absolutely, but that in fact it makes the holder of this truly absolute power stop and realise that there's nothing to be afraid of anymore, that they are totally safe, totally supported, totally abundant and totally free - because the kind of power that lies within the Sanctuary is way above and beyond that which any kind of dictator, serial killer or emperor could ever even begin to imagine or manifest in reality.

If in this environment they then still want to go ahead and rape, burn, pillage and enslave, the amusing side effect will be probably nothing more and nothing less than that they will end up with an outbreak of psychosomatic diseases and horrible nightmares! What a perfect system to learn the lessons of power - and all in the safety of one's own body, mind and soul.

I'm aware of the fact that it is unpopular to talk about the 'dark sides of human nature' in the field of personal development, where all strive to just look on the bright side at all times, but nonetheless I think it's important to acknowledge the realities of our situations, our thoughts and our emotions.

Here is a 'lesson in power' as expressed by one man who allowed himself to let go and play out his darkest fantasies in Sanctuary.

"The three women are absolutely helpless before me.

I want to explode them where they stand, I want to rip them to shreds with a profound longing and the only reason I'm not doing it is because it would be too quick, would be unsatisfactory, would not and could not ever fill my desire to have them be in such pain, suffer so totally that their suffering would somehow heal me, somehow fill my hunger and sate it or even begin to alleviate it.

And the truth is as I have always known, that all the screaming they could do, and not just these here in front of me but all the ones they stood for, worlds upon worlds of these, screaming for all eternities would not begin to fill me, could never even begin to satisfy me."

You, dear reader, might be appalled by this but what this statement represents in truth is an understanding that totally changed this man. His repressed desires to 'explode' the women were never an end in themselves but only a result of something else, a terrible need and hunger that, as he understood at that moment, could never be filled in that way. It opened up the understanding that he needed to find something else in order to fill this hunger. When he did find out what it was, you could say that the very instant it happened he ceased to be a ticking time bomb or a latent threat to the women in society; and that is quite aside from the changes to him and his own life and relationships.

The facts of power are simply that once you have it, you can do with it what you like - there is no inherent link between goodness and the amount of power you are given and indeed, in that sense power is exactly like a knife. There is a hand and this hand belongs always to a single individual who makes the decisions to use the knife to peel an apple or stab someone in the throat.

It is certainly one of the scariest of moments when one realises that one holds such power, and then it gets even scarier as an individual is confronted with their choices in this circumstance and the illusion of 'being a nice person, really ...' begins to crumble under the onslaught of reality.

In order to prevent this from ever happening, people gladly disempower themselves in any way they can, using others to carry their powers for them, abdicate from them, pretend they don't and never did have them and a host of other games designed to defuse themselves.

A very good friend of mine once remarked that: "Power is only dangerous in the hands of an angry man." I am sure he used the term 'man' as in hu'man', to be sure.

Learning about your anger in Sanctuary, as the gentleman who wanted to 'explode women' did so profoundly that day, is a good place to be

214

learning about it, and long before it has reached explosion point and you find yourself with a shotgun on the roof of your local McDonald's.

At the root of most anger, if not all, lie injuries that need to be found and healed from the ground up; and it is my contention that people who are balanced and no longer in an agony of needs, hungers, wants and in constant pain from the injuries that others inflicted upon them are **safe to hold the lightning** of personal power at last.

19/2 - As I Will ...

In English, the word 'will' is most generally used in the context of a future possibility: "I will do this tomorrow", for example.

It also occurs as a verb but is used very rarely that way in ordinary conversation. To will something is the act of making something happen using your **will** or intention, as in: "He willed the traffic lights to change."

In witchcraft there exists the statement, 'As I will, so mote it be,' meaning that 'My will will be done'. That is a very powerful statement of intention and of power which once again, is surprisingly rare in every day life here in the Hard.

I have observed a good many people 'trying' to make that statement of, 'As I will, so mote it be' but failing entirely to make it ring true, have it be what it is supposed to be, namely an unwavering statement of truth that cannot do any other but unfold exactly as the will of the individual decided that it should.

In order to make this statement, conflicts of personal power and should or should nots, can or cannots, am allowed or not allowed and so forth will have to have been **completely resolved** before the statement is made; in the Hard this is not an easy thing to do and the feedback and situations are difficult. In the Sanctuary realms, however, you can learn to do this in perfect safety and with instant feedback on your endeavours.

I have created the following progression to make it easier to attain the 'I WILL this to happen NOW' expression which arises naturally from a state of deep conviction and inner alignment and cannot work in any other way.

I highly recommend you practise this progression on a number of different aspects and desires in Sanctuary; it will make manifesting in the Hard much, much easier for you.

a) The Seed

In order to do something or have something happen, we firstly have to have an idea as the seed to start the process off. For our purposes here, it might be a fairly nebulous idea of a special object you require, a special guide or person, a house or a landscape that would bring you something you really need to be all you were always supposed to be.

b) I Wish

The next step is to 'wish' you had this object, item, energy, whatever. This is not an offhanded thing but a magical state and a very specific request to the all-there-is, and which in Sanctuary is mostly yourself and all your resources, including your Higher Self and all your guides and helpers.

To help you with the 'wishing state', it is very useful to do this in the right place and time. You could, for example, have a wishing well in your Sanctuary, or a special building, a temple or suchlike, where you would step up and make your request, very seriously and very specifically.

You might have heard stories where wishes came true in a very unfortunate way, such as the Monkey's Paw story and the many tales of genies who fulfil wishes in an evil way that ends up hurting the wisher. Now many have taken this to mean that the supernatural forces who grant such wishes are evil bastards who are out to get us and punish us for the act of wishing, but that is not so. What these stories are trying to do is to explain that one should be careful what one wishes for, and to take great care in formulating these statements and requests. In order to be able to do this, it's important to **think about** what it is that you want for a time, and be sure you are wanting this for the right reasons and from the right states of mind.

At the wishing state, a lot of objections become apparent - "Is this really what I want? What would happen if I got that? Would it be good for me?" and so on and so forth, and I'm sure you can see now why it is so important to consider these things and resolve them **before** we say, "As I will, so mote it be" and become your own evil genie who sets in motion a chain of events that leads to nothing beneficial at all.

When these objections or conflicts have been successfully resolved and all feels good and right in all ways, then we step up and officially make the wish.

Now please understand that this is not done in this progression to have the wish be granted magically from within or without, although this might happen sometimes and make the rest of this exercise immaterial; what you might find in Sanctuary is that the result may or may not materialise right away, and it may materialise in such a way that it isn't entirely formed as yet.

We need another stage to bring the magic closer to ourselves and away from genies, angelic interventions and the like, and this stage is to say...

c) I Want

There is a big difference between saying, "I wish this will happen," and saying "I WANT this to happen." To want something is an application and statement of will of an individual; there is a different energy flow, from towards you from the outside, to from you outward into the universe.

'Wanting' something is also, very interestingly, very different from 'needing' something - wanting is something you do when your needs are already fulfilled. This is one of the most annoying problems beginner magicians find themselves faced with and the one which, if it hasn't been clearly understood, causes people to throw the whole magical reality creation away in a huff, namely that when you try to do magic from a place of neediness, absolutely nothing happens at all, no matter how desperately you try.

It seems such a paradox - when you have all the money you need already, then it's so easy to make some more. The same with love, recognition and everything else the universe has to offer to a human being. When you don't have it and you're totally desperate, it really is as though the entire universe deliberately turns its back on you for all your pleading, begging and spell casting.

Yet it is actually not a paradox at all but a simple lesson in how things work. Magic is for people who are stable, balanced, healed and therefore able to handle the energies evoked and involved. You can only get to do it when you are ready to do it, and this means of course having handled the basics of survival on all levels successfully.

The 'I want' stage, therefore, is that declaration of having done the pre-requisite work to fulfil the needs and now being ready for **more and what lies beyond** these basic survival needs.

Before you step up to your place of declaring what it is that you want therefore, be sure to have worked out that you are NOT doing this from a place of need for simply, that's the wrong place altogether and nothing beneficial for anyone concerned can come of it.

It is very possible that at this stage, you might have to take a real break and go back to sort out your unfulfilled needs on every level before you get to step up and declare, "I want..." in the sacred realms of Sanctuary.

d) I Will

Now, to stand somewhere and, from a place of freedom from need, declare clearly that you 'want' something to happen, or change, or manifest is a very powerful thing already. It includes a great many things without which this can't be done at all, and for one it states that you have a right to want this thing. It also includes that you are ready and willing to receive it, and to accept all the consequences this entails.

This is an absolute pre-requisite to stepping up and now, clearly and without reservations, absolutely aligned and absolutely without fear, hindrance or any conflict at all, bringing this desire into being by saying, "As I will, so mote it be."

This is the state of magic and it is perhaps the most powerful state of being for a human to experience whilst we are who we are and where we are.

By all means, take your time before you step up to make your will manifest. Take your time to explore the repercussions and be sure that you are ready to handle what you are calling into being, because make no mistake, when you are making your will thus manifest in the fabric of time and space, it **will** come into being.

A special ritual place and time help give you a sensation of the sheer grandeur of this undertaking and of its importance. You may like to create a surrounding ritual for yourself before you do this extraordinary thing, a truly human thing which so many have attempted over the millennia, and so few have ever achieved.

20 - THE CONCLUSION

Now, here we have the basic ideas of what to do with, in and through the Sanctuary realms. In the past pages I have given you a great many ideas for a very great many applications, experiences and uses of these realms, probably far more than can be processed in one reading of this manual.

I would very much like you to look on this manual not as a book you read the once, but as a handbook or a reference guide you keep handy to dip in and out every so often, to fire some new ideas and remind you of others.

What I have called 'Project Sanctuary' is an ongoing learning experience that becomes more and more intense and rewarding, the more you do of it.

I have really never been without using the principles and learnings from my own Sanctuary explorations and those of others, not for a single day have I not used it in some way since I first discovered the power of learning about the Universe through this extraordinary custom made language each one of us seems to be born understanding perfectly if we just tune in a little and give it some attention.

All my work in the past 6 years, and this encompasses truly unique and extraordinary achievements such as the Energy Healing For Animals and Story Teller courses, the entire EmoTrance system, all the patterns and articles I have written, the songs and stories, the pictures I have painted and not to forget, In Serein - all of these are **directly** descended from Project Sanctuary and what I learned by **doing Sanctuary** with myself and with others.

For this 3rd Edition of 2002, I have therefore included some of the major patterns which have arisen directly from Project Sanctuary, as something you can use and do for yourself but also, and perhaps even more importantly, as a proof of what Project Sanctuary can do - what it can explain, what it can teach, what it can allow us to experience and to resolve.

It has been the most extraordinary experience of my life to be involved in this process and I am absolutely delighted to have been able to share this with you. Now, what you are going to do with this is entirely up to you.

Perhaps we'll see you in Pertineri Market?

With best wishes,

Silvia Hartmann, October 17th, 2002

ADDENDI - ARTICLES & ADD ON PATTERNS 1996 - 2002

Here is just a **minute** selection of the many, many add-ons, discoveries and articles that have literally blossomed out of straightforward, basic Project Sanctuary journeys and applications.

I was tempted to include many more, but the fact is we have been doing this for six years now and some of the more complex patterns are not suitable for someone who is just starting and would probably blow their mind.

I have therefore called a halt at some point and will continue to collect the more advanced patterns for a project which will most likely become Project Sanctuary - Patterns & Techniques Volume II at some point in the future.

There are some add-on patterns which truly enrich the basic Project Sanctuary work for everyone, however, and I have selected 15 of these patterns to join us here in this 3rd Edition.

These patterns are all extremely useful and important in their own right, but if you have time for only one, I highly recommend 'The Gift' which is probably the most wide ranging, simple and useful technique for change and growth I've ever designed.

So now, let us move along and here is the first of the 'Project Sanctuary Add Ons & Articles' for the 3rd Edition.

A1 - 3 Steps To Sanctuary

A marketing man once pointed out that "Project Sanctuary doesn't have an introduction product you can give away for free."

Now, there are many free introduction products for this manual, such as 'The Gift', but I still dutifully sat down and thought about what you could do in the way of such a thing. Eventually, I decided to write a 'Virtual Introduction Evening' for Project Sanctuary, following pretty much what I do when I am given a couple of hours and a group of interested folk to allow them to have a first experience with Project Sanctuary.

I have included this here in case you too would like to try something like that; it really is the most fascinating experience to find out what people do when you give them the basic tools and it is always a mind-expanding experience for the facilitator, too.

A1/1 - Welcome To Project Sanctuary!

If you are fascinated by dreams, symbols and metaphors, you've found the perfect place.

I am very pleased to be able to introduce you tonight to Project Sanctuary.

I could tell you a lot about why it makes you more intelligent to have better understanding and communication between your dream mind and your waking mind, but the best way to understand Project Sanctuary is to do it.

Any questions before we start?

Q - Is this hypnosis? Do I have to be in a trance?

A - Oh no. In a trance, that's where you **are** your dreaming mind. Or when you are asleep. We want to do this whilst we're awake, seeing everything, noticing what is happening so we can talk about it, understand what goes on, learn from it. I often say PS is a meeting place, not quite in here and not quite there, so both partners can step up and have a conversation.

Q - How is this related to the sort of thing where you go to a special place in nature for your Sanctuary?

A - That's a guided meditation - you go to a place you are guided to by an author, or a speaker. In Project Sanctuary, the one who guides you is your own unconscious mind. You and it create the Sanctuary together but that is only the starting point, like a base in a foreign country. When you are on holiday somewhere new, you have a base - a hotel or something. You make excursions from there and return there so you have a place of rest and safety in between.

Q - I'm not very good at making pictures. I can I still do this?

A - Oh yes. Whether or not you make pictures is neither here nor there, although doing Project Sanctuary does make you get better at it. As long as you know if something is green it doesn't matter how you know that - often it is just a feeling.

Alright, so now let us get started.

This is not something where you have to try really hard, or even try at all. It comes quite naturally. Now me, I really like the thought of a 'Sanctuary' - that's why I called it that. Not everyone likes that word, so you can think instead of a perfect place, or a haven, or your dream home, or where you'd really like to be if you could be anywhere you wanted to be in a world where dreams are made real.

Some people like certain landscapes, certain times of the year, so we'll do it step by step and all you have to do is check inside whether something feels right, feels good - that means you're going in the right direction. If it feels wrong or not good, that's the wrong direction. This is how you know which way to go when there's a decision on something, it's not a question of thinking about it or arguing with yourself this way and that. In Project Sanctuary, you can have what you want, eat your cake and never get fat, really everything and you can afford it all.

A1/2 - Exercise 1: A Landscape

Ok, first of all, let's think of a landscape that really pleases you, an environment where you would really feel at home, where you would breathe a sigh of relief and have this sense of homecoming and perfection.

If you get many choices in your head, either go with the first one or just choose one, if you could only have the one, forever.

Don't worry about choosing now. This first one is a start, nothing more. All of those other ones are yours too later on and you can move between them as the mood takes you. For now, just pick a one that makes you go, mmmmhhh .... it feels so good to be here.

A1/2 - Exercise 2: A Time of Year, A Time of Day

What time of year is it in your favourite place? Spring, Summer, Autumn, Winter? And as you are there, what time of day is it? Morning, noon, afternoon, evening, night? Or more specifically, an hour of the day?

This place of yours is in a true sense outside of time and space, but by giving it this shape and time you are fixing it. This is important because it is a meeting platform, as we said, and you need to find it again easily later on.

Now, and for the first real Project Sanctuary exercise, I want you to go and just be there for a time. Walk around if you will and sense the place, make yourself known to it and have it know you in return. Find out what there is, how big this area is, and what kind of boundaries, if any, exist around this your Sanctuary space and the outside universe.

Take your time to do this - I'll give you about five minutes - and when you are done, turn to your neighbour and briefly tell them about your Sanctuary. I know this is exciting but we don't have much time, so please just tell them a brief outline so they get some idea, then hear what they discovered in turn in the same way.

If you are doing this by yourself, please stop afterwards and just tell the room you're in, in your own words, briefly what happened. Saying it out loud makes it more real, connects the reality of the physical world to the system too to make it really span across the layers of all-there-is.

A1/3 - About Change

A lot of people are a bit wary of making a decision about their first Sanctuary one way or the other - what if I get it wrong? Won't I be stuck with something that wasn't as good as it could have been and everything will go horribly wrong from thereon in?

The space of mind and energy where Project Sanctuary lives - at a meeting point between thought and reality, here and there, now and then - is fluid, as fluid as our thoughts and as boundless.

You can change anything at the expense of a single thought. You can reverse things, turn back time, re-shape things literally endlessly and until you are satisfied. You can erase things and start all over with something different at any time.

This is a truly amazing space to learn and try out all kinds of things because you simply cannot make mistakes here at all and everything you do is perfect. Even the things that are not perfect are perfect for teaching you something about understanding perfection and yourself better.

So go ahead and do and dream and make whatever you would like.

Are you ready for Exercise 3?

A1/4 - Exercise 3 - Personalising Your Sanctuary

Now, and as you have become accustomed to the space to a degree, the next question is, if you are to spend some time here on a regular basis, what would you need to have here to be truly comfortable in all ways?

Shelter, support, company perhaps? Do you need entertainment, stimulation, what **do you personally** need and want around you to be really happy, really feel fully supported and so you can let go totally in trust and relax into enjoyment in all ways?

As you consider these questions, and in response have your first attempts at manifesting these things in your Sanctuary space, you get to practise one of our first and most important principles.

With each new creation you add on, always stop and check back how this changes things and take a moment to consider how your feelings have changed, deepened, become different because of that addition.

It is also very interesting and important to check out how the addition has affected the Sanctuary itself. As you are here and doing these things, your dreaming mind is on the other side and it is watching with interest. At some point it will come forward and make changes from its end - perhaps not right away but soon enough, you might find a structure, plant, part of the Sanctuary that you didn't put there!

Your dreaming mind put it there for you to see and to show you some of its desires and ideas - and this is the magic of Project Sanctuary.

This is when the process becomes interesting and takes on the life of a conversation, played out by two who are not yet talking properly but who are engaged in a mutual landscaping and design project.

To proceed with give-and-take when this happens, to try all sorts of things until a compromise and satisfactory outcome have been achieved, and, in doing so, learning about this other you never see and can't talk to in words directly because they speak a different language, is perhaps the most central point of Project Sanctuary and this is where its potential for true magic, healing and restoration lies.

When the two of you have learned to co-operate, have found out how to speak to each other so you can understand each other, and when you can come together to co-create with all your many and varied resources shared, you will have access to levels of thought, effectivity in the real world and abilities you can't even imagine as yet.

This is only an introduction, and time is pressing on, so let's get to our last exercise.

With these few basic tools, you have a beginning in that realm. If you like the ideas behind Project Sanctuary and feel this might be something that could really enrich your life across the levels, help you with topics such as 'self sabotage' and 'unconscious resistance' and all of that, I'd encourage you to go on to the full Project Sanctuary set.

But even if you choose not to do this, I would strongly suggest that you **use** the basic Sanctuary we have established today. With the fourth exercise in place, there is a tremendous amount you can already do with this - from a 'time out' by thinking about it and going there for a while, a storage place for favourite items that can never be taken from you, to a place to have fun in mind for a while. You can also share these basic four steps to Sanctuary with others, even young children; it is an easy thing to do and comes naturally to most humans I have ever met.

There is a deep yearning, a deep desire for more unity, more communication and understanding within ourselves; for why we do what, why we don't do things we should or thought we wanted, and the answers to these kinds of questions cannot be had in any other way but to go to the dreaming mind and know what it knows, get to understand what it can see, feel and experience - we are truly bereft if we remain with what our conscious mind alone has to offer. It has much to offer, for sure, but to ask it to truly give us everything we need in this life and give us all the answers is an impossible demand. Our logical mind has only access to half the pieces of the jigsaw puzzle.

A1/5 - Exercise 4: The Emissary

Even if your Sanctuary is not ready yet - and indeed, it could be said that it is **never** ready as your time of life moves along and your desires and needs change from day to day! - with the landscape set you can invite an advisor to come and be there with you.

The purpose of the Advisor is to be an ambassador, an emissary from your dreaming mind with whom you can start to have communications and conversations, or interactions if your emissary won't or can't speak in words that make sense to you.

In order to do this, all you need to do is to have a space in your Sanctuary, to go to it and to invite a first emissary to come and be there on behalf of your dreaming mind.

Try and accept what comes to you without reservation.

Some people hope for a wise native Indian guide and are most disappointed when a small off-yellow duck turns up instead.

Emissaries come in all possible shapes and forms, and some come in impossible shapes and forms, too. The important thing is that they **are** and that they **have come**. I know there are some amongst us who are hungry for immediate success and utter perfection on the first try but lay that aside in Sanctuary. It doesn't matter if your first emissary appears as a lump of coal, your Aunt Betty or a floating angel - there is no-one here who gives prizes for the 'most worthy emissary'. Indeed, and if such things are generally a consideration with you, I wouldn't be surprised if your dreaming mind would test you by sending an emissary that is absolutely not what you would have chosen for yourself, just to check out if you have at least learned enough by now to be worthy of giving you its time and attention.

Also note that I said your **first** emissary. There will be many more manifestations as the system comes into operation more properly, and what I would call true spirit guides come quite a bit later and no sooner than you are ready from your side to cope with them.

Try to find out what you can about your first emissary. Just learn about them and your responses to them. Say something and note what they say or do in turn.

Lastly, you can exchange gifts with your first emissary.

This is a time honoured strategy when dealing with the messenger of a powerful kingdom - to give them something unique and very precious as a token of trust and the desire for mutual co-operation and respect.

We will close with this exchange of gifts now. You start by offering a gift from you to the emissary and when this has been received, just extend your hands and wait if they will give you something in return.

Try and expect nothing, and prepare to be surprised.

This concludes our first experience of Project Sanctuary.

Three Steps To Sanctuary

Here are the basic 3 steps to Sanctuary once more in brief to help you remember:

> You create a space, time, place for yourself that pleases you immensely.

> You personalise this space to your likings, wants and desires.

> You invite a First Emissary to be there with you so you can learn about your dreaming mind.

If the experiences you have had during this introduction were such that you are now finding that this is something that excites you and you want to explore your fascinating mind further, I am looking forward to welcoming you to the Level 1 Project Sanctuary course when you are ready.

Either way, I thank you all for your attention and your time tonight.

Remember what we have said, and what you have learned.

There may well come a time when you or someone else requires this very special form of integration and exploration and when it does, come along.

It is a unique journey for each individual.

With best wishes for your road,

Silvia Hartmann

A2 - Grovian Metaphor Therapy

Named after its originator, David Grove, this is a very interesting and complex way of working with client generated metaphors to firstly find, then to undo deeply repressed traumatic memories.

There are two aspects of GMT (Grovian Metaphor Therapy) which are of great help to Sanctuary processes and I would share these with you as well as an add-on to the central body of patterns and techniques.

A2/1 - GMT Metaphor Elicitation

The first is GMT's simple and straightforward elicitation of metaphor from a feeling, problem, blockage, illness or sensation which is easy to do and proceeds like this:

"If this x (pain, problem, feeling, challenge, limitation, blockage) had a colour, what would it be?"

"If this x had a shape, what shape would it be?"

To clarify the image, the first two attributes are now repeated:

"So it is blue, and triangular, and ..." then we ask about the next attribute, such as weight, size, or location if appropriate.

If a metaphorical description has still not been found and you still only have a blue, triangular, huge, dense and heavy something, you use the repeating of the attributes as before but this time, add the question, "And what else can you tell me about it?" which tends to elicit more and more information until eventually a metaphor appears: "Well it's like, stuck in the ground, and huge, like a really big sword made of blue steel ..."

As Project Sanctuary interventions can take things from there, the rest of the complex process is not applicable for duplication here; for serious students of therapeutic metaphor, this is a very interesting and highly idiosyncratic process I would recommend.

Now to the second and even more useful aspect of Grovian Metaphor Therapy which revolves around the moving forward in time of 'stuck' metaphorical or even real situations by simply asking the question:

A2/2 - "And What Happens Next?"

This is profoundly simple yet also profoundly useful with any stuck situation, even with situations that seem to involve absolute endings, such as a character's death. Pushing it on with "And what happens next?" (and even what happens next is worm fodder and decomposition) EVOLVES the problem beyond the fearful states EVENTUALLY if you force enough time to pass.

What happens next? After the worm fodder stage?

The body becomes one with the earth and dissolves.

What happens next?

Parts of it are absorbed by other life forms and are integrated into their living systems and if you wish, you can take this to the end of time and back again, which entirely changes the perception of the original event by taking it beyond a threshold state which **seemed to be the end** .

By all means, try this very simple question on all and any stuck Sanctuary scenarios.

It is really amazing 'what happens next' in many cases.

It is pertinent to note that to ask, "How did this come to be?" is also an interesting connection-movement that completes the flow of events in the opposite direction.

A3- Growing A World From Seed

A3/1 - A Seed Painting

Have you ever made a seed painting?

It's one of the most natural and instinctual forms of art and expression and one you can find in every culture, no matter where, no matter when.

This is how you make a seed painting.

> You start with any shape, any squiggle, or even a little coffee stain in the middle of an otherwise blank piece of paper.

> Now, you simply add something to this - a line or a shape, a geometrical pattern, another squiggle, anything really.

> As the name suggests, you just allow the seed painting to grow until it fills the entire page, or creates a shape of its own, or simply until you've had enough and it seems complete.

In the process of making a seed painting, nice and usual patterns emerge that can become the core or a component for future drawings, designs or ideas and it is a great way to loosen up a bit and gain confidence in mind-hand-eye co-ordination.

A3/2 - Fantasy Seeds, Maps & Connections

A3/2/1 - The Need For Maps

If you have ever read any decent fantasy story, you'll notice that they are often accompanied by a map of the world in which these events take place. Indeed, sometimes these maps are the starting point for the story tellers, as was the case in Robert Louis Stevenson's 'Treasure Island', for example.

There is a good reason for this.

'Making up' a world that has never been inside your head, even a small island, is not quite as easy as it may seem. When you are telling a story you need to be quite specific as to what is where, and it is important for the cohesion of the story that it doesn't take 3 days to travel from A to B on one occasion, and half an hour on another. This is known as 'continuity' in movies and plays; in the context of a Project Sanctuary realm, we speak about 'locking down' places and their relationships to each other so we are clear and precise about where they are and we can find them all again later.

Drawing maps of your Project Sanctuary world is an important and fascinating time in the development of using these realms.

When you work with children, it is a most excellent starting point to engage their interest right from the start.

A3/2/2 - Making A Project Sanctuary Seed Map

As with our seed paintings, you can develop the most complex and elaborate construct starting with the smallest squiggle - a single item, a single component of a landscape or even a dwelling, or a single person, creature, event or occurrence around which the rest of that world begins to grow organically.

For slightly older children, a wonderful start is a 'Treasure Chest'. If there was such a thing, and it was especially for you, what would it look like and what would be inside it if you opened it?

What kind of ground is it on, what is the landscape around it?

From a single object, a ball, a tree or a cat or a more complex object-collection such as a house, a car or the above mentioned treasure chest, an entire world can grow to remarkable proportions and clarity in half an hour or less.

Drawing it at the same time and adjusting it, bringing it 'into the Hard' by placing areas on a piece of paper is an example of acting in accord, a sign and symbolic action to the unconscious mind that we are willing to listen, that we are willing to engage in a communication and most importantly, that we are willing to LEARN about the way in which metaphorical language and interface devices are used to communicate extremely important insights, learnings and concerns which we really need to know about.

Whether you are a professional therapist working with children, or you would just like to brighten up a rainy day with a little game of seed-world, I promise you, you will learn something new in the act of doing this.

And, let's not forget all those inner and not so inner children who have been reading this and for a while now, have been tapping with excitement to have a go themselves.

To those, I'd say, "Go for it! Make a seed-world and find out what it contains. It is probably going to be more fun than watching **someone else's world** be described on the TV, yet again."

A4 - IMAGE STREAMING

A4/1 - Introduction To Image Streaming by Win Wenger

Image Streaming is a conscious-unconscious communications training device that can really help Project Sanctuary users supercharge the clarity of their internal representations, heighten their experiences and help with problem resolution.

It is also said to make you smarter and more creative, so get Image Streaming!

Here is a message from the inventor of Image Streaming, Win Wenger, as to where to go to learn this technique and how and when it originated:

"I was playing with forms of image streaming without realizing it in 1973 and first identified it as such in about March of 1974, and have been learning about it ever since. My first publication of it was in a booklet called Voyages of Discovery, in 1975, later subsumed into the 1979 book Beyond O.K.--Psychegenic Tools Relating to Health of Body & Mind (both publications--Gaithersburg, MD: Psychegenics Press)."

Many thanks,

Win Wenger,

Founder, Project Renaissance,

main website at http://www.winwenger.com

A4/2- The Basic Imagine Streaming Process

A4/2/1 - Summary Of The Process

Summary of the process from:' The Einstein Factor' by Win Wenger, PhD, by Silvia Hartmann, PhD.

The procedure of Image Streaming is deceptively simple. You sit back in a comfortable chair, close your eyes, and describe aloud the flow of mental images through your mind. Three factors are absolutely crucial. I call these the:

Three Commandments of Image Streaming:

1. You must describe the images **aloud**, either to another person or to a tape recorder. Describing them silently will defeat the purpose of the exercise.

2. You must use **all five senses** in your descriptions. If you see a snow-covered mountain, for example, don't just describe how it looks. Describe its taste, its texture, its smell, and the sound of the wind howling across the peak.

3. Phrase all your descriptions in the **present tense**.

A4/2/2 - Tips For Beginners

Close your eyes and describe out loud anything you can see. To begin with, this may just be sparkly bits now and then, swirls, a colour going by, that kind of thing. If you have sincere trouble with getting the process going at all, use an after image from a bright light to start you off on this first step.

Keep describing out loud what you see, this aspect is vitally important to engage certain parts of your neurology.

Do this for about five minutes at a time, then stop.

Do not censor what you see to begin with, and do not try to control it.

Do not be disappointed if at first all you get are vague impressions; this process improves immeasurably with very little practise.

Taping your Image Streaming sessions on an audio recording device and playing them back later, allowing pictures to emerge as the process is reversed and fed back upon itself, is a further application of this.

Later on in the process, you can use it for problem solving and a great many other things besides; and it has been said that doing this on a regular basis makes you smarter and opens up whole new channels of communication within your own neurology.

A5 - THE GIFT

A5/1 - Introduction

The Gift is the most popular of all Project Sanctuary patterns so far and was first formally published in July 2000. It arose straight out of Sanctuary events which included the exchanges of gifts in order to achieve a healing, or a communication; this was so useful that I began to think of this as an **energetic intervention** that could be extremely subtle yet amazingly easy to do.

The Gift is also the first time that we come out of the realms in which Project Sanctuary lives and go straight into the Hard with it - sending energy for real, to a real person or occurrence or animal with volition to make immediate changes to **their** energy systems in a very practical way.

If you are new to Project Sanctuary, use The Gift first in Sanctuary to get a feel of how it works and what it does. Then use it in Sanctuary AND in the Hard and just notice and observe what happens. Now, on to this pattern which many thousands of people all over the world are using already on a daily basis and that has remained a firm favourite even with those who don't know a thing about the finer points of causal planes work or would look at you in astonishment if you mentioned energy interventions and magic.

A5/2 - Welcome To The Gift!

Welcome to The Gift - a simple pattern that is ancient as well as modern, with a thousand and one uses, that can make the world a different place for you, for the people you love, for the people you don't love, and for those who you haven't even met yet.

It may be that the act of giving The Gift can make changes at a far wider level too; as more and more minds become involved in this wonderful process, we might well have the opportunity to permanently influence matters on a profound plane of reality.

Having worked professionally with Energy Therapies for many years, I am very aware that we receive far more information and insight about the nature of reality around us than we could consciously ever understand, or evaluate, or even respond to.

Much of this information is invisible - but you can still feel it and it certainly has the power to make you happy and bright, or to bring you down; it is this information or knowledge that makes the hair on your neck rise on entering specific buildings; that gives you a strange feeling in the pit of your stomach before the telephone has even rang, and that accounts for 'gut level responses' to people, situations, proposals and ideas.

When you are engaged with another in any kind of healing relationship, and this could be either as a professional therapist or just listening to a friend who is in trouble and trying to help them somehow, both you and I have the power to help in a most profound way - if only we knew how to transfer our invisible and unspoken understandings into action in some way.

The Gift is the bridge over which your deep and unspoken understanding and your knowing about how to help can travel to the other person. It is easy to give, any human alive can do this - children are especially good at it - and you will know that a change has occurred when you have given The Gift.

What exactly happens when you give The Gift is a mystery. It has been suggested that you could be making a healing adjustment to the other's energy system, or maybe that you adjust the flow of the meridians through their bodies, or perhaps align a chakra or two in just the right way. I'm not sure what happens, only that something happens, that it feels wonderful and right, and that it creates positive change for both the giver and the receiver.

I invite you to try it for yourself. It's a simple thing, yet endlessly applicable in its very simplicity and profoundly useful and helpful in many situations.

A5/3 - How To Give The Gift

Very simply, we are going to ask for a metaphorical representation of our unique contribution to the person to whom we are going to give The Gift.

The name metaphor means a container - and in the case of The Gift, our metaphor will 'contain' whatever the person needs from us at this precise moment in time and space. It could be an understanding, a special vibration of love, something that might remove a certain negative energy, something that could unblock something, or provide nourishment in some way, support, an embrace, a space of silence or perhaps sanctuary or sustenance.

We do not need to consciously understand what it is that we are giving; and I am saying 'consciously understand' because when you have given The Gift, you will have a different kind of understanding - you will know that it was the right thing to give, because it 'feels right'. You might not be able to explain in words how it was the right thing - but then, metaphor and intuition are from the unspeakable realms, where what exists is beyond words, and that's just fine.

So, for a moment, consider a person to whom you might like to give The Gift.

Allow yourself to consider them in all ways, and beyond the face they may be wearing, beyond their social status and clothes, beyond their problems and successes, beyond any love or jealousy you might have for them.

Consider them and then ask yourself this question:

At this time, at this moment, I ask what gift I can give to this person.

Relax and let an idea or image bubble up in your mind. This image, sound, feeling or idea is the container that will carry your unique gift to the other.

Here are some examples of gifts that appeared when the question was asked:

A small blue and red bird

A multi coloured spiral

A small tree in a flower pot

A pair of wings

A huge field of green grass

A luminous white dove

A warm blue cloak to wrap around your shoulders

The sound of ocean

What looked like a beach ball, then turned out to be Planet Earth.

Now, take your time to consider the person and find a gift for them.

Don't argue with your choice, accept whatever springs to mind - your conscious mind doesn't know enough to know what would be the perfect gift but your unconscious mind does, and that is the place from where the metaphor arises.

Most people more than readily can think of something. Should your mind go blank, you can either leave the request to keep working on it and send it to you as a 'flash of insight' at any time within the next few days; or you may consider which colour might be good for this person, and then just imagine a gift box with a matching ribbon on top in that colour and trust that your perfect gift will be inside that box.

Now, imagine the person and imagine offering the gift to them. This part of the pattern creates the transfer from you to them and represents your intention to be of help.

That is all you have to do. From then on, whatever happens next, will happen under its own processes as the interaction unfolds and the changes are made.

Some things you might notice or come across when you give The Gift are as follows:

Sometimes when you think of the person, they appear very different to what they normally look like - they may appear older, younger, may be dressed differently than in 'real life', or may be expressing emotions through their body postures that you are not normally aware of. This is perfectly normal and it is a sign that you are seeing who they really are.

Often, you might experience strong emotions yourself when The Gift has come to your mind. Again, this is in a way the correct reaction to this process and it tells you that it is working. Emotions and energetic states are inextricably linked in a single system.

So far, every person who was offered a Gift received it most gratefully - some with tears, some with astonishment and gratitude and some with childlike delight. It is conceivable however that a Gift might be rejected. Should this happen, you could ask what they would prefer to have from you instead - there is something that is absolutely unique to you for them, that they cannot get from anyone or anywhere else. If you feel you can fill the request, go ahead; but you also have the right to not fill it if it seems inappropriate or feels less than good to you.

Pay attention to your self when sending The Gift. It is often as profound an experience to give it as it is to receive it.

It is not necessary to tell people about The Gift, although with good friends it adds another dimension to the process and if you can discuss the nature of these Gifts, you can gain tremendous insights into many things.

You can give The Gift just while talking to someone and without their knowing anything about it. Briefly focus on a place beyond their physical body, and you may be able to imagine an astral copy of the person to whom you will give the gift. When you do this, pay attention to how the other person responds when The Gift is given. Some people lose their train of thought, some look over their shoulder; they are aware that something has happened which, indeed, it has. Note also how after a giving of The Gift the nature of the whole interaction seems to change for the better.

Remember that The Gift represents an energetic exchange, in spite of the often seemingly simple or mundane metaphorical object that carries your intention across. Energetic exchanges are **felt** not heard or measured with a Geiger counter; pay close attention to your feelings and your emotions when giving The Gift because that is how you will know that you have done something important.

The original pattern of The Gift was developed for healers and therapists who were suffering from extreme overwhelm when faced with deeply unhappy, physically and mentally scarred people who were suffering from a lifetime of neglect, terrible trauma and lovelessness.

The Gift creates a straightforward method for their unique healing energies and intentions to go the right places for that individual, and most importantly, helps them to no longer feel overwhelmed and helpless.

The negative emotions of helplessness and conscious overwhelm disappear when you use The Gift to help others, and in so doing, are a gift to you.

A5/4 - Gifts For All Occasions

A5/4/1 - A Gift For You

Interestingly, sometimes it happens that a person to whom you have given The Gift will offer one in return to you - and I don't mean people who you have told about having sent them a gift and who will nearly always reciprocate likewise automatically, but those you imagined offering a Gift to.

Needless to say, please receive it in gratitude. As we have said before, this is an energetic exchange and energy needs to flow freely both from you to them, and from them to you.

You can also give yourself a gift in the same way as you would another person.

This is an interesting exercise on many levels and it is intrinsically very different from other people's gifts as it will be your own energy you are using instead of a different flavour which comes from another person.

You may consider gifts for 'past selves' - perhaps there was a time in your life that was very traumatic, or you 'used to be a different person', which usually means a worse person. To give those parts of yourself Gifts can help to re-align them, ease their suffering and to help them grow and heal. It is possible that there are certain 'past you's' that cannot be healed by anyone other than you yourself.

A5/4/2 - The Mirror Gift

As it is the case that people pop up in our lives in order to be a mirror to us and our own problems, and as it is also the case that my sister-in-law always gives me presents **she** would liked to have received, you might consider when you have given a few gifts to your loved ones, which one of those gifts you would like to have received as well, and give yourself the same one, too.

A5/4/3 - Gifts For Strangers

As my intuition increased, I used to find it harder and harder to travel on public transport or be in crowded places, simply because of the general unhappiness, loneliness and suffering that was emanating from the people around me.

For example, I saw an Indian lady with many heavy bags at a train station. Although I helped her carry the bags onto the train, there was so much sadness and physical suffering around her like a dark grey fog that she hardly seemed to notice me. I gave her a tropical garden, and she took a deep, deep breath and seemed to become alive and aware of her surroundings.

I then went through all the passengers of the train compartment, one by one and felt myself getting lighter and more comfortable with each Gift given and hungrily received.

I received a number of Gifts in return also and left the train full of energy and brighter than I had been in years.

What I believe is that The Gift is a stepping stone, a learning process that will allow us to do this type of work automatically and without us having to even give attention to it once we are fully familiar with its workings.

I would invite you to try it for yourself, and note what difference it makes to you and your individual dealings with strangers and passers by.

A5/4/4 - Gifts For Animals

Animals (wild animals and domesticated animals) are extremely aware of energetic shifts of all kinds, and they too can receive The Gift. Further, their feedback to receiving the gift is immediate and clearly visible in their physiology, their body postures and their subsequent behaviour. Here are a few examples of gifts for animals:

A gift bow (for a dog which later turned out to have been 'an unwanted gift').

A foal (for a mare who was highly strung - as soon as the owner thought of the foal the mare stopped dead, relaxed right out and stood very quietly, with her head drooping).

A blue green blanket (for a dog who then came into the room "for no good reason" and lay down, at full stretch, exactly in the spot the blanket had 'appeared' to the owner).

A5/4/5 - A Gift For The World

If you remember, the original Gift pattern was designed to help with overwhelm.

What can be more overwhelming than global issues such as world pollution, world hunger, the suffering of all the children, all the animals, global warming, wars and famines, and so forth?

What causes depression and overwhelm is the thought 'There is nothing I can do'.

With The Gift, there is something you can do now beside recycling and donating to charity, and I believe that every one of us who addresses such issues at the energetic level in this way actually does make a difference.

As The Gift pattern does not require much meditation, time or effort other than conscious volition to **do it now**, it is a perfect beginning to start to use our abilities to make changes at the energetic level on global issues too.

What Gift will you give to the world today? To The Children? To Humanity? Whatever you have to contribute, know that it is uniquely yours to contribute - no-one else in the world can give this Gift the way you do - and that it will make a difference.

A5/4/6 - Feedback

Here are some stories received about using The Gift in practise.

"A friend came to visit me who is in a very unhappy relationship. I listened to her for a long while but began to feel more and more uncomfortable in the face of her anger and couldn't think of what to do other than to just go along with it and hope she'd tire of it soon. I remembered The Gift from the newslist, and focussed on what I could be giving her. As soon as I thought of it, a white dove appeared before me. It was carrying a long flowy red ribbon in its beak, and fluttered in midair. I stared in awe. After I got over my surprise, I gave it to my friend, mentally released it to her. Instantly, she stopped talking. The entire mood of the room calmed, and she tied up a few loose ends and left, calm and confident."

"This metaphorical gift giving solves a huge dilemma I have had weighing on my heart. I recently spent time with some very old friends and was quite disturbed by the way they are treating their children, and by their troubled 13 year old son. These are not people I can confront or help right now, and their kids live across the country from me so I can't establish a relationship and help that way. But I CAN go inside myself every time I think of it, and send whatever seems appropriate at that moment. It has been a wonderful relief to me."

"I heard that a dear friend's father had died suddenly. I wanted to do/say something to help but was in a spin, couldn't find the right words, so I settled myself down and pictured my friend and his father, immediately I knew that the 'Gift' was a very special poem about laughter.

Later on I was tapping for my friend but it just didn't feel right, I couldn't find the right thing to tap on....until your mail arrived. It was so obvious I couldn't see it. Now I know that the greatest gift that I can energetically send at this time is laughter. Thank you for putting into words what I knew but couldn't see."

"I have been troubled by feeling very negative - hateful - towards a certain person recently. When I got the message about The Gift, it occurred to me to try it on that person to see if it would make any difference. Immediately, a huge black raven sprang to mind. I was worried that it might be something bad and hesitated, but it looked very beautiful and powerful so I decided to trust my unconscious mind and send it anyway. I felt better immediately as I 'saw' the raven flying away all purposefully and actually found it hard to get back those feelings of negativity about the person. Later, someone told me this: "The raven on the Shamanic Medicine Wheel is the guardian of in absentia healing and its medicine is considered needed to bridge the Void, to reach the collective unknown." I had no idea of that but WOW. What a Gift - and just what that person must have needed. And what I needed to do to regain balance in my mind."

"The Gift I gave to a friend I did give to myself too and quite a few spooky things have happened to me since, including a change of attitude to food, frequently I am 'energised' by some 'energy' which leaps out of me, and feeling at peace and full of self-love and kindness. I also had a weird experience of finding out I share a past life memory with a friend!"

"Today, a friend stopped by. He was tripping out, exploding with ideas, and I began to feel overwhelmed with his energy. I thought of The Gift, and a small speckled egg appeared in front of me. It was a lovely greenish bluish greyish color, with brownish spots. I just stared at it for a moment, sort of cherishing it. Then I released it to him. I was watching his face as I gave him this egg. He stopped in mid word and just stared at me, and asked me what he'd been saying. He said, "Something just happened. Everything is different." So I told him about the egg. He teased me about having 'egged' him. Then he said that the sensation he was experiencing was a sort of encapsulation. About a half hour later, he was again escalating his thought process, and my attention drifted back to the egg. I replayed it in my mind, and as I did so, he again stopped, looked at me, and asked if I'd 'egged' him again. I hadn't meant to! We laughed about it. Now I can't wait to use this with my kids, and my ex when he stops by & begins to attack me. This is truly the simplest thing I've ever done, and the results are remarkable."

"I was in this doctor's office with a replacement doctor because the regular one was on holiday. This was a woman of about 50. She spent the first ten minutes apologising to me that she wasn't the real doctor and kept asking me if I wanted to wait until the real doctor was back again. I thought of The Gift and what came to mind was a single red rose. Whilst she was still apologising, I imagined a ghost shape of me giving the rose to a ghost shape of her, it took it and said quite loudly in a tearful voice, "No-one has ever given me one of these before." At that moment, the real woman stopped talking and looked over her shoulder, in the same direction where I was seeing the ghost shape. She took a deep breath and seemed confused for a bit, then she smiled at me and said, "Well, let's find out how can I help you."

"The morning after I received The Gift on the list, I was out walking and saw a woman shouting and screaming at her dog in the park. For some reason I wondered if I could give a Gift to the poor dog and I thought of a big red ribbon, like a gift bow. I send it to the dog and then went on to say hello to the woman and stop her somehow. She was very angry at first but calmed down, and then told me that dog had been 'an unwanted gift'. I nearly burst out into tears on the spot."

"One of my best and oldest friends is dying. I lay in bed and couldn't sleep for tears although I kept telling myself it was all for the best and that he was going home. I was exhausted and at 3am, I called up an image of my friend and began to give him all sorts of Gifts, dozens of them, until he smiled and stopped me and gave me a gift instead - it was a big white Indian blanket with symbols painted on it which he wrapped about me. I don't know what happened or how but I felt really warm all of a sudden. I stopped crying and went to sleep. Thinking about it now, I think The Gift was always about me."

As you can see, The Gift is a great introduction to Sanctuary style work for beginners as well as a very powerful intervention in its own right, with literally innumerable applications in every conceivable area of internal, external and transpersonal relationships.

Please feel free to share The Gift with anyone you would like; this pattern is specifically 'public domain' which means that payments or copyright fees for its use are waved. I would like to see The Gift taught especially to small children as a first introduction to the realms beyond the visible, and their own abilities to make changes to the world in this unique and very wonderful way.

A6 - LoveLine

A6/1 - Introduction

LoveLine is another classic Project Sanctuary pattern which, like so many of these patterns, simply **happened** one day with one particular person, and as soon as it did, opened my eyes to a whole range of possible interventions, lessons and learnings about a great many things.

I have called this pattern 'excruciating' in the past and I stand by that. It is extremely emotional and extremely powerful. The energies raised here can also be painful instead of being experienced as healing or beneficial; if this is the case, you need to use EmoTrance in conjunction with this pattern to be able to handle these very powerful energies of human connection and of love.

Conducted with an open mind, however, LoveLine can change your mind about who or what you really are in a way that is more profound and long lasting than just about anything else I've ever encountered.

With these caveats, here is LoveLine, first published in January 2002.

A6/2 - Introducing The Concepts Behind LoveLine

Feeling unloved, sometimes?

Do you wonder sometimes if you are at all lovable? Feeling lonely even inside a relationship? Misunderstood? Alone?

Well, I think we can put an end to that. And a beginning to a completely different understanding of how and what love has been in your life, what really went on and how you could, if you wanted to, begin to think of yourself in a whole new way.

There is just one pre-requisite you need for this journey, and that is a measure of courage.

Loving is not at all as easy as it may seem or as is generally preached about.

This is because if you love and lose, there is tremendous pain involved, and this pain gets linked back to the decision to love, like an allergy. Just think about that. There are so many people out there, allergic to love. Many more than are allergic to peanuts, only that love is somewhat harder to avoid and a shortfall in the supply will cause various forms of energetic scurvy. If it was a substance, you could sell it with the slogan: "Love. Nothing else will do."

As a way of protection, it is often easier to make it so that you never really loved this (awful) person at all, that you were just deluded or very young or drunk or didn't know what you were doing; that's a process I've seen many times and of course, it's designed to make it hurt less when you think about that (awful) person. Sometimes it is not a deliberate choice but something that just seems to happen - you look at the person and whatever there once was is no longer there and you really wonder if anything you thought or felt before was ever real at all.

We need a measure of courage for this pattern because we are going to revisit a time, a moment, when you were **in love** with the people in your life you ever were **in love** with - all of them.

You see, there are dimensions beyond what we can perceive here in The Hard.

Some of these dimensions have different laws of nature, and in many of them, time does not procede linearly as it does here, with one sunrise after the other, here today and gone tomorrow.

Indeed, there is a level of reality where **any event** that ever happened sets up a standing pulse and remains, to all intents and purposes, infinitely.

So, when they said to you, "I will love you forever" - they did. And still do.

Sure, here in the Hard they may be dead, or gone or packed up and left and did all these things but this pulse is still there.

If it was ever said, felt, experienced then it **is**.

And it is forever.

Infinity = 1.

What in effect we will be doing when we undertake the LoveLine journey, is to get in touch with those standing pulses of love. These are as good as it gets, and the ones we are going to re-visit to remind ourselves of many things are not occasions when we received those, but when we **gave them**.

Our moments of "I will love you forever" are also standing pulses in a Universe much greater than the eye can see or the mind can hold in consciousness. They are very particular focus points of power and of understanding, space time events when you are all you can be and more, much more than you probably think you are right now.

I have a sign on my door that says, "You are not who you think you are."

It is a reminder of the fact that our so called self concepts are such puny, whimpering, twitching miserable little things, formed from habit and unknowingness, and that whatever you think you are, that is not beginning to scratch the surface.

But enough of the introductions.

This is what we are going to do.

A6/3 - How To Do LoveLine

First, you need to create a space, a meeting platform, where we will meet with the people we once loved and where we set up a standing pulse of inordinate resonance that still sings in the Universe, and will continue to do so, and has always done so, from the end of time to the end of time.

This space would be a wide sweeping landscape, as far as the eye can see and the colours and textures would be radiant and soft, entirely to your liking. It would be still there, and if you stood on this plane we have specially constructed to bridge to other realms of understanding, you would feel the stillness and clean clarity that surrounds you, from the virtual ground to where the virtual sky meets the horizon.

Slowly, turn on the spot and have your plane be clear in your mind and body, too. Know it and be familiar with it, remember it on a level because you have been here before, perhaps not in awareness, but there are stratas within you that well recognise this place.

Now, invite a one you once loved to be here with you.

One will come, and might be the one you thought it would be, or it could be another altogether and you would be very surprised.

All I want you to do is to step up to them, to look them in the eye and give a small nod, a small acknowledgement that indeed, you did love them.

That is all for now.

There is more that could be done if you wanted to. You could speak with them, hold them, be with them but that is not the point of LoveLine.

For you see, LoveLine is an unfoldment and a reminder.

In this space and on this plane, where you stand would be the moment of your conception and out in front of you, stretches invisibly across the open landscape your time of life.

There are people standing quietly - you cannot quite see just yet who they are and that is right and as it should be at this moment. These are your loves through your life so far.

These represent not themselves but your own ability to love, to make a connection, to understand something about the nature of the universe that is truly **holy** and profound, something no-one, but no-one can tell you about but only you can feel, know, experience - understand.

In your own time, step forward and begin to walk towards the first of these. Don't be too close, remember this is just a recognition. For each one, halt, stand in front of them and acknowledge them, remember them, recognise them and touch the standing wave that you yourself created in that moment that is with you once again as you gaze at them, quietly and steadily.

Make your acknowledgement and continue on.

As you do this, you will find surprises.

You will meet loves that you did not remember, did not recall, had forgotten or repressed.

You will be amazed how much you have loved, how many of them there are and how deeply you loved them.

Not a one with whom I have shared this basic journey has not come back astonished, sometimes appalled that they just didn't recognise or realise just how much they had loved and how many times. How much love there had truly been in their lives when they really thought there was none. How absolutely they knew how to love already if only they would remember and retain.

From here, the LoveLine journey can develop and take a life of its very own.

You might like to go to the plane with the intention of meeting those who loved you once, and thus for all infinity.

That is the moment, that is the manifestation, not what went before or what came after, it is that moment where the standing pulse comes into being that is here with you in this spaceless space, this timeless time of truth which is by no means an imagining but just a seeing, a translating of an energetic Universe that is beyond our eyes in every way.

You might like to do this more than once; indeed, there are so many there to meet you that to walk the LoveLine in its totality on one single visit has been proven far too much for anyone who has attempted it thus far.

When you do, allow events to unfold and interact with the feedback you receive.

You might want to hug a person but they would back away, and tell you they're not worthy of your love or that there is too much of them that can't be loved at all.

And yet, the standing pulse of love loves **all of them** at once, all they are and quite regardless. Sometimes it is enough to tell them that and other times, they need to hear it said aloud on this meeting plane between the levels and the layers.

Let your desire and intuition be your guide on this journey of discovery, or should I say of re-discovery, for of course, there's nothing new here at all.

You already knew all of this.

Of course you did.

The LoveLine pattern is nothing but a much needed reminder of a truth about love, and loving.

A7 - How To Make Organic Tesla Machines

This is a nice training pattern for time control, originally written for Mindlist in September 2002 which utilises the possibility of the 'Project Sanctuary Computer' generating the outcomes once you have programmed the details in and set the scenarios to run in their own time to make causes and effects become visible.

I'm sure you all heard about Mr Tesla and his amazing machines, that he built and ran in his mind in quantum time, then went back to check and measure which parts had worn out and when he came to build them for 'real' they functioned beautifully, the problems having long been found and ironed out in the mindspace trial runs.

I've heard it too and just put it aside, as something Mr Tesla could do, being a genius, but not available to me as an ordinary human being. But actually that's not so. This is actually something everyone can do, and it isn't even that hard.

What it needs is some attention and intention, and a **starting place** to practise the basics before we go on to such finely calibrated precision items as mechanical turbines made from tooled brass.

In the context of Project Sanctuary, what I'm thinking is as follows.

1. You need to create a kind of space-time platform where the events to unfold will take place. A specific location of some kind that you can find again later on and easily so. For beginners, that is best done by locking down the aspects of such a space with a landscape, a time of day and a time of year. (It's a long story, you'll just have to trust me on that bit.)

2. Now in this space, I would put something simple, like a box or any object that won't change, and visit this repeatedly to make sure the platform is stable, you can find it again and you're getting a feel of how time is moving there - whether it changes at all in between visits, for example. Most people manage a perfect encapsulation of the original space and there's no movement of time in the space at all - it is always afternoon, around 3pm, in late spring and regardless of whether the last visit was three months ago, 5 weeks ago, 10 days ago, one hour ago, time never changes.

3. Here comes the interesting part, which is to introduce a straightforward object that naturally has phases which indicate its passing through time, if you will. Let's say a candle that burns down, or a water clock, a ripe banana or even a machine that clearly **shows in**

its states how time is progressing. Don't make it too complicated or else you'll lose the whole point of the exercise, namely which is to practise in readiness for No. 4 - we are introducing the component of time passing in that space.

4. Now the next thing that's needed is to **control** how time moves in the space. Forward, backward, fast and slow. This is simply a practise matter which gets much, much easier over time and in the case of working with Tesla constructs is of the essence.

5. I would then highly suggest practising with an uncontrollable system, such as planting some seeds, or introducing some creatures which will interact, to bring the systems on line that are basically plotting the evolution of **unpredictable** system groups over time and to begin using wider time movements - moving things on by a year, 100 years, 1 million years and back again.

Organic systems are **much, much more** complex than mechanical systems and once this evolution and observation ability is on line (which is actually quite easy, amazingly enough, it just happens!) you should be ready for your own first simple Tesla machine.

As I said, start with something simple. And don't confine yourself to machines. You can make absolutely anything in that space. Musical notes appearing on a sheet of paper, trainings being conducted, received, criticised, refined, and honed until there's a standing ovation every single time; structures of databases, management systems, computer programmes; building houses and living in them; living entire lives in many different incarnations - all of these things are, essentially, Tesla machines.

It's a pretty incredible thing, worth getting familiar with.

A8 - STAR SEED

This pattern was first published in June 2001. It is amongst my favourites and as well as giving a very nice insight into the nature of energies and people's reactions to energies, it is also an excellent example of how Project Sanctuary can come to the rescue, quite automatically, when such knowledge is needed to solve a problem if you have bothered to practise it and made it come alive within you.

Star Seed

I was reading over a meditation set designed to bring light to someone who lives in loneliness and darkness.

At the time, I was playing some pleasant music and mentally drifting, just kind of relaxing after numerous hours spend wrestling with various MicroSoft products in one form or the other, surfing the web and following without much thought from link to link.

And there was this meditation, and I read it and as soon as I did, such a person came right to my mind and instantly and without any further doing on my part, I send them a ray of light into the shadows amongst which they dwelled.

However, rather than a good response and a nice feeling as such exercises are expected to produce, the intended recipient responded very much like a vampire when the curtains have been drawn on a sunny day - they raised their arms to protect themselves from the white light and where it 'hit' them, it caused them excruciating agony and instant radiation burn.

Startled, I sat up straighter in my chair, shut off the love light with haste and considered the situation.

As I did, the process that had started in my mind took on its own life and had me walk lightlessly into the deep shadow where the recipient of my good works lay writhing in agony. I cautiously applied some cooling, soothing and healing and extended my heartfelt apologies which were accepted quite graciously, given all the circumstances.

But still, here we were and once I was to leave, the person would be all alone in the darkness once more and I did want to express my regard for them in some way, do something for them before I went back.

Quite without my doing anything other than desiring to do something, a tiny star appeared, small enough to fit into the palm of my hand easily. It wasn't white either, but softly shone in muted rainbow colours. I offered the tiny star to the person and they could look upon it without its light hurting their sensitive eyes, and they thought it was absolutely beautiful and they loved it.

So I left the tiny star with them and returned to the here and now, extremely moved and quite shaken up by the whole experience which had taken no more than a minute at the most in 'real time' and over which I had had very little control.

It set me to thinking about many things.

Firstly, how it seems that I was shown there that you cannot just chuck light and love at people who may not have any way of dealing with or processing this kind of energy. It is a startling thought but one that actually tallies well with my previous experiences on the subject. Like, for example, at one hypnotherapy training I attended there was a lady who really responded very badly to being told to imagine a white healing light. At the time, I thought her response was due to perhaps a bad experience for real in the presence of a bright light, such as in an operating theatre, police interrogation or in the dentist's chair. I have also observed on numerous occasions that real love energy is not a mushy, fluffy pink thing but indeed, a force of such power that it would rush through your mind and body like a storm and sandblast your self from your self.

Further, recently I had a bad experience personally at an abysmal seminar, where the workshop leader told us that coloured "lasers were coming from the stars and piercing our chakras". Eeeeow!!! An appalling sensation on every level, viscerally painful and undoubtedly, not a good thing for anyone's energy system at all. Be careful with that light ...

I guess there's so much in the way of entrainment that light=good and that you can't ever have enough of it, I had never really consciously considered before that at the energetic level, structures need to exist that can handle, channel, process such incoming energy for it to be beneficial to the intended recipient.

Those of us and those parts of us who really do 'reside in forever night' most certainly cannot handle any of it.

The Star Seed is a beautiful thing. It's an ecological thing, a small something that doesn't hurt, confuse or destroy but that very respectfully and mindfully of the existing conditions offers a starting point to begin

258

to re-awaken and to stimulate the receiving structures of the energy exchange systems.

It might be a very useful thing too. Many more of us than believe it do suffer from a 'fear of love'. It is interesting to muse that this might once again turn out to be not evil unconscious self sabotage at all, but an essential protective device to stop us from burning up like vampires under the noonday sun.

In this sense, I would offer you a Star Seed or many, to take to parts of you that might require such a thing, and to keep around if you should meet another who would be glad of one, too.

A9 - THE DIAMOND PYRAMID

The Diamond Pyramid pattern is called thus because we actually constructed one from the many 'diamond splinters' we collected from across our worlds in the Sanctuary realms. The principles behind this pattern were once again learned during a Project Sanctuary exploration and this article explains these things in such terms that someone can begin to think about how this may apply to them without any knowledge of the Sanctuary realms.

Where this article ends is where this pattern actually starts. I highly recommend this for a little play, it is truly beautiful when the sun comes up and lights up your own 'acres of diamonds'.

The Diamond Pyramid

One day, I was speaking to a friend on the phone.

I was telling her about thoughts and experiences I had whilst driving at dusk on a country road the day before, how I was not enjoying the driving at all and how sad that was really because I remember well that there used to be a time when I loved to drive.

I used to drive for no good reason at night, get the car out, fill it up with petrol and just drive.

Where I used to live at that time, there were mountain roads and back roads that were totally empty of both traffic and traffic cops and I used to really race and just love it - I'd do it for hours, stereo blazing, the sports car responsive and roaring, nice leather covered steering wheel responding to my every touch.

What happened?

Twenty years on, I'm tense.

Back hurts, eyes are smarting, I wish I was home instead, the gear changing has become a chore and I'm afraid that night will fall soon and then I'll be panicking if someone forgets to turn their main beam off and blinds me.

Now I'm not some sort of OAP or doddering octogenarian. I'm forty, for God's sake, in my prime, far more so now than I ever was back then.

What happened?

My friend laughed a little sadly and she said, "Well, I guess it's like that. Stuff happens, traumas of one kind or the other, and they all pile up on top of each other, and you just break down under the weight of it all. The older you get, the worse it becomes."

I sighed in return and said, "I guess you're right. I've had a couple of really bad accidents and at least a dozen truly terrifying near misses. And all the times I had to drive vast distances and got so totally exhausted and fed up I just wanted to cry."

We were silent there for a moment and then all of a sudden, I had a thought and said,

"Wait a minute."

"Wait a minute there. What is this? Ok so there's - lets say, 32 trauma incidences to do with driving a car. Fair enough. But what about the other types of things? I've won ralley and street races when I was younger, for Heaven's sake. I had some of the coolest moments of my life in a car. Like making love in a car. Like driving somewhere and it is totally beautiful, the countryside or the weather or even the guy in the seat next to you? Like getting into your car and you're hopping with excitement because you're on your way to the coolest place, time, date, festival, party, show, whatever? What about those kinds of things?"

We thought about this for a moment and the fact is, I've had really good experiences in, with, around and even on top of cars, just as powerful in emotional charge terms as the negative ones and I would have thought, loads more of them!

Yet these experiences were not being 'piled on on top of each other' in the same way the 'trauma' experiences were.

We set to wondering what would happen if they did. If you have enough trauma experiences, eventually they tip the balance and you end up with a 'nervous breakdown'.

I laughed and said, "Well I guess if you pile up your fun experiences in exactly the same way, well, you'd have to have some kind of 'nervous breakthrough'!"

We fell about laughing for quite some time but you know, that is a most fascinating idea, indeed.

I wonder what a nervous breakthrough would be like, look like, feel like?

When you really break through and you go, goddamm it, I can't stand it anymore, yes, it's true, I love driving and I'm a great, safe driver with fantastic reflexes. Cars are brilliant, wonderful things, travelling is the coolest - oh dear God, there's no more denying it - I give up, it's the truth, there we have it.

A real moment of bright day of the soul, if you will :-))).

So, I would put it to you that there is a mechanism in your mind, as there is in all our minds, that collects evidence from our lives.

As it stands, especially the people who are unhappy with themselves, in therapy, therapists themselves, in personal development and all such folk might well be there because this mechanism is collecting their failures and traumas faithfully and stacking them up, but somehow failing to collect their triumphs and their 'diamond moments'.

There may be a societal entrainment component to this unfortunate strategy whereby you get love and attention when you fail miserably and get excluded and discriminated against when you are too outstanding, too 'show off', too 'fond of yourself' and all of that, nicely entrained in so that most folk cannot tell you about their merits rationally and without writhing at all, not even small children.

So, what happens to the moments of anti-trauma that I call diamonds structurally?

They are not being collected in a special reservoir of connected memories, thoughts and feelings (also known as a 'gestalt') but instead, seem to be scattered about randomly, like a host of diamonds scattered all across a huge landscape that is your time of mind.

Just to be fair and to even the score so at least we have some form of balance between bad experiences and good ones in our mind, I would say that there is much merit in starting to bring some of these diamonds together so we can have a collection point to start us off in the right direction.

How do we do this?

Firstly, I think it would be good to have the desire and intention to be doing this in the first place.

You may well, when faced with your 'acres of diamonds', feel a strong reluctance to setting this process in motion at all.

This reluctance will reveal to you just why in your particular case it was ok to collect the sticky coals and make them into a huge black wall or pile of shame, failure, inadequacy, misery, and non-deservedness but it was not ok to collect your diamonds and build them up into a sparkling pyramid of success, pride, capability, perseverance, love and joy.

Why wasn't it ok to collect your successes and moments of high esteem?

Who said it wasn't?

What made you feel that it wasn't?

When and how did you decide that it wasn't (safe, right, good, perfect, acceptable) to collect your successes like trophies on your life's shelf?

With those questions answered and dealt with, you can then literally instruct yourself to keep an eye open for all the diamonds - big and small alike, little splinters sparking the sunlight for they are valuable too and all and every one helps with building the pyramid that will balance the slag heap on the other side.

If you are metaphorically inclined (and if you are not, start being so because that is the royal road to communicating with your unconscious selves) you can send someone out to start collecting your diamonds while you eat, sleep and play.

You can use BSFF, EFT, hypnosis, NLP procedures, Sidereus techniques or even just think about your diamonds and your new collection - all of these things will help to get you started on the way towards having some serious nervous breakthroughs on such topics like what kind of person you are, how efficient and effective you are, how well you have done in your life so far and many, many other things beside.

Those who have applied the 'Diamond Pyramid' construction scheme will tell you that it is a very emotional thing, a very freeing thing, but more importantly, it brings back justice to a system that has been incredibly unjust and hurtful in the process to those who have been running it.

It doesn't make you a better person, it doesn't make you a worse one.

It doesn't make you into anything other than exactly what you already are - but you will have a totally different understanding of what exactly that might be in terms of self concept and understanding than when you started out.

And, that, my friend, can only be a good thing all around.

A10 - A NEW ALONE

This is a classic Project Sanctuary pattern which involves a very important **movement**, namely that of zooming out to the greater ecology beyond the problem. This is a good example of this movement which I employ often to help myself and others regain a sense of perspective and re-frame the entire situation into a new, bigger and far more holistic understanding. See also 'The Zodiac Cage' for an example of this movement.

A New Alone

This lady, Sophie, was overcome by feeling alone, overwhelmed, black. It was a true crisis and this crisis did not respond to the application of advanced energy therapies, so I went to Project Sanctuary for aid and clarification as I so regularly do and asked her, "Where are you?"

Very distressed, Sophie expressed that it was all black, terrifying, a terrible sense of dread so she could hardly breathe - she was in a black cave, cold, wet and entirely dark.

I asked her to find a way out and although she did manage to get outside, the feelings of panic and dread did not recede at all and this was rather strange and unusual - as soon as she had gotten out of the cage I would have expected for the feelings to be different but they were entirely unchanged. So I asked her to rise up into the air, high up to be able to see and then describe the outside countryside.

It was a beautiful valley encircled by mountains with a nasty black mount in the middle which was the entrance to the cave of doom.

I suggested to blow up this cave but Sophie did not want to do so, it seemed that there was something important inside the cave which needed to be explored, found somehow, learned about. She said, "There is no way you are getting me back in there. It's too scary. Once I'm in there you might not be able to get me out again ever - I'm not going."

In spite of this forceful declaration, she knew full well that this was a typical Sanctuary style 'test' and so we discussed what resources she might need in order to be able to re-enter the cave. Two powerful guides eventually were called upon and all three, with strong bright torches, then entered the cave again.

Sophie was still extremely scared and could hardly breathe; they went into the dark tunnels and eventually found a chamber in which there lay an abandoned baby, all alone in the dark.

It had been here for a long time, it seemed, long enough for it to no longer cry or whimper, or do anything at all. As soon as Sophie saw the baby, she rushed to it and picked it up carefully.

"It was terrible," she said. "The baby wasn't moving at all, it was limp, cold and completely unresponsive." The fear had gone, for her fear had been about not knowing what she would find; now she felt terribly sad and terribly sorry for the baby, and angry too at those who had abandoned it here in this dreadful place.

She held the baby close and took it outside into the sunshine and sat with it. She and the guides gave the baby healing and love, and it began to warm up and move about a little.

Then Sophie went ahead and did three things. The first was to realise that indeed, this was a beautiful place to be alone, protected by the mountains and with the beautiful valley stretching out towards their snow capped peaks.

The second was that it was now the right thing to do to blow up the caves of doom and the black mount above them; she did so immediately using a Solus device and so there was nothing left, only grass, not even a faint rising would have told you there was ever anything there at all.

The third was to find a younger self, a woman who loved babies and children and was delighted to be able to be allowed to take care of the baby, to take the little Sophie and live with her in a comfortable cottage in this Sanctuary space, so "she could grow up loved rather than left and abandoned."

Now, being alone meant something completely different and it felt different too and that is why this story is called 'A New Alone', as relaxing in the valley Sanctuary replaced the caves of doom in actuality.

A10/1 - Learning To Fly

Sometimes and too close up, problems are truly overwhelming as they are all around and all the eye can see - where you are is **all there is** and this of course, is not a good place to find holistic solutions to our internal conflicts and problems.

In Sanctuary, one of the first and best movements to master and learn is that of flying.

Truly, and in the right spirit of things, I believe that learning to fly by oneself and not any longer with the aid of dragons, balloons or machinery of any kind marks a truly important turn of events and opens up a different kind of working relationship with the Sanctuary realms.

It is a turn towards freedom and exploration because when you learn to fly, you can truly go anywhere - even where the solar winds may take you when you are ready to give up control in trust to the underlying trade winds and tides of these realms.

Sophie was an experienced Project Sanctuary student and knew she could fly - and the Zoom movement of literally zooming up and out of a situation to take in the bigger perspective on the situation.

Of course, the further away from a situation you are, the less emotionally involved you become; this is well known and has been used in hypnotherapy for many years and represents a form of disassociation.

When we do this zooming up in the Sanctuary environment, we are not really disassociating from the problem as in moving away and not being able to be aware of it or feel it anymore; rather we are taking note of the problem in the context of the wider ecology and that is the aforementioned bigger perspective. This gives, as in Sophie's example, the opportunity to remember wider resources and call them in, to understand something about the problem which could not be understood from the 'close up' perspective - Sophie noticed that the valley was a perfect place for someone who wants to be alone for a time and so it wasn't the being alone which was the problem as such, a breakthrough insight in and of itself which changed as much as did the very real and effective rescue of the abandoned baby from the caves.

A10/2 - The Zoom Pattern

Here is the Zoom pattern in a practical step by step format for your own solution exercises.

With a problem state or emotion, tune in and/or name or label it.

Ask, "Where am I?" or create the representation or interface devices to show you these problems in Sanctuary.

Zoom out until you can see the totality of the situation or an overview of the place where this is taking place.

Zoom out even more to see the wider landscapes beyond and to understand the greater ecology.

With what you have learned, decide on the resources (help, tools, magic, support staff etc) you need to do what needs to be done to resolve the problem.

Go ahead and make the intervention.

When you are satisfied, run on time to check that all will evolve to your satisfaction and that the changes you have made are steady and how you want them to be.

A11 - THE ZODIAC CAGE INDUCTION

As a trained hypnotherapist and also a dedicated story teller, I often combine the components of a Project Sanctuary realms intervention with story and hypnotic delivery.

I have included the Zodiac Cage induction from November 2000 here as an example of the 'zooming out' movement from 'A New Alone' which we looked at earlier; but also of how what is in essence a pure Project Sanctuary happening turns into a hypnotic induction, simply by describing the pictures and occurrences carefully and with a rhythm to entrance the listener or reader and help them make the new changes for their own internal worlds.

The Zodiac Cage Induction

One of the weirdest forms of post hypnotic suggestions for limiting beliefs I've recently come across (again) is the whole New Age fascination with soothsayers, crystal ball gazers and, in this particular case, astrology.

God didn't give us the neurology we are blessed with, all our life's experiences and Free Will AND the new Energy Therapies on top of that to have us sit in a corner and believe we can "never" (get rich, stop being a hypochondriac, get to learn to control our tempers, find true love with a Virgo, etc etc etc etc etc) because of what star sign we were born under.

Truly, it didn't.

I was talking to a success counselling person the other day and they are pretty switched on in most ways. So it did astonish me to hear them make the comment that "Of course they were a coward and a weasel because they have seven water signs"!!

This reminded me of a personal experience with a horoscope by a famous British astrologer which was given to me as a birthday present - full chart thing, quite expensive and quite pretty looking. I open it up and the very first line in the damn thing reads:

"You're not very smart so you've got the make the best of it."

I tell you I was pretty depressed. The fact that I am pretty smart had kind of been my saving grace up to that point, and actually, it really depressed me at the time.

I've also had many clients who in the past have made references to similar experiences - one actually was so afraid of going out anywhere because he had been told by a tarot reader that he "would spend five years in an institution" and "would die by drowning" that I had to do a kind of hypnotic de-programming exercise with the guy, back in the days when we didn't have MTs to take the sting out of such things.

It is remarkable how such things can really get right down into your unconscious mind and stick there, so I think it might be neat to visit with that area and delete any and all limiting beliefs arising from the topic.

For practise groups, here's a cool little mediation I came up with for the "seven water signs" person. You don't have to do any formal trance inductions, just speak this little hypnodream quite slowly and with some intent in your best resonant voice.

Beyond The Zodiac Cage

It is true
that at the moment
you were born,
certain planets were aligned
in the starry skies
above.

It is true
that a certain kind
of attributes
was given
to those planets
and to those
constellations.

But you know,
the people who
came up with that,
they stood on the Earth
as they looked up
and it was all they
could perceive
at this their time
from where they were.

If you were to
move beyond that now,
were to rise
straight up,
soar to the sky
and up and through
as you rise right above
this Zodiac Cage
that might indeed surround this Earth,
and you were now so high
that you could see it from the outside
and beyond,
then you would see and know
that
ALL THE STARS
AND ALL THE GALAXIES
AND ALL THE UNIVERSE
were present at your time,
your place of birth -
all of it, all that could ever be,
of course, it was all there and
all of it gave you its light
and welcome
at that moment.

And all is there
for you to draw from,
all of it, with no exception
nothing left behind
and it is all for you -
your heritage, your right
in its immensity
and its entirety.

You are free.

A12 - Sereya's Song

This story is an example of a Project Sanctuary derived fairy tale, sparked in true seed fashion by a young child's comment that they felt as though no-one could see them at all.

Project Sanctuary is about **stories** - unfoldments of events, cause and effect, as I'm sure you know. When you take the therapy out of it, when you take the meanings out of it and just observe and write down what happened, of course you will have a brand new story that has never been before.

I can't know what your views are on creativity, writing original works such as novels, poems, songs and the like; but for me, being able to write something like Sereyah's Song just like that, sitting down with the idea and having the entire thing unfold so beautifully without having to do **anything other** than try and keep up with my fingers on the keyboard is a priceless gift indeed.

I have included this story here as an example of a pure Project Sanctuary application, and I hope you will enjoy reading it as I enjoyed writing it.

Sereyah's Song

Once upon a time, in a very far away land indeed, there lived a little girl who didn't speak.

There was nothing much wrong with her, or so we would have thought. She once had a voice and although there was no-one now who would remember how it once had sounded, it might have been quite sweet.

She once had words, too, but now there was no voice, no words, just silence.

No-one noticed this, however. There were many people in the town where she lived. There were mother and father and brother and sister and uncle and aunt and cousin too, and neighbours and people in the church and in the school and in the market square but all these people were talking loudly and living loudly and thinking not at all, and least of all about some little girl that was seen yet never heard.

One day - it was late summer - she stood, as she did, in the shadow of a tree and looked and watched and listened and drank the world all up with her big eyes as she always did. On this day, there was nothing special. As always, people were going about their people business, and

273

the little birds in the tree were going about their bird business, and a dog and a cat in an alley were going about their business, and the tree beneath which the little girl stood was going about its business too of growing and of groaning a little in the wind and of shaking its dusty leaves under the sun. You could say that it was a day like any other but on this day, the little girl came to noticing that no-one knew she was there and that she might have been a rock, or a little tree herself, or perhaps a fence post or a letter box.

This made her sad and she walked away from the town that day, out into the open road and past the fields that were bare and stubbly, with the straw bunched up in rows and scare crows standing all alone, once in a while, and birds sitting on their broomstick shoulders.

She walked for a long time and slowly, it got darker and the sun went down, red and round and then the sky began to show the stars, first the big ones and then the small ones too as all the light went away, as all the colours went away and it was very black and very still.

The little girl was very tired by then and hungry too and her feet hurt from all the walking. She knew she should probably be afraid, all alone out on the dark road with no light to show her the way and the night sounds all around. But she wasn't afraid at all and as it was too dark to see the road now, she went and sat down on the verge amidst some dry grass that smelled nice and was soft under her bare legs and bare arms as she lay down and curled up and thought to go to sleep.

Now, we can't be sure what happened next. Perhaps she slept and dreamed and perhaps the light she saw approaching on the darkened road was real - who knows? But there was the light, far away and to the left, just a shine that lit up the tops of the little trees and the higher bushes that lined the road and it moved this way and that as it followed the winding country road and came closer, closer, towards where the little girl was lying in her nest of late summer grass.

She watched the light come closer and sat up, then stood up to see it more clearly, to see what might be making this golden bright shine in the night that was not at all like any lamp she'd ever seen, much brighter it was and big and round, and finally, up the road came a figure and it was the figure itself that was the light, like the shape of a person but all lit up from within, and the little girl felt a shiver of excitement because she understood that this was an angel, passing by on this road tonight.

The little girl had never seen an angel before but that didn't matter for there is something about angels that is very special and you recognise it right away, even if no-one ever told you that there even were such beings, or if you'd never met one before, or if you didn't even know the word.

When the angel saw the little girl, it stopped in the road and turned to look at her.

It was quite big and it didn't have any wings. It was hard to tell if it had eyes or a nose because it was made all out of light, a light that was alive and bright, swirling and yet it didn't hurt your eyes at all to look at it, which is very different from the light of a fire or a lamp.

The little girl who didn't speak lifted a hand to give a small wave so the angel would know that she had seen it and that she wanted to say hello. She wished she could say something to it and she was afraid that it would think her dumb or stupid and would move along, just like all the people always did, without really having seen her at all.

But the angel did see her, and it raised a shining hand and waved right back at her, and it smiled, too, not in a way like people do but it smiled and she could feel the angel's smile touch her on the shoulder and brush a strand of wayward hair from her face.

Oh, but the little girl wished that she could speak! Oh but how she wished she could tell the angel something, just a little something from all the things that were locked up right inside her mind and in her head, behind her tongue that wouldn't move and her teeth that were like prison bars and held all that and so much more behind them, but it had been such a long time that now she didn't even know how to speak anymore and no words came, no sound was made and she got so afraid that the angel would just drift away from her that she had to cry.

That is when the angel spoke to her, but it didn't speak in words or voices but in colours and they made a sense and came straight across to her so she would know its meaning and its purposes, and what the angel said without a word or voice was this:

"Why are you crying, Sereya?"

The little girl Sereya, for that was her name, didn't know what to do because she couldn't speak and didn't know how to make the colours that would tell her story in return and so she cried more, she cried harder, and her hands made strange and pleading gestures to the angel who stood and watched her for a time and then it came forward and picked up the little girl Sereya in its arms of light and lifted her easily off the ground, held her close and without a further word or sound or colour, began to move on, first along the road and then Sereya became aware that they were no longer on the road exactly but gliding above it, and then she could see from the light as it passed below along the road that they were flying, higher and higher still until the land of night lay dark below and there were just the clouds, and high above, the stars bright and white, so many there were, so beautiful they were, and the angel was warm and the little girl Sereya felt entirely safe and entirely enchanted, held close and tight and soft.

For a long time they flew and Sereya might have slept, snuggled close to the warm angel and the music of the stars a rushing that was soothing all around, but then there came a time when they moved in closer to a sense of blue and green, and not long after that, the angel came to set them down on a green hillside somewhere, beneath a blue, blue sky, by the side of a small brook that leaped and bubbled clear sweet water.

Sereya was very thirsty and she drank from the brook, washed her hands and face and all the while, the angel was watching her and once again, she wished so hard that she could speak, that she could ask about this land, where it was, why they were here, ask the angel's name, tell it how wonderful it had been to fly amongst the stars, to thank it for taking notice and taking time - oh! So many things! But still, she couldn't speak and all those things inside of her that wanted to come out, they made a heavy pressure on her heart and although this time Sereya didn't cry, she sat down on the wonderful green grass and wished she was another, any other, someone who could laugh and dance with the angel, someone who could be worthy of its time, someone who would be interesting, and loved, instead of being good for nothing and with a stone for a heart and the silence.

So she sat and waited for the angel to turn away and fly away but the angel did not turn away, nor did it fly away. Instead, it came and sat down next to the little girl so both of them were sitting in the grass, looking at the little brook as it leaped with joy and bubbled clear bright water.

They sat for a long time, and at first, the little girl was very uncomfortable and got more and more unhappy, thinking that the angel must surely have much better things to do than to be here, and wondering what it might want from her, and how she was doing wrong by not doing anything, and how she didn't know what she could do to please the angel, and all the while hoping, praying, that the angel would stay and not leave her all alone her by this brook, for the truth was that she liked the angel more than anyone she'd ever met and she wanted it to stay very much indeed.

More time passed and Sereya got so weary with all the worrying that she couldn't worry properly anymore. She found it hard to keep her thoughts as they used to be, here in this beautiful place, where the brook made its little water sounds and sparkled diamond bright in the sunlight, beneath the sky so blue and on the grass so green, and in the grass were little flowers, half hidden, half peeking out with their flower faces, looking at the little girl and the angel who were sitting side by side and watching the brook flow by.

More time passed and the angel hadn't gone away. Sereya glanced at it once in a while but the angel sat beautiful, calm and flowing light right by her side and said nothing in word nor colour, and it didn't even seem as though the angel was waiting for anything, it was just there and seemed to be happy enough to just be there and in no hurry to be going somewhere else.

More time passed. Sereya yawned and stretched out her legs, wriggled her toes and came to think she would like to put her feet into the sparkling brook. She looked to the angel but it was just sitting there, so she thought perhaps it wouldn't mind if she did and so and very slowly and cautiously, she crept closer to the brook, close enough and dipped her toes into the cool and bouncing water. Oooh! It was cold but really nice and Sereya put her feet right into the brook, until they touched the round cool stones at the bottom and it felt so wonderful that she wanted to laugh and splash, but she wasn't sure if that was alright and she looked to the angel, for she was afraid that it would leave if she did the wrong thing, but the angel was just sitting and looking at her and the brook and it said nothing and did nothing, so she gave a careful little splash with the tip of her toes at first. The angel didn't seem to mind, and Sereya thought that perhaps it was alright then and she splashed very carefully and slowly at first, but it was too much fun and she stood up in the brook, held her skirt up high so it wouldn't get wet and splashed for real, being real careful not to splash any water into the angel's direction because she didn't want it to be angry or upset with her.

But the walking on the smooth stones and the splashing in the brook was too much fun and Sereya forgot for a moment and she jumped up and really - SPLASH! - made a big splash and water went everywhere, including on the angel. She stopped immediately and put her hand to her mouth but the angel just reached up and caught the water droplets in the air with its shiny hands, threw them up even higher and let them rain upon itself like diamonds falling that melted into its warm skin of light and it was laughing!

Sereya watched the angel and very cautiously, very carefully, put her hand in the brook and splashed a little more water across to the angel. The angel bent forward to catch the splashes as before and it was happy and so Sereya was happy too and splashed the angel more, and then the angel got up and put its feet of light into the brook and all the brook became both water and light and they splashed each other, laughing out loud in sound and in colour, and it was wonderful and so much fun, much more fun than Sereya could ever remember having had before.

Exhausted from the splashing and the laughing, Sereya went to the bank of the brook and collapsed into the grass and it was then she noticed that she, too, was now glowing with light across her skin, everywhere where the light water had touched her and that was everywhere, because she and the angel had been splashing real hard and slipped and fallen in the water too between times.

The angel still stood in the brook that was living with its light and it looked to Sereya and then it came across and carefully touched a light finger to her arm and as it did, something happened and she knew the angel's name, and that its name was like the Sun but smaller and more joyous too, and it wasn't a word at all but something else entirely and she found that she could think the angel's name and when she did, it made a sound that was the angel's name and it was here, and real, and you could not just hear it but really feel it and you knew completely that it was that one angel's name out of all the many angels, all across the universe.

And then the angel said Sereya's name, and her name too wasn't a word at all, but it was like a small star of many colours, bright and beautiful it was and it too was what you could feel and know that it was her, just her alone, the name by which she was known entirely and it was the only name like that amongst all the many, many children there had ever been across the time and space of all the universe.

So they said their names to each other many times, and other things besides, and at first Sereya would listen to learn how to say things in this way but as the angel told her many things and showed her many things in its language of light and colour, sound and feelings, Sereya recognised that she already knew this language well, that she spoke it in her dreams and that it was the way that people's words were dead and dull compared to this that had made her give up on human speaking in the first place.

And when she recognised this, and remembered the angel language not just in her mind but all of her, the angel told her that the time had come, and that she was ready once again to come to that very special place of old where truth is told and listened to and where a little girl can tell her story in the language of light.

So they bade goodbye to the brook and the brook sang its delight at having been right there for both of them that day as they rose and travelled, purposefully and with knowing, hand in hand, across the time and space it takes to go to where there is a place of old, a very special place, high on a rounded hill beneath the stars so bright and watchful there, the sky a colour you have never seen and all the suns of all the time are here, each one a star.

On this hill there is a temple, round it is and bordered by white columns that indeed are shafts of light that talk to the myriad suns above each one, and it was here that the angel and Sereya came and went right to the center of the temple, and this is where the angel sat down at Sereya's feet and where she stood and looked around and then, she told her story in the language of light, and it was a story such as had never been told before in all the times spent, all the days of all the worlds of all the universe, because it was her story and it was unique, as unique as her name in the language of light, which was just like a star of many colours, bright and beautiful.

And the angel listened to her story, and so did the stars above, and the ground below in silence and in reverence and Sereya sang in many colours, many lights, her one voice soaring clearly through the heavens and all the worlds, and it found its place, its rightful place that had lain empty and waiting for her true voice, for her true song, for her true story.

When she was done and all the universe stood first in silent devotion, then vibrated back in reverence and gratitude for all she'd done and when she knew that her voice and being had become recorded in the fabric of time and space exactly as it should, Sereya took a deep breath and knew that she was free and all was right and when the angel took her back to her life in the little town, there was no sadness, no regret and she could speak the words of human language once more, could speak them freely and with ease because she no longer had to try to make it be that language of light she needed to have sung the song of Sereya.

And on a still night, or in a still place, if you just care to listen, you can hear her song, and you can hear the angel's song and all the other songs, each one a miracle and each one so beautiful, it fills your heart with gladness and if you listen even closer still, and if you pay attention, you can tell that one, that very special song of light that is your own.

A13 - THE MULTI-TASKING PERSONALITY PATTERN

(Or, how to be in many places at the same time and do many things all at once.)

I have a system in my mind that runs various different case scenarios when faced with a problem. For the past few years, mostly since Project Sanctuary, there is the Sidereus response generator to add input on what one might do in order to overcome something, change something, sort something out.

Here is the story.

I am in the middle of writing my first ever full length novel and totally obsessed.

As a result, I'm writing all day and all night long and NOT doing a whole load of other things that I should be doing, one of these being washing up the dishes.

After three days or so, we have no more plates in the cupboard and dishes absolutely must be washed now or we have to eat the fried eggs off the counter top, which is the point at which I draw the line.

Being still in 'that state of mind' I noted with interest the various resistances I had to washing up.

Believe it or not, I had treated washing up traumas of a different kind some years previously with EFT quite successfully and the resistance was fairly mild in comparison to how it used to be; on this particular evening, there was quite a lot of resistance to tackling the task.

I asked myself what the main resistance was and what came up strongly was that my time would be much more happily and profitably spent continuing the novel - it was at a very interesting stage and there were 'parts of me' that couldn't wait to get back to it and considered it far more important than the plates and forks.

I then went on to consider what action I might take.

I could just simply override myself and make myself wash up. That would be easy because there was a lot of pressure from the mess in the kitchen and the knowledge that visitors were due.

I could tap myself for the resistance and make it easier for me that way.

I could take my mind off it altogether by putting on an interesting lecture on tape which would lead me to be in complete trance and unaware of what I was doing until it was all done.

And then the Project Sanctuary generator kicked in and suggested to send off the part that wanted to write the novel and just have them do that - just get on with it, have it there and when I get to sit back down in front of the keyboard, I'd just have it dictated to me and I would then physically write down what the part had come up with whilst I was washing up.

This brought me up short because it was so not with the whole wholeness programme that it actually shocked me to consider that idea. It was also an interesting and instantaneous insight into the wholeness programme itself, how exclusive and pervasive a map of its merits and necessities existed in my mind and the fields in general. Everywhere you go, everyone will tell you that 'wholeness' is the name of the game, re-integration what you should do, and parts 'conflicts' are a very bad thing.

However, I was very intrigued by the idea of sending off a part and decided I should try it.

Should it turn out to be a total catastrophe and I end up with writer's block and no more creativity after this intervention, we can reverse time and retrieve the part if necessary.

"Ok," I said to myself, "Ok, go then. Go write. I'll be with you later."

It was a very strange sliding energetic release sensation, reminiscent of what sometimes happens in Reiki or MET interventions, complete with yawning and tearing of the eye.

I remember after that, standing in the kitchen, feeling quite confused and then seeing the dishes again with a whole new sense of **reality** about them and starting the job in silence.

As I do, I discussed this pattern with various colleagues and had them try it out. Here are a few of the interventions, mostly used with our classical Project Sanctuary metaphorical interface device:

 A lady therapist trying to do her book keeping and finding resistance from a part of herself that manifested as a young student who wanted to party rather than study and do research. As soon as she gave permission, the younger self manifestation rushed away so quickly it "made her head spin" and the book keeping proceeded smoothly.

 One gentleman had a conflict over creativity. He represented the part that didn't want anything to do with creativity as a man in a white shirt and tie, ca. 1950, in black and white and said that when he sent the part off to go where it was happiest, it went to some kind of 'It's A Wonderful Life' scenario that would be threatened with dissidence if someone started to be colourful and creative and **other**, yet had all kinds of other merits such as acceptance in the community, family, church and neighbourliness instead.

Another gentleman sent off the part of himself that was an idiot to a country where the lamp posts were made of rubber, as were the roads and many other idiots happily stumbling about all day in perfect harmony and mutual admiration and support. We laughed so much it hurt after that one, but it's true, I haven't heard him call himself an idiot since that day and can't say I've heard any further tales of idiocy by or about him - and that was approximately a year ago now.

One lady also applied it to housework and had a young beautiful teenage part of herself leave and go to a beach complete with palm tree and handsome lover on a rug beneath it, holding two glasses of champagne and said she felt incredibly relieved and happy for that part of herself who could never be at home with rubber gloves.

My observations on this way of dealing with so called parts conflicts were that there seemed to be occasions where a 'part' would just rush off to God knows where the very instant it had received permission.

On other occasions, the 'part' seemed to be unknowing as to where to go and it was necessary to find it somewhere where it would **fit in** and be **perfectly happy** - the 'It's A Wonderful Life' world, the country of the rubber lamp posts, the holiday beach.

The next part of the experiment was to observe the changes in behaviour or thought this intervention would bring about.

What makes me think that something very real takes place when you do this is the exclamations of the people when the parts leave. They go, "Whoa!", "Wow!", "Bloody Hell!" or suchlike verbal expression of an internal sensation that you could call an energy shift, if you will.

This is followed by a momentary confusion and often further insights on the topic. Also, this is quite an emotional intervention. Whether people laugh or cry, there is a response that is very similar to MET treatments - including my tearing of the eyes and yawning which I take to be indicative of an energy shift strong enough to affect the physiology directly.

Because I had come up with the pattern as a response to procrastination, and told my fellow experimenters much the same as I have told you here, naturally they remembered to try this pattern when they were having procrastination problems of their own.

The result seemed to be that the task became simpler, easier, or they simply forgot what the procrastination was about and got on with it.

Some people had more than one part strongly objecting to the task in hand and with some, conversations and trial and error discussions as to just where these parts would go needed to take place - five, ten minutes at the maximum.

So, the MTP pattern was effective for people familiar with mental interfacing work in the context of procrastination or internal resistance to undertaking a specific task.

The other safety question, as to what happened to these parts and if their 'going' constituted some kind of damaging loss, was easily settled.

Only an hour after I had sent my novel writer off to prepare the next chapter in my absence, I sat back down at my desk and there was not a moment's resistance or hesitation as I returned to the document and the words and scenarios simply came alive again in my mind.

I also had feedback from one of my colleagues who actively called on his 'Wonderful Life' character for support and sent his artist off to do some major sculpting during an interview with a bank manager, which proceeded smoothly and on a whole new level of rapport and mutual friendliness from thereon in.

It seemed that rather than try and integrate the two, having them **both** as a kind of fancy dress costume for special occasions was a very effective way to go about things. It also, interestingly, underlined and demonstrated the theory that what we are is not any one of our constructed sets of attributes, talents, abilities. Further, by moving around these attribute collections or personae at will, we found that we actually had a great many more personae at our disposal who could all **act quite congruently** when the other personae who were uncomfortable or objecting to the task in hand were no longer there to have conflicts with them.

A13/1 - The Guardian Angel

Sending off parts that are hindering congruency is one thing and very useful.

There are many more possibilities to this pattern.

If you remember, I did not just send my writer part away to lie on a beach, but indeed, to keep on writing. The 'Wonderful Life' gentleman send his artist part to do a sculpture. These things were going whilst I washed up and he talked with the bank manager.

That is some time saver!

If you use the modular personae system, you can literally be in many places at the same time and do many things at the same time.

It is even my supposition that there may be a strand of 'that is **exactly** the purpose of parts & personae formation' on some level.

Here is an interesting, classically multidimensional example of this.

As me and my colleagues were experimenting with the MTP pattern, one of them had a child who was sick in bed with flu. The colleague was trying to do some essential work with the child resting upstairs but felt there was "a part of her that wanted to hold vigil by his bedside, fluff the pillows constantly and administer all sorts of things", although she was consciously aware that this was not only entirely unnecessary, but would have been quite counterproductive in driving the teenage boy to distraction - which is never beneficial to anyone's immune system.

She sent her part off to do all the healing it felt were necessary, all the fluffing of pillows and as soon as she did, blew out a deep breath and said, "That is so much better. What a relief."

We then went on to consider the possibility as to a healing servitor part that would indeed, be **in actuality** upstairs with the boy, making interventions at its own level and safeguarding him in a very special way.

A custom made Guardian Angel, if you will.

What a nice idea that is. Do you have any friends, children, relatives or any one or any thing at all that might benefit from a Guardian Angel? Might it help you with a helpless sense of responsibility that cannot be fulfilled in the Hard?

A13/2 - Projects

On the time saving front, having a personae/part/number of personae/parts working together to accomplish something in absentia, as it were, whilst 'you' go on with your daily business, is also a fascinating thing.

Here are just some ideas as to what you can do with this.

> Set tasks such as problem solving, brain storming, art creation and so forth on any topic and either ask to be informed when a result has been reached so you can take this further, or just to make it physically manifest in due course and automatically..

> Send servitor personae to perform symbolic acts on your behalf - Red Cross missions, fact finding, communicating with single people or whole groups of them, negotiating for your projects, outcomes and desires.

> You can set personae to do work in and with your own neurology - rescue and retrieval, repair, maintenance.

On major projects, this following is a pattern that is very unusual but has turned out to be quite extraordinary in its repercussions and results.

A13/3 - The Class Of Self

Assemble all the personae that have a say or effect on the forthcoming project into a class.

Now, rather than preaching at them, ask them firstly what kind of environment they would prefer to be in, and secondly, what activity they need undertake altogether in order to help with the project in hand.

Prepare for a surprise, for when this pattern was tested, one gentleman's class of self rushed off to the nearest international airport for travel and excitement; another's class decided they wanted to play football. One lady's class wanted to sing together and another lady's class wanted to sleep in a forest grove and share their dreams.

I consider the Class of Self to be one of the ways in which different personae can find common ground and begin to have a new relationship with each other in a suitably ecological and of course **entirely personalised** way. This reduces stress and conflict and cannot help being a nice thing.

A13/4 - The MTP Pattern - How To

It helps when there is a reason to do this, so consider a conflict of interest that exists in your totality at this point.

Decide what it is that you want, because these conflicts are not theoretical, they arise when different actions and courses of action need to take place but the question is which one and perhaps also, which ones in which order and sequence.

Find the major opposition to the proposed plan of action.

Ask what they would like to be or do instead, then simply give them permission to be and do exactly that, in a place where being and doing exactly that is perfect in all ways.

If they absolutely refuse to go, it may be an indication of a possible danger with your proposed course of action and it might be wise to look into it more before setting out on this; in this case, the MTP pattern is a useful safety device.

If they go, let them go and observe your responses and how this has affected your outcomes, plans and actions.

A14 - CORPORATE ENERGY CLEARING - WHITE FISH WITH WINGS

I had the unusual experience some time ago of being asked to assist in the clearing of the energy field of a global company which was in serious trouble following a failed take-over that had resulted in a number of the main managers leaving and the remaining ones feeling disillusioned and disenheartened. Nothing much was being done, there was no enthusiasm in the corporation at any level.

I called on the help of a fellow energy magician, and together, we set to work.

We tuned into the company's energy field and clearly perceived that the company **as an entity** was injured and that its unique field was disturbed, distorted, unclear and dissipating.

We asked for a Sanctuary representation of the company to help us consciously know what was happening and what we found was a white neo-Grecian building representing the company in a very pleasant green garden scape but it was deserted because it had the energetic equivalent of a stink bomb set off in it at the time of the take over in-fighting.

So now there were people wandering about aimlessly in the grounds, talking amongst themselves here and there but not getting anywhere because inside the building were left abandoned a great many resources such as:

Their original intense enthusiasm about building this global organisation;

A true feeling of connectedness and brotherhood amongst the managers and staff;

Excitement and energy;

Co-operation and harmonious sharing of resources;

The true desire to make a change in the world for the better which was the vision of the company.

There were many more such resources in the building which now stood abandoned and dusty.

My partner and I firstly established a boundary about the whole garden made of an energy field (looks vaguely like a soap bubble, shimmering soft rainbow) which would make it impossible for further negative energy or negative people to enter but would allow energising passage to everyone else - present and future staff, management and customers who are **true of heart** and in alignment with the company's vision, which was so important to the entire operation. This boundary of coloured lights can be seen from far away by night and it would further serve as a beacon to draw the right people to the company as well as keeping the wrong ones away.

Then we called for cleaning, cleansing and restoration of the building.

Above the building, the sky opened and a spiral of what looked like opalescent white fish with wings came streaming down and into the building which, after a short time, began to glow and light poured from the opening windows on all levels.

We were both sighing with pleasure and felt that we had done what needed to be done. At that time the white beings were still involved in clearing the building, a process which is now entirely completed.

The white building is sitting on the green gentle hill, shimmering gently as the dusk falls.

It is now ready to be re-occupied. The people who had wandered about lost in the gardens can now return and would have full access to all the resources that lie within.

From here, messengers and visitors may come and then leave, go beyond the rainbow curtain and bring back with them many more to help with the company's mission, contacts, customers and staff alike. The lost managers were having a good time familiarising themselves with the building, finding their new offices and support staff and were taking a tour of the many magical features designed to make our work easy, enjoyable and extremely effective.

When we were done, I laughed and said, "Will they put this into the minutes?" I am not sure if they did or not, but the company is doing very well indeed and the management talks in terms of their firm having received an entirely new lease of life.

I have included this example to remind you of the possibility of clearing, restoring and repairing energy fields of all kinds using the Sanctuary interfaces; I called the company an 'entity' which had an existence beyond the mortars and bricks, computers and people of its physical dimensions. There are many entities out there with energy fields in need of repair - countries, organisations, groups of people of all kinds and many, many more besides.

A15 - DREAM LOVERS

(Or, Why Autogenic Relationships Give You Wings!)

We have learned by now that we have a range of needs that cannot actually be fulfilled in the Hard, but are and always were **energetic** in origin and need to be addressed energetically. This is an essay on unfulfilled human relationship needs and how to go about making use of the human ability to create neurosomatic responses - in other words, how to make all parts of you be happier and give you what you really need, through the medium of the Dream Lover.

If it is the first or the last thing people do when they start to play the Sanctuary Game in earnest, sooner or later we will get some form of love and or sex turn up.

After all, what are sexual fantasies? Romantic daydreams?

What happens when you do those, and how are they different from actually interacting in a Sanctuary habitat with those energies we call in and which present themselves in metaphorical form?

I have profoundly misunderstood how sex et al works at the Sanctuary realm levels for - well for as many years as I have been engaging in various fantasies, ideas, role plays, game plays and true-blue triple-x - rated activities 'in my head'.

I have profoundly misunderstood it as being second best and indeed, some form of admission of failure to be doing this in the first place.

This is based on deep societal conditioning that, quite regardless of whether or not you were a child of the 60's or you grew up in the strictest of Mormon communities, is in full on effect and action across the globe and rests on a number of taboos, principles and a great many misconceptions and scare stories about the nature and expression of sexuality and romantic love.

When we enter the Sanctuary spaces, we take this conditioning with us, of course, and here it interferes with what we manifest and what games we play in the most profound way, of course.

Even when the 'counteractive' Sanctuary features kick in and present us with situations, set ups and characters that we didn't call upon and did not expect, our reactions to these developments hog tie and warp, displace and distort any further ongoings.

Now, let's back up here and consider the phenomenon of stigmata.

This is when a very religious (Christian) person manifests real wounds in the palms of their hands and in their feet, corresponding to the nails used to affix Mr. Jesus of Nazareth to the cross.

This particular physical manifestation is very well known and very well documented across the ages, including with photographs and video tape in these latter days, and ranges from what look like scars to full on open wounds that bleed profusely and cannot heal, no matter how many antibiotics or bandages are employed.

It is an example of a neurosomatic manifestation. I prefer the term neurosomatic to psychosomatic which you might be more familiar with as it does not carry with it the 'stigma' of someone's just being insane or making it all up; a neurosomatic manifestation is simply a physiological occurrence **in the absence of a material influence which could have caused it**.

At my very first hypnotherapy training, I saw a woman's hand turn red and the skin begin to bubble as she thought of being burned.

It shocked me profoundly and I have never forgotten this.

Our minds and bodies can and do instantly manifest changes in the physiology in the absence of any kind of 'real' fire, real nails or real anything being there to cause it - that is the core of neurosomatics and a fascinating field it is, in every way.

Now, let us switch back to Project Sanctuary.

As you will know, the more you engage with the Sanctuary processes and the more real they become, the more effects they have on you and your entire neurology, and this includes the more effective they become on your body as the neurosomatic manifestations kick in.

You may be familiar with autogenic training techniques, also sometimes used for weightloss and other types of performances, whereby the person who seeks to perfect a skill or improve their fitness levels vividly imagines exercising, or scoring the perfect goal, or diving the perfect dive.

There is a world of research into the phenomenon of how autogenic training techniques physically and actually improve a person's performance in the Hard, right down to such a person's having physically acquired extra muscle tissue, lost weight and indeed, manifested a variety of physiological, measurable changes in their body composition and chemistry.

The core principle, just to state it clearly here, is that when events are created in the neurology, the body responds to this as though they were happening in actuality - and the more intense, or real, if you will, the neurological event can be made to be, the more direct the effects become on the physical body.

So let us stop for a moment and consider the uses of this simple principle in terms of practicalities.

When I was a beginner at hypnosis, I caused a friend of mine to get sick for a fortnight because I told him at the beginning of the session that he was asleep on a night beach but failed to instruct his neurology to keep him warm and comfortable.The induction was an hour but in the mind space, over 8 hours had passed on a freezing cold beach and this person was stone cold, shaking with cold, near hypothermia when I finally got him out.

Blankets and rubbing and hot cups of coffee did little to make matters any better, and he went home and duly got a serious cold two days later.

This person, in the hands of a total beginner at hypnosis, got hypothermia in a warm room.

The opposites of this are those Tibetan monks, who, as a part of their initiation rites, get to sit on a glacier with freezing soaked bed sheets wrapped around them, to dry them with their body heat, and then they can go home.

Basically and at the most basic level, a control over one's neurology in that way overrides external occurrences entirely - being hot or cold is a very, very simple example of a realm of possibilities that reside in the simple fact that neurosomatics create a physical reality for the body in which we live.

Simply put, you can exercise better and harder and faster than any athlete could for real in the Sanctuary realms.

And, to bring us back to the original topic of this story, you can have sex in Sanctuary and experience all the releasing, relaxing, healthful effects of this natural occupation for which our bodies are set up in exactly the same way.

A15/1 - How To Make Neurosomatics Work For You

Now, the monks and the Eastern athletes spend a lifetime practising their version of autogenics and they get reasonable results.

The rest of us can manifest neurosomatics as a byline to misery and sometimes, to joy and happiness as well but the whole thing is completely out of control and left to chance and accident.

Clearly and irrefutably, there is the central link of making so real it becomes reality for the entirety of the neurology.

That is what creates the measurable results, that and that alone.

When someone first starts playing in the Project Sanctuary spaces, dabbling with bits here and there, there is very little difference between that and just a bit of off handed day dreaming.

However.

When one does it more, pays more attention, takes the processes and the habitats and the developments just a little bit seriously, Project Sanctuary makes a quantum shift in **how real an experience it becomes**.

People who have been doing it for a while know this very well.

Jenny, for example, re-created her father's funeral in Sanctuary. As an experienced PS player, it became very real indeed and in fact, it is difficult for her now to get a sense of the original, real funeral in the Hard as being any realler in any way than the actual Sanctuary event.

It is at this reality point that the true benefits of Sanctuary become revealed.

It is here that we are now talking that all important bridge into neurosomatics, a place where not just the energy states are deeply affected by what you do in Sanctuary, but the physicality follows suit immediately - with pheromones, with hormones, with heart rate, with alleviation of symptoms, with practically measurable changes.

So the question must be, how can we make Sanctuary manifestations so real that they have an immediate knock on effect on the energy system and the physicality, the neurology and indeed, what I call the totality - all the many bits on all the many layers and levels that make up a human being?

What has to happen for this to be so, to become so, and in doing so, actually get to be **in charge of what happens to our totality** and

entirely regardless of the actual presentations of the Hard in which we find ourselves at any given point?

What has to happen is that one does it **wholeheartedly** - engages in the process totally, without reservations, without holding back, without arguing with it, without putting shields around certain parts of the self which sit there and go, "Oh its just a fantasy, nothing real here ..."

That is what blocks true neurosomatic manifestations from taking place and Sanctuary becoming as incredibly effective as it actually can be in alleviating all sorts of needs, wants, survival necessities for an individual in their totality.

And here's the revelation about "Sex and love in the Sanctuary".

I have never been able to do any Sanctuary relationship of that nature wholeheartedly. I have always had strong reservations about all of them and encased and enclosed them, stepped them off and physically prevented from ever becoming too real, too all encompassing.

Here are my major reasons for doing so in hindsight.

The first one and for me, the most important one, was the societal entrainment that there is something seriously wrong with you when you have invisible friends.

Consider, for a moment, a typical American mom's and dad's response to the discovery that their five year old son has an 'invisible friend'.

With or without the help of a handy psychiatrist or psychologist, the first response is a heartfelt "Oh no!!!" - clearly, there's something seriously wrong with this kid, they probably have misformed societal peer bonding structures because they should be having **real** relationships with **real** kids instead.

The next step will be to wean that kid off their invisible friends as quickly as possible. Now the kid will probably resist this, and if the parents/psychologists involved are a bit kindly, they will plot to do this "gently and over time" - perhaps even "playing along a little" to keep rapport with the kid, but absolutely dead set on the long term iron goal of mental and societal health and acceptance, namely the place where there are no more invisible friends AT ALL but only lots and lots of real ones to make sure the kid is popular and happy.

That's the baseline blocker to all Sanctuary type relationships and is played out in every home around the Western world over weaning the kids off having relationships with teddy bears, their skate boards or their ponies and into "real relationships" as quickly as possible.

But now, puberty looms and we get into the territory of sexual fantasies, where exactly the same contortion that applies to teddy bears and invisible friends exists just the same.

Sexual or relationship "fantasies" are the societally held hallmarks of those who are unsuccessful at real relationships - those failures, "wankers" who no-one wants, who are deficient, unattractive, undesirable.

Indeed, the very act of engaging in such "fantasies", most guiltily and never talked about, hidden behind vaguely acceptable activities such as hero worship or being a member of a fan club (but even that is already very dodgy behaviour and not one expected from either homecoming king or queen!), is by now a clear sign to the person themself who is engaging in these activities that they are indeed, "losers in the Hard".

So, sexual and relationship 'fantasies' have big time stigmata attached to them, even and especially for the person who engages in them.

In the 19th century societies, it was held to be terribly bad to masturbate and so people didn't for real and true fear that they would go insane and to hell.

They didn't and as a result, would 'spasm' - uncontrollable outbursts of sexual feelings, orgasms or activities, often during sleep for the lucky ones but sometimes in the street or in society which would lead to spending the rest of their lives in an institution. Others would sublimate instead into severe neuroses and the most severe neurosomatic illnesses and diseases possible, and some would turn rapists, sadists or simply go insane.

Nowadays, we don't spasm so badly anymore, and yet at more subtle levels, these same problems are still in action. This is not just so for sexually related manifestations but for a great many others such as personal power and creativity; but the topic of this article is sexuality and the merits of being able to have perfectly healing autogenic sexual and love relationships in Sanctuary; to avoid 'real time' spasming, insanity or sublimation into illness, and to be able to run an overall totality where all needs and survival needs at the energetic level are entirely fulfilled.

A15/2 - Autogenic Relationships - The Rules

Now what would happen if one were to make a conscious effort to understand the following real and logical rules relating to this system?

These are the rules.

1. There exist sexual and sexual relationship needs in every single human, no matter how gloriously satisfying a 'Hard' relationship they are in, which cannot be fulfilled 'the Hard way' because of the limitations of the societies and worlds we live in.

2. Not fulfilling these needs - these SYSTEMIC needs - leads to problems including inappropriate expression of energies that have nowhere to go as well as malnutrition situations on the other hand.

3. These needs can be completely fulfilled in Sanctuary, balancing the energy system perfectly and having direct repercussions on the physicality through the neurosomatic systems of the totality.

4. These needs and imbalances can only be corrected through the neurosomatic system and via Sanctuary experiences **if the go-ahead is given by the conscious mind to allow them to become entirely real**.

A15/3 - Overcoming Objections To Having Reality Fantasies

There are some core objections that get in the way of allowing oneself to have one's neurosomatic relationships be as profoundly real in every sense as the athlete's autogenic perfect goals he practices on a regular basis.

The first one is the 'invisible friend' objection - namely that fantasies are second best to the 'real' relationship.

The fact is that to try and milk any one 'real' relationship for the wants and needs that specifically exist in any given single human being, shifting and changing as they do from moment to moment, from day to day, from year to year is to ask the impossible of any one single human being.

It is completely impossible in the Hard to fulfill every want and need with, through and by a human being - it is a structural impossibility.

The promise of this, or the expectation of finding one single other human being that can indeed fulfill all these multi-level shifting needs for the rest of your life, is one of the very core reasons for millennia of suffering, misery and disappointment, of wasted lives waiting for "the one" who will make it all alright and most of all, for judging and condemning real people who have failed to make the impossible happen.

Every human being, from a Taoist monk to Don Juan, from a mother-of-five to granddad, happily married for 64 years, from tough gang banger to a Roman Catholic nun has structural and energetic needs that can ONLY be fulfilled in ways that are **other** than human generated.

That's a simple fact and if we as a species would get our heads around this, a whole heap of suffering and misery would simply implode and cease to exist from this moment on.

"Invisible Friends" and "Fantasy Lovers" are not second best to real people at all - they are **other** altogether and serve completely different purposes in all ways; indeed they are by definition what makes a person happy and balanced enough to even be able to relate to people at all in the first place in many cases.

The next objection is that of "getting lost in fantasy" - namely that the fantasy will replace real people and real relationships and indeed, make the one who is engaging in these autogenic relationships incapable of having Hard relationships with anyone.

This indeed happens when someone makes a conscious decision to give up on Hard relationships, or Hard people as a whole, and withdraws entirely into neurosomatic or autogenic relationships instead.

However, to take these occurrences as a reason to declare autogenic relationships to be a bad thing and have them be forbidden would be to declare cooking utensils illegal because some highly disturbed and confused individuals use them for self mutilation.

You can kill yourself with Vitamin C or carrots if you overdose - but that is no reason to ban Vitamin C or carrots, for that matter.

As autogenic relationships are so deeply misunderstood and so strongly discriminated against by societal entrainment, this very entrainment forces people who have discovered the very real benefits of such relationships, and with no hope or previous experience or indeed, help and logical advice on how to actually use autogenic relationships to have a better life all around, in the Hard AND all the other levels, to make that choice of "either-or" in the first place.

Ordinary people - like we are - who are intelligent, rational and deeply committed to personal development and being the best we can be in this particular incarnation have no problems at all in understanding the differences between Hard and autogenic relationships and allowing both to be the rightful sources of inspiration, lift, energy and experience in their rightful realms.

We can both deeply love our spouses and our children in every way and on every level AND have an intensive and intensely nourishing autogenic relationship with a Sanctuary lover or very many of them at the same time - indeed, it is my proposition that if we do, and do this deliberately and entirely consciously, we take a huge, huge burden off our existing relationships with the 'real people' in our lives and find that it becomes very much easier to appreciate them, to love them and to find contact with them entirely satisfying and perfect too - because simply, we no longer have the false expectations and needs we thought we could fulfil through and by them when that was never a possibility in the first place.

A15/4 - What Autogenic Relationships Can Do For You ...

First of all, autogenic relationships, if conducted with absolute forethought and being very clear about the fact that you are doing more than making use of your neurology to balance yourself perfectly, put yourself into a better condition and making yourself far, far more effective in daily life, are deeply charging and energising.

If you noticed, there were a lot of disclaimers in that sentence above - "If conducted with forethought ..."

There is every world of difference in our neurology, and in the resulting manifestations in thought, behaviour and physiology, between creeping off to the bathroom, redfaced and ashamed, with a sex magazine under your arm for a bit of evil, sad, forbidden, guilty, shameful nastiness because you got the urge, and basically rubbing your hands with glee, looking forward to having a very cool and balancing necessary experience as you dance off with your sex magazine for a bit of much needed fun, rest and recharge.

This, in a nutshell, is the difference that needs to be achieved with autogenic love and sexual relationships in Sanctuary. For those amongst you who are baulking at the term 'relationship', be restful in knowing that this relationship engagement with an autogenic lover may as be as brief as a nude model of your choice bending over a log before you get stuck in and vanishing immediately afterwards in a most satisfactory implosion.

If you can say "Yes!!" to the entire autogenic experience, leave all thoughts of doubt and shame at the door completly and engage in these activities, these feelings, these contacts with your autogenic sex partners, lovers, romantic heroes, prostitutes or whatever, willfully and totally positively in all ways, it WILL be a totally different experience and the results on the Hard will be totally different in all ways as well.

We are not just talking about results on your own mind and body here in the way of more energy, more joy about being alive, more grinning to yourself and feeling better all over.

Consider this, for example. Have you ever known a person who was desperate for a 'Hard' relationship but couldn't even get the neighbourhood dog to take a sniff?

Then, miraculously, they did get into a relationship and all of a sudden, all sorts of people come out of the woodwork and started making offers - including strangers in the street!

What do you think has caused this to happen?

Of course, they're happy. They're more relaxed, they are broadcasting desirability and health - it makes them a hundred times more attractive.

Can you create this effect with the help of autogenic lovers?

Of course you can!

If your autogenic experiences are real enough, your pheromones will broadcast your satisfaction at the most basic of Hard, measurable levels for all to smell - for half a mile, if not more, even with our rather limited and most unconsciously routed sensors for smell.

But there is a lot - a whole lot! - more to achieving 'in love' states with autogenic lovers.

We have, of course, talked about the balancing effects on your energy system, making it shine more brightly, and thus in and of itself becoming far more attractive to all and sundry.

Have you heard this one? Someone has a neat sexual experience at the weekend. Glowingly happy, they return to work the next day - and all of a sudden, their sales records goes through the roof.

I know of a woman who, after not being able to get a job for six months, aced three job interviews in a single day after a weekend with an Internet Romeo.

It's amazing what a little re-balancing of the energy system can do for you!

I bet you have in your memory banks examples of this - of how easy life was when you were in the first flush of romance, after a great outing to a dance club where you got flirted with or chatted up, of a time in your life where your relationships were great and everything just flowed happily.

Is that sounding like something that might motivate you to have a real go at making a bright new start with your autogenic relationships?

To let go of all and every reason why they can't be completely real, completely energising, completely relaxing and take that tension, stress and worry from your weary shoulders?

Why they can't be exactly what you have been waiting for, possibly for your entire life?

Completely real in all ways - yes, you were with three beautiful women and they absolutely DID admire you and wanted to please you totally, were totally delighted by what you had to give them in return and took it gladly?

Can you really allow yourself to have it be so, to understand that it is not or never second best to anything you might get up to in the Hard, but indeed, a foundation and springboard for all your activities in the Hard, from the energy level up?

If you can, I think I can promise in return that your days will be quite different in every way imaginable.

Have fun.

Allow yourself to make it really, really real.

You'll be surprised at what 'autogenic relationships' can do for you!

A16 - YOUR PERSONAL HELL

Now, this heading doesn't sound like too much fun but actually, it is a very pleasing pattern that lays many needless fears to rest. It is a very beautiful and profound Project Sanctuary intervention which might do a lot for your future; I recommend it most highly.

A16/1 - What Is Your Hell?

Most people can readily describe a place they would consider to be 'hell' to them specifically; you can elicit this place quite easily by asking the following questions:

Is it bright or dark?

Wet or dry?

Hot or cold?

What kind of landscape?

Who else is there?

What else is important about this place?

How do you feel being there?

Once you have fixed your place of hell in time and space and you know what it is like, you can consider making some changes.

A16/2 - Getting Out Of Hell

There are many things you can do to change your personal hell in any way you choose. Most people, however, like to spend at least a little time taking a good look around in consciousness for the first time as they become aware what frightens them the most and what they might have silently, darkly been dreading probably for most of your life.

This is an example of how when you bring these things up into Sanctuary where the conscious and the unconscious mind meet the wider realities of the Universe that it is usually nowhere near as terrifying as one might have expected it to be. Still, the term 'hell' is never to be used lightly and if it doesn't really give you a deep sense of fear or dread, you might be in an antechamber to hell rather than the real thing for you. Not to worry, changing antechambers is a good move in the right direction and if nothing else, essential practise you need before you feel ready to tackle even deeper, darker places in courage and with a sense of being able to succeed in owning them, then changing them.

Of course, you can bring light to dark places and soothing shadow for endless deserts; call in friends or helpers; just leave the place behind and choose to inhabit a different place or go there and rescue any parts of you who seem to be stuck; but I wouldn't want to inhibit what will really happen and take place when you meet your personal hell.

Here is an example of one such development. This hell belonged to a young man who we shall call Tony. It was dark, endless, composed of razor-sharp stones that would trip you up, slimy; cold night winds howling all around, no shelter of any kind and he was there entirely alone and entirely terrified. He tried all manner of changes that simply wouldn't happen - guides refused to materialise, no light appeared and he was about to give up and declare he would have to stay in hell forever when he had a flash of insight that showed him how to resolve the situation.

What was required was a sunrise that had been overdue since the "dawn of time" - the whole planet seemed to have become stuck and did not revolve as it should. Now that seemed rather a huge task, moving an entire planet and yet as soon as he had thought it, he could feel the ground beneath him begin to tremble and already the first faint glow to be seen in the blackness. Not much later, and the sunrise really happened - the whole landscape was flooded with the light and Tony could see the landscape at last. Hell was no more, just day and night. There were the most wonderful things revealed to him now that the sun had finally risen again, treasures and riches of amazing beauty and proportions - he was stunned, and profoundly awed by what had been "his personal hell".

A17 - NEVERLAND

A17/1 - The Problems With 'Building Heaven On Earth'

As you can guess from the last pattern, I have often wondered what true Hell on Earth might be like. What it could be that would make someone "be in hell" in their own lives and with little chance to escape.

For a time I thought it must be prison or torture camps but then I read Victor Frankl's books and changed my mind about that. Once in a while I'd see something terrible and thought that could be it - the Dying Rooms for girl babies in China, the horrendous conditions of so many women in the World who suffer unnoticed and unprotested by anyone, it seems - so many options.

But it was not that. It wasn't about physical suffering and hardship, about what evil others or the environment perpetrate upon you. That's life, there is nothing anyone can do to entirely end that.

The moment when I met a true hell was when I met a very rich man who had **built his Sanctuary in the Hard**.

He indeed had made all his dreams come true - literally. He had bought a vast area of land and there, he had build what I can only call "a Sanctuary" for real, complete with all the features you find often in people's Sanctuaries, such as the gardens, the water features, the treasure vaults, the castle and the summer houses, the ponds and lakes, the libraries and tower rooms - all of it and then some.

When I arrived at his estate and saw this, I had a revelation on the nature of how not to live your life and also made immediate connections to this very process that I had observed before, both in reality and in tale.

This is absolutely "Citizen Kane" - this man build his own Xanadu and then became a prisoner inside this what was supposed to have made him happy, and brought him nothing but heartache and pain but this time, there was **NOTHING** he could do to change it anymore. There was no money that could buy more, other, bigger objects, animals, people, whatever to make it any better.

This man, call him Max, was perhaps the most unhappy person I have ever met. The desolation in which he wandered amongst his illusions of joy, of power, of happiness made HARD was simply heartbreaking. His entire life had been spent chasing this dream and making it come true -

only the dream had been the wrong dream, dreamed for all the wrong reasons, and none of it should ever have been made real because none of it was about REAL swimming pools or giraffes or shiny cars, but what they **represent** instead.

Now, I have learned many an important lesson about the nature of reality in my life but this one really shocked me, really brought me up sharp and it also put another facet on the diamond that is Project Sanctuary for me.

Many's the time I have heard "The Healer Illusion" expressed by so many different people, men and women alike. You could call it a dream, you could call it wishful thinking but in the end, I'd say it is an illusion because it doesn't work in the Hard, which is where we are and in my opinion, it is HERE that we need to work and play, live and learn something very, very important that most possibly cannot be learned in any other realm, or in any way.

The Healer Illusion revolves around the idea that enough money should be earned to create a holistic treatment center somewhere in beautiful nature, preferably with a brook nearby. This holistic treatment center has various rooms where people get healed in all sorts of holistic ways and in serenity and beauty.

Only, when you come to question this a little more closely and bring in the matters of the Hard, (such as long lines of sick people queuing at the door, or the fact that there isn't that much public transport to allow the poor to partake of this because it's way out of town in a nature reserve) the Healer Illusion becomes uncomfortable, not at all as satisfactory to consider as it does when it is very much a "Sanctuary construct" - an idea, a sense, a feeling, a quality rather than a hard building with hard bills and hard customers.

Personally, I had for a very long time the illusion of wanting to retire to Tuscany and live in an old pink stone villa there. I'd think about it often with a sense of deep longing, imagining myself there on the terrace as the night falls over the unkempt olive groves, with candles in coloured glasses softly flickering and the heat of the stones giving way to the cool night breeze.

I'm sighing happily even as I am writing this - that's my idea of bliss, of happiness.

For many years I didn't have a hope in hell of making this come true. There were entanglements with people, my children, not enough money, and so on. As I began to earn more and technology advanced, the Tuscany Illusion moved closer to becoming real. With a portable satellite receiver, I can access the Internet anywhere in the World and do my work wherever, it doesn't matter anymore. There are many such buildings in Tuscany and they're cheap enough, and I even found a local person who was happy to help me through the ins and outs of negotiating in a foreign language and sort out the legalities.

But luckily for me, I met Max, desolate and worn down by the deepest forms of unhappiness and unfulfillment you could ever want to imagine.

And I understood that Tuscany cannot make me happy.

The sense of relief and relaxation inherent in the fantasy is only a temporary response to my needing something like that once in a while - a space of grace and solitude.

But I cannot live there.

What would I do there? The hard practicalities of this are ridiculous. My friends and my family are here. I don't speak Italian. There are long days, every day, to be filled with something - should I be waiting for the sunset and that moment that probably would never match my fantasy at all?

The Tuscany Illusion is exactly that - an illusion. Or we could call it a Sanctuary construct, a particular energetic habitat which gives me what I need in moments of need but that should **never - NEVER! - be confused or mistaken for a GOAL**, something you really have happen and something you spend many years of your life organising.

If Max (or Citizen Kane, for that matter) had built their respective Xanadus in the Project Sanctuary realms first, moved in and lived that for a while, they would have **KNOWN** that it wasn't what they wanted - at least not **in that way**.

Citizen Kane says as his last word, "Rosebud". This is a reference to the day when last he was happy, as a young child sleighing without a care in the world near his poor parents home.

It is possibly so that where we all go wrong is to try and make happiness last; that we don't see "being happy" **as a state of being which is brief and flows through us,** unexpected and often entirely unrelated to the people, objects, or situations we seek to surround ourselves with and the people, objects or situations themselves.

I have entitled this article 'Neverland' because that is much the same in a sense - a young boy's fantasy or illusion of the perfect place where you might be happy, with Indians and pirates and being able to fly. This is fun **for a time** but not a goal, not a life - you live in that life and you have the desolation and loss of hope again which Peter Pan feels just the same as Max or Citizen Kane.

I actually believe that many of us are protected from making this kind of dreadful mistake by the absence of funds to make it come true, to build Neverland in the Hard. As long as we can't do that because we haven't like Max made millions upon millions at clever computer trading, we can still live, dream, hope and struggle even.

Further, I believe that people who are on a personal development path which includes spiritual development are already aware of this on some level and their lack of prosperity or power to make illusions become entirely hard and entirely real is absolutely not self sabotage, but on the contrary, a very important protective device designed to put the hell of Neverland out of reach **until** a level of maturity has been reached where this is simply not going to happen anymore.

With Project Sanctuary, we have a real device to short circuit these learnings and have them be fast and very effective - so we DON'T have to make these terrible mistakes for real and waste a lifetime until we get it, how it works, and what "Rosebud" means for all of us.

We also have on our hands the opportunity to begin to understand the relationships between reality and illusion, how we do both, how they interact, intermingle and cross-fertilise each other and how you really do have to understand both in order to have a true sense of reality at last.

'Neverland' is a perfect case history of how **important** an understanding of these topics is for every single one of us who seeks to make this incarnation count, have it be all that it could be, have it be a splendid one, rich and deep with moments of experience, sensory impression, creative expression and in truth, really **having lived your life**.

PROJECT SANCTUARY - CONCLUSION

So now, you know what a Project Sanctuary Interface to the unknown realms is, how to build one, and you have been given many beginning ideas as to what you can use this for, and how to use it. We've discussed how to co-create in the quantum realms and to use the processes that then unfold in different ways, for different reasons and purposes but always with the intention to learn more about these realms, about the universe, about ourselves.

You've read many examples, and you've met many very different people on a very personal level - all the names, of course, have been changed to protect their anonymity.

I know that you couldn't help but resonate to some of the things that you've heard, felt and seen along the way, and that you have been awed and surprised by your own explorations, learnings and insights.

In view of all of that, I think we can now agree that to call this chapter a 'conclusion' is a joke.

There can be no conclusion to the PS Interface system as a representation of the infinite space of your mind, nor the possibilities there lie within - and without.

Exciting as it is, this is ***just the beginning***!

In the course of deliberately creating an internal world which can provide a unifying framework for all your experiences, your dreams, all your past selves, all that you have done so far and all that you want to become, you have learned something that is, of course, much beyond the exercises, techniques, personal insights and fascinating experiences you have had along the way.

You have begun to understand your self.

In doing so, you have begun to admire yourself and re-evaluate your previous understandings of who you are, and what you can be and do.

This is the morning, the dawn.

All lies before you.

Now, it really begins.

Share your experiences with other Sanctuary builders - your special landscape or problem overcome might be just what they need to fill in a blank space or to give them ideas as to how to proceed.

You can post your experiences on the Project Sanctuary public forum at http://ProjectSanctuary.com and exchange ideas with others.

"A Reality Shared Is a Reality Expanded"

Further Information

About The Author

Silvia Hartmann, PhD

Silvia Hartmann is a highly qualified and experienced trainer of Hypnosis, Hypnotherapy, Energy Therapies and Neuro-Linguistic Programming, author, international lecturer, ordained Minister and mother of two.

With an extensive record in trainings design, she is well known for her outstanding ability to create trainings that allow the participants to understand and integrate even highly complex materials, and for making them easy to learn, easy to do and easy to replicate.

She is the author of numerous highly acclaimed original works in the field, including 'Project Sanctuary' and 'Guiding Stars 2002'.

Silvia Hartmann's best-selling EFT Training Manual 'Adventures In EFT' has to date been translated into four languages and is acknowledged to be "The Best Book on EFT".

After studying and researching Energy Psychology & Meridian Energy Therapies approaches in-depth for four years, Silvia Hartmann created EmoTrance, a truly groundbreaking and entirely innovative approach to working with the human energy system.

Silvia Hartmann – Bibliography

Books/Manuals 1993 - 2003
The Harmony Programme
Project Sanctuary
Adventures In EFT
HypnoDreams
Adventures In EFT - 6th Revised Edition
In Serein Trilogy
Oceans Of Energy

Trainings Designed 1995 - 2003
Hypnosis For Healers
Introduction To Energy Psychology
AMT Practitioner Certification Training
MET For Neuro-Linguists
AMT Advanced Practitioner Certification
AMT Trainer Certification Training
Energy Healing For Animals
The Story Teller
Sidereus Energy Healing - Basic Set
True Web Magic
EmoTrance - Self Help, Practitioner Level, Trainer Level
Intensive Energy Field Clearer
Mind Million Energy Intensive

Papers / Special Reports / Projects 1996 - 2002
EFT & NLP
The Gift
Energetic Relationships Paradigm
PowerFields
The Multi-Tasking Personality (with James Masterson)
Guiding Stars 2002
The Wisdom Of The Water
Developmental History Of EmoTrance

Misc. Lectures / Presentations 1993-2002
Healing Words
Energetic Relationships
True Magic
Myth & Metaphor
The Missing Archetypes
Metaphor In Cultural Transmission
Metaphor In Energy Therapies
Advanced Patterns In Energy Therapies
On Creativity
The Sidereus Universe
Millennium Healing Patterns
Oceans Of Energy

Silvia Hartmann's HypnoDreams - With Sound Healing by Ananga Sivyer
The Wisdom Of The Water (2002)
Heart Healing (2003)

Silvia Hartmann Related Websites
Complete Catalogue of Trainings & Manuals - **http://starfields.org**
Hard Copy, CD & Video Orders - **http://dragonrising.com**
Adventures In EFT - **http://1-eft.com**
Project Sanctuary - **http://projectsanctuary.com**
German Language Versions - **http://emotionale-freiheit.com**
Spanish Language Versions - **http://tecnicas-tapping.com**
News, Articles, Downloads - **http://sidereus.org**
EmoTrance TM - **http://emotrance.com**
On-Line Distance Trainings Catalogue - **http://sidereus.org**
Introduction To EFT - **http://123eft.com**
Live Think Tank/Newsgroup -
                    http://yahoogroups.com/group/starfields

Further Reading

Adventures In EFT

Adventures In EFT is the World's best selling guide for beginners in Gary Craig's Emotional Freedom Techniques (EFT).

Now in its sixth fully updated, enlarged and revised edition, 'Adventures' does not require any previous knowledge of healing, counselling, psychology or human health or changework at all - anyone who can read can pick up this book and start to make their lives feel a whole lot better, right away.

Yet, in spite of 'Adventures' easy to read, friendly and informative style, all the base patterns of EFT are here - modelled on Gary Craig himself and with additional modelling from the leading EFT therapists of the world, Adventures is also a fine handbook for any healer or counsellor wishing to begin to make use of the extraordinary powers of EFT to make profound changes in people's lives.

Sparkling with ideas, enthusiasm and lively suggestions for how to take the Classic EFT protocols and make them come to life for you.

Adventures In EFT

The Essential Field Guide To

Emotional Freedom Techniques

by Silvia Hartmann, PhD

ISBN 1 873483 63 5

Available from
http://DragonRising.com - +44 (0)1323 729 666
and all good bookshops.

The Advanced Patterns Of EFT

Primarily for professional therapists, psychologists and students and researchers in the field of Meridian & Energy Therapies, The Advanced Patterns of EFT, by Silvia Hartmann PhD, re-writes the limits of what used to be.

The first part of this advanced manual concentrates on the EFT treatment flow and describes essential patterns, techniques and variations on the Classic EFT process which move an EFT treatment into the realms of true quantum healing.

The second part consists of the advanced patterns themselves - treatment guides, techniques and approaches for guilt, bereavement, high end addictions, parts healing, shamanic applications and the original Guiding Stars patterns, released for the first time.

'The Advanced Patterns Of EFT' is an outstanding, original contribution to the emergent field of Meridian & Energy Therapies and an invaluable resource to any serious student, practitioner and researcher in the field.

The Advanced Patterns Of EFT

by Silvia Hartmann, PhD

ISBN 1 873483 68 6

Available from
http://DragonRising.com - +44 (0)1323 729 666
and all good bookshops.

Oceans Of Energy -

The Patterns & Techniques of EmoTrance Vol.1

For most people, EFT is all they could ask for and all they ever need to smooth out their lives and be able to do and be so much more than they ever thought possible.

I've learned so much by working with EFT this closely for four years, and as a result of what I have learned, I have designed EmoTrance - a stand-alone Energy Healing system for those who wish to work with the human energy body in a more personal, more intimate way.

EmoTrance re-connects the user with their body and their own being in a profound and lasting way. It is an outstanding self help tool, not just to remove old injuries, but also to manage new states that arise all the time, there and then, so they need never become future incidents for us to have to tap on.

EmoTrance is further a superb healing technique when a healer and a client align in their intention to produce a change - entirely client driven, entirely respectful of one individual human's personal perceptions and experiences in this world, it is fast, gentle and deeply profound in all applications.

Lastly, EmoTrance is designed to teach us about our own intuition, our own energy systems and those of others, our 'energy nutritional requirements' and what energy healing really is at the end of the day.

If you have worked with EFT and you are ready to step beyond into a whole new world of living today and creating tomorrow, we invite you to take a closer look. EmoTrance Level 1 is also the pre-requiste for managing the more advanced energy healing, reality creation and magickal patterns of Volume 2.

Oceans Of Energy

The Patterns & Techniques Of EmoTrance - Volume 1

by Silvia Hartmann, PhD

ISBN 1 873483 73 2

Available from

http://DragonRising.com - +44 (0)1323 729 666

and all good bookshops.

The Wisdom Of The Water - Audio CD

Developed in parallel with the breakthrough techniques of Energy Flow of EmoTrance, 'The Wisdom of the Water' is a fantastic collection of healing dreams, each one evoking a rich tapestry of healing energies, of states and of experiences.

You can simply allow yourself to relax and feel or you can actively use the journeys in conjunction with EmoTrance to run the energies being evoked smoothly and powerfully.

From the simply wonderful energy clearing and recharging experience that is 'The Wisdom Of The Water', used around the world by practitioners and teachers of EmoTrance with their clients and students, to the powerful and truly amazing 'Darling', this full length audio CD is a truly stunning experience.

Silvia Hartmann's masterful evocation of energies, subtle and extremely powerful, multi-layered and multi-ordinate is raised and supported by Ananga Sivyer's original music, using traditional healing instruments from shamanic cultures across the World. Additional background vocals by Pia complete the extraordinary depth and richness of texture as three master healers align to prepare your energy system, your body and your mind for deep healing and for transformation.

The Wisdom Of The Water
by Silvia Hartmann, Ananga Sivyer & Pia
Audio Self Healing Guide On CD
ISBN 1873483 08 2

Available from
http://DragonRising.com - +44 (0)1323 729 666
and all good bookshops.

Heart Healing Audio CD

A superbly healing energy experience awaits you. Three master healers, one intent - to help you heal your heart, contact your soul and to celebrate your uniqueness and the precious gift you are.

Use these powerful healing evocations to balance you, to lift you, to support you or simply as the perfect holiday in mind, body and spirit.

7 + 1 unique dreams of healing, 7 + 1 absolutely personal experiences of re-alignment and expansion. From the pure power of 'Heart Healing' to the celebration of 'The Child', we are immensely proud to present 'Heart Healing' with and by Silvia Hartmann, Ananga Sivyer and Pia.

On this fantastic CD for you: Eight wonderful healing dreams, to engage with and experience time and time again - and each time afresh:

- Heart Healing
- Receiving The Colours
- Celebration
- Ocean Wood
- Resonance Connection
- Morning Light
- Precious
- The Child

This extraordinary collection of mystical healing dreams was especially written for those who wish to both release the injuries of the past and to prepare for the new dawn of a different way of feeling, being and doing. Evoking powerful energies and images, sensations and emotions, 'Heart Healing' calls to your heart, your mind and to your soul and guides you towards reconnecting within yourself, and with yourself to the Universe around us.

Incredible experiences - as often as you need them, and fresh and different each time you embark on the healing dream. Each healing dream is an absolutely unique energy field restorer in its own right and for its own purposes. All eight sessions together make up a healing journey like you have never experienced - gentle, loving, and yet powerfully moving as master healers Pia, Ananga Sivyer and Silvia Hartmann combine their intent to raise you, restore and empower you, their unique words, visions, music and vibrations becoming the powerful wind beneath your wings.

Align YOUR heart, YOUR mind and YOUR soul in a whole new way. Pure Energy Healing, Pure Energy Magic - The Heart Healing Journey Complete.

Heart Healing
by Silvia Hartmann, Ananga Sivyer & Pia
Audio Self Healing Guide On CD
ISBN 1873483 09 0

Available from
http://DragonRising.com - +44 (0)1323 729 666
and all good bookshops.

The In Serein Trilogy - FREE Web Book

In 2001, Silvia Hartmann took an entire year out of her life to write a full length fantasy trilogy - 'In Serein'.

At the top level, this an exciting fantasy fiction novel set which is easy to read, fast paced and in typical Silvia style, enchants the reader and draws them deep into the story, sharing the triumphs and disasters of the main characters from the first person perspective.

But In Serein is more than this.

The story interacts with the reader, challenges them to have an emotional response and does not hesitate to confront sometimes very frightening scenarios.

Yet, and on still further levels, there are many lessons about thought, about magick, about reality, about healing, about soul to be found here - and these are not taught but individually experienced by the reader. Project Sanctuary players will easily find many settings, experiences and scenarios which they themselves can interact with and in doing so, enrich their worlds.

A masterpiece of experiential writing, In Serein is available by the author's request free of charge on the World Wide Web, as an open web book, to be found and interacted with by those who would.

The In Serein Trilogy
Book 1 - Sorcerer & Apprentice
Book 2 - The Cage
Book 3 - End Of Dreams

Available as a free web book from
http://InSerein.com